THE GNAWA LION

PUBLIC CULTURES OF THE MIDDLE EAST
AND NORTH AFRICA

Paul A. Silverstein, Susan Slyomovics, and
Ted Swedenburg, editors

THE GNAWA LIONS

Authenticity and Opportunity in Moroccan Ritual Music

Christopher Witulski

Indiana University Press

This book is a publication of

Indiana University Press
Office of Scholarly Publishing
Herman B Wells Library 350
1320 East 10th Street
Bloomington, Indiana 47405 USA

iupress.indiana.edu

The paper used in this publication meets the minimum requirements of
the American National Standard for Information Sciences—Permanence
of Paper for Printed Library Materials, ANSI Z39.48-1992.

Manufactured in the United States of America

Cataloging information is available from the Library of Congress.

ISBN 978-0-253-03679-7 (cloth)
ISBN 978-0-253-03675-9 (paperback)
ISBN 978-0-253-03678-0 (ebook)

1 2 3 4 5   23 22 21 20 19 18

Contents

Acknowledgments

IT WOULD BE impossible to recognize all who shared in the process of bringing this project to fruition, and for those who are not listed here—especially the innumerable people who welcomed me to Fez and into their homes time and time again—may God repay you and your families.

I owe a debt of gratitude to colleagues and friends in Florida, New York, Ohio, and Morocco whose insights strengthen the pages that follow, including Roger Anderson, Russell Brown, Hicham Chami, Daanish Faruqi, Jack Forbes, Tyler Graham, Sarah Hirsh, Jessica Lambert, Philip Murphy, Josh Neumann, Kendra Salois, and Matthew Schumann. The hours spent conversing over drinks, sipping mint tea, in conference hallways, and over email were invaluable. I want to thank Larry Crook for his mentorship, guidance, and detailed readings of these chapters as they developed. To those who took valuable time to read and respond to this document in its entirety or in part, I am appreciative, especially to Ellen Koskoff, Fiona McLaughlin, Phillip Naylor, Andi Ongoiba, Alexander Smith Reed, Philip Schuyler, Jonathan Stock, Welson Tremura, and the anonymous peer reviewers who responded to different versions of sections of this work. A previous version of chapter 4 appeared in *The Journal for North African Studies* (Witulski 2016a) and a version of chapter 6 appeared in *Ethnomusicology Forum* (Witulski 2016b), both available at http://www.tandfonline.com. A version of chapter 7 appeared in *Ethnomusicology* (Witulski 2018).

Paul A. Silverstein, Susan Slyomovics, and Ted Swedenburg, the editors for Indiana University Press's Public Cultures of the Middle East and North Africa series, provided the inspiration for this project that helped me to undertake the process of turning it into a book. Dee Mortensen's generous direction, Julia Turner's and Mary Jo Rhodes's editing, and the thoughtful responses from the anonymous manuscript reviewers were transformative in connecting disparate thoughts into a cohesive whole. Of course, even with the help of these individuals, mistakes will make their way into this work. Any such errors are solely my own.

I would have never made it through this project had it not been for the support of others. Jill Sonke, Jennifer Lee, and Chuck Levy led me in inspired new directions both within and outside of this research. My colleagues at Bowling Green State University and Florida State University gave me encouragement as I worked through the writing process while also providing opportunities for me to learn new skills as an educator, musician, and researcher. The project resulted from the generous financial support of many, including the Fulbright Student

Grant Program and the Moroccan-American Commission for Educational and Cultural Exchange's wonderful staff, led by Jim Miller; the University of Florida's School of Music, Center for African Studies, and Alumni Fellowship Program; and the Department of Education's Foreign Language and Area Studies program.

There were many who worked closely and patiently with me throughout my time in Morocco. They deserve special recognition for answering my constant questions, even the most banal. They include M'allem 'Abd al-Rzaq; M'allem Aziz wuld Ba Blan; 'Abd al-Rahim Amrani and the members of his ensemble; Mohammed Sousi, his son Yusef, and the members of his ensemble; Fredric Calmus; Yassine Boudouaia and the members of his ensemble; Ahmed Shiki and his son 'Abd al-Salam; Ahmed Aydoun; Fatima Zahra and the staff at Subul al-Salam; Majid Bekkas; M'allem 'Abd al-Qadr of Rabat; Hamid al-Qasri; M'allem 'Abd al-Latif Makhzumi; Mulay al-Tahir; Adil Walili; Omar Chennafi; and so many others. To Mohammed Boujma' and his family, 'Abd al-Hafez and his family, Sandy McCutcheon and Suzanna Clark, and to my friends and neighbors in Fez, thank you for opening your homes and lives to me.

Madeleine, Julia, and Elise, you have given me so much joy and support, even if only through hugs, smiles, and sweet cooing. Finally, I want to thank my wife Jessica: your love is a gift from God.

Notes on Transliteration and Transcription

Systems of translation repeatedly fail to maintain the nuanced complexity of what they portray. I make use of two such systems here: the transliteration of Moroccan Arabic and the transcription of musical sounds. While both are flawed, I aim for simplicity by adapting the transliteration system of the *International Journal of Middle East Studies* and, for musical transcriptions, closely approximating the performances from my fieldwork recordings and other sources in musical notation. I omit all diacritical markings in proper names, but otherwise use ' for *'ayn* (ع) and ' for *hamza* (ء) throughout the text. In the case of common English words or place names, I use those in place of a strict transliteration. In this way, I prioritize readability at the expense of some consistency. For example, the city is Fez, but its residents are *fassi*. Similarly, musical notation is meant to provide a rough outline of the sounds I describe. Rhythms and pitches are notoriously difficult to precisely reproduce in writing, and those moments of uncertainty are where many of the most interesting things happen.

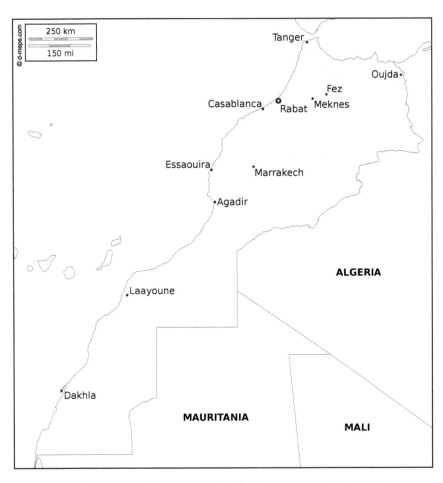

Map 0.1. Map of Morocco and the Western Sahara with major cities. © Daniel Dalet, http://d-maps.com/carte.php?num_car=22751&lang=en.

THE GNAWA LIONS

1   One Minute in Meknes

Less than a week after arriving in Fez in November 2010, I made sure to visit 'Abd al-Rahim 'Abd al-Rzaq, a gnawa ritual leader with whom I had worked during my previous two summers. His joviality shone through as I sat down in front of his "office" in the Blida neighborhood of Fez's walled medina, the old city. The smell of the nearby leather tanners wafted through the courtyard where he was sewing gnawa paraphernalia and meeting with prospective clients. The noisy setting made it difficult to converse, something that I had grown used to. His "day job" was as a guardian for the funduq, a collection of workshops and storage spaces where laborers pounded away at brass plates and teapots, making piles of new goods to be sold in the nearby tourist markets. 'Abd al-Rzaq was surprised and happy to see me. He immediately stood up and handed me a piece of thick cardboard to sit on so that I would not have to be on the stone floor. After the onslaught of introductions that opens so many conversations in Morocco, he invited me to a gnawa 'ashiyya in nearby Meknes. An 'ashiyya, like a lila, is a healing ceremony animated by the music of the gnawa tradition. Unlike the lila, which extends from the night into the next morning, an 'ashiyya begins earlier in the evening and concludes soon after midnight. It is shorter and, therefore, costs the hosts less for the musicians, any space rental, and food preparation for guests. We made the appropriate plans, and I quickly became excited about an auspicious start to this fieldwork visit.

The event took place in a second-floor apartment in a poor neighborhood between Meknes's medina and the ville nouvelle. After a delicious chicken couscous meal provided by the hosts and shared by the musicians, we descended to the street for the opening procession, called the 'ada. Accompanied by a pair of large drums (tbal) and four or five sets of iron castanets (qaraqib), 'Abd al-Rzaq's brother Hamid, serving as the leader of this event, the m'allem, lit incense, wrapping the hosts and a young woman in aromatic smoke. As she fell into and out of a trance on the dirt road, the sound of the music and singing attracted a large crowd that, eventually, encircled the central participants. After an extended procession and blessings of the instruments, flags, candles, people, and sacrificial animals to be used later in the evening, the large group of musicians, participants, and spectators made their way through the small door, up the steep, tight staircase, and back into the apartment. The musicians then began performing, inviting the spirits of the gnawa pantheon to join in the event and calling for blessings from Allah and prayers from the Prophet Muhammad. Incense and sound together thickened the air, making it heavy with odor and vibrant with motion.

Over the past two generations, gnawa music moved from an existence that primarily served enclosed rituals to one that engages new contexts across Moroccan popular music. The gnawa are a population understood in contemporary Morocco to be descendants of West Africans, having come to the Maghreb[1] through the slave trade. Their music is now heard on the streets of Marrakech, at festivals in Essaouira, in Fez's cafés and Casablanca's nightclubs, and in the bars of Rabat. The gnawa music that appears in these public spaces large and small is based within the constructs of a healing ritual, but the artists filter it through audience tastes as they adapt it to new settings. Different artists take any number of aesthetic paths through this creative process while audiences and individuals choose their favorite singers based on some combination of aesthetic pleasure and perceived authenticity.

With the growth of the music's popularity, listeners hunt out new opportunities to hear these powerful sounds. They return to the rituals, events that continue in both the poorest neighborhoods and the richest. It is the listeners who, when ill or in need of rejuvenation and catharsis, hire musicians and outfit their homes with the trappings of ritual ceremony. (Respiratory issues, arthritic pain, and mental illness are common health concerns that bring people to the gnawa.) They are the ones who watch the events unfold, smell the incenses, wear the colored fabrics, and trance in tune with their possessing spirits. They hire their favorite singers and ask for their favorite songs. They choose to request the spectacle—the burning of candles against the skin of the possessed dancers, the slicing of flesh with knives—or they decide to hire musicians who avoid this kind of ritual manifestation entirely, preferring a quieter, more subdued ceremony.

The gnawa ritual is an event led by and oriented toward the paying host and the present audience of listeners. Although musicians and ritual leaders direct the proceedings, they also defer to the tastes and requests of those present in the room. Musicians and others who work within the ritual economy fight to be hired by potential clients, catering to their preferences. Performers must choose how to adapt and adjust to compete for a limited number of engagements. As younger musicians enter the scene, this competition only intensifies. These musicians, both young and old, use ritual and musical authority strategically to warrant their hire or their fees. As listeners hear popularized versions of these songs and look for their favorite star musicians to lead their rituals, popular aesthetics creep into ritual settings, changing the way events look and sound. The lines between sacred experience and entertainment blur as each follows personal taste to guide his or her engagement with the sounds, scents, and spiritual practice.

In the following pages, I examine different ways that ritual leaders engage their changing audiences by negotiating, performing, and asserting their own authenticity. Most find a point at which they are comfortable balancing the wants of their audience against what they discern as the needs of the spirits and the integrity of the ritual. The increasing influence of popular music aesthetics is dramatically changing this debate, while the professionalization of the gnawa requires musicians to at least consider prioritizing their listeners' requests.

Zakari, one of the ensemble members, often makes the long train ride from Mar-rakech to Meknes to perform with 'Abd al-Rzaq or Hamid. He dances for some of the more virtuosic and acrobatic segments of the ceremony, taking advantage of skills that he developed as a kid when break dancing with his friends. His ability has put him in demand with a number of different gnawa troupes. When the time comes for Sidi Musa to enter the ceremonial space, he overtakes Zakari's body, causing him to get up from the group of musicians, stand facing the ensemble, and ease into a trance. Sidi Musa, Moses, has control over water. He is the blue spirit. Those whom he possesses are draped with blue cloth by the muqaddima, *the woman in charge of the event, as they fall into trance. Sidi Musa's newly inhabited body enacts an intricate dance that mesmerizes the surrounding spectators, and his presence becomes an early dramatic highlight of the ceremony.*

This evening, as Zakari is falling into the trance, holding his head above the incense burner, feeding the spirit with its smoke to entice Sidi Musa to take firm hold over him. Zakari begins to move, bending deeply forward, syncing himself into the music. A small bowl of water appears, brought out by the muqaddima *while the room holds its focus on Zakari. He takes the bowl, balances it on his head, and begins to spin. The dance that follows includes rolling on the ground, twisting, and jumping, all with this bowl perched atop his head. He mimics swimming motions while lying on the floor, contorting his body to keep his head upright, holding the bowl. But at one particular moment, he is swaying in front of the incense burner when the sound of the* adhan, *the Islamic call to prayer, drifts in through the open window.*

When one hears the adhan in Morocco, the most appropriate action is to si-lence any music, stop speaking, and listen, waiting for its conclusion. Once the adhan ends, the practicing believer has a period of time to complete her prayers. Some immediately cease any current activities and begin praying. I have been in taxis in both Morocco and Egypt when the call came, and the driver pulled over, opened up a prayer mat, and prayed on the sidewalk next to his car before getting back in and continuing the drive. But many gnawa, and many Moroccans more generally, do not pray so dutifully or at all. Some do; some don't. It is a matter of personal religious practice, a daily decision made by believers each time they hear the adhan. Most, however, do respect the explicit sound of the religion, turning off music and waiting patiently for it to pass before continuing their activities. This act of reverence marks the day, with each pause becoming a signal for the passage of time. Hirschkind (2006) notes instances in which the adhan even interrupts other religious sounds, as those listening to recorded sermons pause their moral educa-tion during these few minutes while the call to prayer is audible.

Despite attending a number of lila and 'ashiyya ceremonies, I had never experienced this moment, the conflict between the gnawa's religious sound and the audible institutionalized Islam of the adhan. Lila ceremonies, long and loud, usually occur in the evening, when there are fewer instances of the call to prayer, or they are so loud that they simply cover all outside sounds. Here, though, was an intimate moment as Zakari quietly settled into his possessed state, standing next to an open window in an apartment that happened to be in the proximity of the neighborhood mosque. The second-floor apartment stood above any hindrance from walls or buildings between the mosque minaret's electronic bullhorns and us, lending both a beautiful view of the outside sky and an unimpeded path for the sound of the adhan's "Allahu akbar . . . ," God is great.

Success within the gnawa musical community is increasingly defined by the commercial standards of the music industry rather than by ritual criteria. Most performers and journalists locate ideas of ritual efficacy as the result of an effective command of two distinct sources of authenticity: Muslim piety and African heritage. While there are many other potential interpretations for gnawa authenticity—age, experience, knowledge of various regional styles, or professional networks, for example—these two consistently came up in conversations with practitioners, listeners, and people from both within and outside the gnawa community. That they are conceived in opposition to each other was often demonstrated when I introduced my topic of study to most Moroccans; the common reply was some variant of "Oh, why are you studying that? Just know that it is not Islam," or "You know that the gnawa are from Africa, right?" By "Africa," people are referring to sub-Saharan Africa and using the gnawa community's history of slavery as a marker, positing them well outside of a Moroccan identity. Musicians highlight specific performance characteristics or personal narratives in an effort to claim effective authenticity as Muslim or African, usually opting for a combination of the two sources, intentionally locating themselves as possessing both Islamic piety and a personal linkage to sub-Saharan Africa. I heard a number of examples for this, including a variety of references to the recently deceased Mahmoud Guinea of Essaouira as a "true gnawa" because "he is so black" or 'Abd al-Kabir Marshan's self-identification as part of a sub-Saharan lineage despite his lighter complexion because of his "black wet nurse." Conversely, in other interviews, elders like Mulay al-Tahir of Tamesluht highlight an ideal gnawa singing voice as resembling the sound of someone reciting the Qur'an. Similarly, Aziz wuld Ba Blan of Fez, whose dark skin and clear lineage prove his heritage to others, cites his recent pilgrimage to Mecca as demonstrating his Muslim piety. These outwardly performative and personal attributes emphasize the gnawa community's internal debate between the Sufi and African sources of their authenticity and thus their ritual power. *Sufism* itself is a problematic term; it serves as an umbrella for a number of local and transnational practices—"mystical Islam," if you will. Some of these attributes are highly contested while others are respected, erudite, and able to be traced back to the earliest intellectual histories of Islam itself. Other symbols include the importance of prayer and pious behavior: the sound of the performed music, residence in a city that was a known slave trade post, correct pronunciation of Arabic texts, use of non-Arabic words, age, chain of lineage to previous gnawa musicians or identifiable slaves, and so on.

After just over fifteen minutes of music for Sidi Musa, the room fell into silence. Hamid, the m'allem, had softened his playing and came to a terse stop, the qaraqib had already been at rest. The nasal loudspeaker nearby is barely audible on my recording, but it speaks loudly in the absence of all other sound. As the long syllables of the muezzin's *recitation come to a close, Hamid signals to his musicians and, rising from the quiet, dovetails the music of his ensemble back in, rising against the interruption's final notes. He reengages the room and the spirit, who spent the minute waiting patiently, bent in half at the waist. Zakari's body reanimates, stepping back into the groove of the ceremonial music.*

The moment, a literal suspension in time and space, displayed the web of performative acts that stretches between many Moroccans' spiritual lives. The gnawa, self-identified Muslims, defer to the adhan, an aural symbol of their faith. Sidi Musa, like many other gnawa spirits, is respected as a holy figure, either a prophet (nabi) *from the Qur'an or a local saint descendant of the Prophet Muhammad, depending on whom you ask. Sidi Musa is joined in the ceremony by other literal or spiritual ancestors throughout the ceremony. Mulay Ibrahim possessed the host of that evening's* 'ashiyya *later, as she picked up a Qur'an and prayer beads, reciting verses. Saints and spirits join the gnawa ceremony each time it is held, but here, in Meknes this evening, Sidi Musa showed patience and deference, becoming a meditative listener along with the rest of us, experiencing the adhan.*

Negotiating Gnawa Authenticities

There are a number of stories, of narratives, about who the gnawa are, where they come from, what they do, and whether their practices are morally appropriate or even permissible. Or Muslim. Questions—or, better put, declarations—about who the invited spirits are or how the music comes from "Africa" peppered my conversations with both fans and disinterested listeners. These conversations did not always go in the same direction, however. Markers of effectiveness within ritual were widely different. What some participants were willing to ignore as unimportant—training, for example—were held up as pillars of authority by others. Authenticity in the contemporary gnawa community exists as a meeting point between performers and listeners. It can mean many things, depending on who those performers and listeners are, just as it can look very different as the meeting point itself shifts. Authenticity is therefore unpredictable and constantly in flux. There is no urtext, no wide communion of opinion that deems certain performers or styles "authentic." It exists in a marketplace—an exchange—and appears within the agreement between a performance and a client's expectations.

This vision of authenticity does not imply that it is exclusively monetary, that is, always a commodity, though as the paragraphs and chapters that follow make clear, this is certainly a component of the discussion as money changes hands, social capital gets wielded, and power over spirits and listeners asserts its significance.

In Morocco today, clients hire musicians to welcome spirits into a ritual for healing purposes. Other clients, notably concert producers or promoters, hire musicians to entertain crowds. Both sets of clients might demand performers who are authentic. The "inauthentic" may be unable to facilitate the cure of an ailment or may poorly represent what the client or audience expects as "gnawa tradition" on stage. In some cases, authenticity may be benign, unimportant. I attended a birthday party for an expatriate teenager in which the entertainment was a local gnawa troupe. The small group of friends in attendance, mostly young, white, and foreign, knew little (if anything) about the potential ritual power of the music. They danced and enjoyed themselves, and the event was a success. Each group of performers and listeners approaches an engagement, whether ritual, commercial, or otherwise, with expectations. When the listener's expectations for the ensemble are not met, claims of inauthenticity result. This is hardly unique to the gnawa. In a TED talk, Nigerian author Chimamanda Ngozi Adichie relates a conversation in which her writing was deemed inauthentic because her characters were not the impoverished Africans that a professor had expected.[2] When there are singular expectations, authenticity can be fairly simple, even binary. When there are a number of expectations, a performance can meet some or otherwise elicit a measured response. For example, the playing of Earl Scruggs, Pete Seeger, and Dink Roberts speaks to entirely different sets of expectations about American banjo playing. The symbol and sound of the banjo go in even more diverse directions within the music of artists like Sufjan Stevens or Beck. (I remember being struck by the banjo's role in his song "Sexx Laws" the first time I heard it.)

In the case of the gnawa, as with conversations of authenticity elsewhere, it's not just that there is a moving target: there is no single target authenticity to seek out. Experiences from diverse audiences result in a wide variety of expectations, many of them conflicting or even irreconcilable. Perhaps luckily, there are equally diverse performers ready to meet the needs of those potential clients. While there are hierarchies of success based on each of these measures, they are not identical, but they may overlap. Certain measures of authenticity map well onto others, opening areas of opportunity for those who identify and effectively occupy them. In gnawa music, authenticity revolves around ritual practice, skill with "working the spirits" (Kapchan 2007). But just as all spirits are not equal, every trancing body is different. Further, the trance takes place in the center of a room encircled by family, friends, and neighbors. At this point in history, especially with the extraordinary fame and familiarity of gnawa music within

Morocco, those listeners' experiences need to be accounted for as well. This leads to a wealth of measures by which a client can select a performer and a similar wealth of different local performers from which to choose. Money can certainly play into the equation, and does (see chap. 4), but taste matters as well. And taste is not easily defined. The available authenticities have largely mapped onto two narratives mentioned above: African heritage and Islamic piety. A third is growing in importance, and for some it has overtaken the others: the ability to engage an audience of listeners, trancing bodies, and spirits.

My effort here is to explore how authenticity is created and wielded in a specific place and time. The term *authenticity* is a slippery one, much in the way that *hybrid* can carry a range of meanings, each with powerful political connotations in the postcolonial world (Kriady 2002). Michelle Bigenho (2002) outlines three forms of authenticity: experiential authenticity, cultural-historical authenticity, and the authenticity born of uniqueness. These three conceptualizations conflate in the narratives I describe in different ways and for different reasons. The first two prove to be the most influential, however. Experiential authenticity describes the moment of engagement in which a music or ritual effectively moves a listener. It may be a matter of aesthetic taste or even that the listener was in the right emotional and spiritual space to receive and connect with what is happening. Cultural-historical authenticity articulates a sense of truth derived from a valued contextual positionality. This may involve placement within a historical trajectory or one's status as a representative of a community. By following the discourses, definitions, and debates that pepper casual conversations within the gnawa community, I aim to foreground the process by which these modes of authenticating people, sounds, styles, regions, and experiences happen. The narratives of authenticity that I outline, especially where commercial success is concerned, grow from this ethnographic experience and arise where theoretical models can break down. I use the narratives not as a generative model of authenticity but as descriptions of what people are saying, doing, and paying for. This approach centers claims of authenticity and their maintenance firmly within the hands of listeners, performers, and others, like journalists or members of the music industry, who hold the power to control discourses. It also pulls the term *authenticity* away from its common usage as a marker employed by or about nations and communities. I see authenticity as determined by individuals. People's own values about their cultures and histories—influenced as they may be by others—are balanced against experiences, memories, tastes, and any number of other priorities when they make judgments about a new encounter.

In this sense, authenticity integrates into a relational understanding of music and meaning (Guilbault 1997). It is the point of articulation, the meeting space between performed and personal values about truth and authority, that generates a sense of authenticity. This view of it supports its importance within conceptions of music and identity that are grounded in and influenced by feelings about the nation (Stokes 2010; Wade 2000), a given experience, or the merits of an individual artist, among other things. This generative moment brings Bigenho's three types of authenticity together to create the singular and slippery concept. It is used by various actors in diverse ways, and the diverse goals that practitioners or listeners bring to their conceptions of authenticity dramatically influence the balance of values that engage this point of articulation (Fiol 2010). A musician aiming for a career on Morocco's festival stages may emphasize connections with media representations and audience notions of gnawa heritage. Another looking for a career in the music industry may highlight virtuosity. These are certainly not mutually exclusive; more frequently a performer will adapt his presentational style depending on the audience and context in an effort to meet audience members' expectations through dress, repertoire, the use of dance and gesture, or discourse about the music. Although this type of audience engagement on stages may seem obvious, its persistence within ritual settings—as ritual performers compete for clients—struck me.

The negotiation of these narratives of gnawa authenticity, especially how they engage the community's past, is the subject of much of this book. This population locates its own history as sub-Saharan. Its instruments bear close resemblances to those of West Africa (see Charry 1996) and many of its songs include texts that highlight its history of slavery (see chap. 2 and El Hamel 2008). The sound of gnawa music centers on a low bass string instrument called the *hajhuj*, *ginbri*, or *sintir*—depending on where you are and whom you ask—accompanied by iron castanets played by an ensemble of men. A leader, called a m'allem, sings while playing the hajhuj, loudly declaiming calls or verses that are punctuated by responses from his male percussionists.[3] The music is born of and central to a possession ritual, a ceremony in which women and men give animal and financial sacrifices to maintain a relationship with a possessing spirit and fall into a trance-dance when the spirit takes over the body, joining in the celebration. Spectators watch and listen, supporting their friends and family while enjoying the music, food, and community. Some are attracted to the tradition even in the absence of a personal relationship with a spirit. As the music rose from marginality to prominence during the second half of the twentieth century, some gnawa musicians began seeking out fusions with other musical traditions in Morocco. Many choose to focus on local or national genres, like those I describe in chapter 5. Others, especially the younger generation of musicians, orient their sound toward their own tastes and enter into the worlds of hip-hop or rock.

A few gnawa musicians have attained a high level of attention internationally, becoming national superstars in the process, but I concentrate on those who focus on domestic markets and local neighborhoods instead of international tourism and major music festivals. Many gnawa ensembles have begun touring internationally and performing on stages alongside international stars like Wayne Shorter, Randy Weston, and Pat Metheny. They participate in festivals domestically that cater largely, though not exclusively, to tourist audiences while they continue their own ritual work to maintain their credibility and perceived authenticity. Although some groups navigate the industry in an effort to achieve international successes, something that they often dream of and reach for, the vast majority of performers focus exclusively on local and regional opportunities. When reorienting performance practice and self-representation for a wider, non-Moroccan audience, these groups add interesting nuances into their staged performance as they work to appeal to what they understand to be the aesthetic tastes of an audience that does not have a lifetime of experience with these musical traditions.

A number of histories and ethnographies of the gnawa exist throughout the scholarship in both English (see Kapchan 2007; Fuson 2009; Sum 2011 and 2013) and French (see Pâques 1964 and 1991; Chlyeh 1998 and 1999; Hell 2002). What struck me during past research trips was the claim, by elder practitioners of the gnawa, that within their lifetimes they saw normative ritual practice shift from a rare and identifiably Sufi ritual to an Africanized "spectacle" that bore little relationship to their own religious values, musical tastes, and memories. They saw saints, living figures in Morocco's history, become known as frightening *jnun* (spirits, s. *jinn*) brought from sub-Saharan Africa while they also witnessed the importation of spirits from other local religious traditions into the gnawa ritual. A debate ensued regarding ritual aesthetics and musical performance practice, a discourse that struggled to codify, change, spread, or resurrect a gnawa authenticity. Authority and ideology came into question as performers reacted to each other's musical, ritual, and commercial moves. The history and ethnographic clarity that I had naively expected was largely in flux, pulled into currents of heritage creation, nostalgia, and neoliberalism. The front lines generally split across two faults: first, a generation gap between elder and younger performers, and second, perceived intention. At times, as outlined in the chapters that follow, cultivating good intention—demonstrable through measures of piety, consistent ritual performance, or participation in the heritage economy—could alleviate criticism based on age or lineage. The reverse is also true. Authenticity as a gnawa musician is negotiable. Furthermore, it is increasingly born of messaging and the careful curation of a performer's self-identity. Authenticity is granted by listening audiences, hiring clients in need of ritual healing, and media influences, some of which are closely related to state power structures.

This, of course, brings up a changing relationship between listening as ritual experience and listening as entertainment, a shift generated as much by listeners as by performers. I suggest that audiences have adopted listening strategies from the realm of popular music and link their experiences of concert and staged settings of music into ritual settings by dancing, chatting with friends, and requesting popular songs of the musicians. The pressure on musicians to appease both audiences and spirits, instead of focusing exclusively on the spiritual and physical health of those present, is the impetus for the widespread nature of musical change in this tradition. Although it is true that the performers—especially those pursuing careers in the commercial music industry—are often the promoters of creative developments, those who are able to find economic success and stardom do so because innovative changes are best adapted to the desires of ever-changing Moroccan and international audiences. In interviews, performers frequently mentioned their efforts to keep up with the "changing taste of the crowd [*jamhur*]." The jamhur decides. The second half of this book, chapters 5–9, looks at these rising pressures and the ways in which musicians accommodate them in an effort to build authenticity alongside, and even through, audience engagement.

Previous gnawa research has accomplished a great deal through extensive efforts to locate the musical and ritual practices within historical and current circuits of migration, most frequently recognizing and pursuing African lineages while analyzing their contemporary manifestations within Moroccan society. Schaefer's (2009) nuanced dissertation explores a variety of historical influences that led to the gnawa's self-identification within the terrain of Moroccan conceptions of race and ethnicity. Jankowsky's (2010) work with the *stambeli*—a group similar to the gnawa in Tunisia—locates that community's potential linkages with sub-Saharan groups that share specific ritual or musical practices. These characteristics infer a cultural family tree in which the gnawa comprise a large branch. But just as these writers do not cite specific and documented lines of lineage, the gnawa themselves do not maintain direct knowledge of their trans-Saharan history (see Kapchan 2007, 20; J. Becker 2004; Ennaji 1999; Lovejoy 2004; Pâques 1991). African identity is one born in a distant past that is remembered in legend and reiterated and embodied through song and dance.

Despite the lack of a documented link, however, the shared characteristics noted by previous scholars do provide evidence for the African forms of authenticity that dominate gnawa scholarship. Kapchan (2007) notes a number of sub-Saharan Islamized populations that also utilize possession ceremonies, including the *bori* (Masquelier 2001) and *songhay* (Stoller 1989). Most of these scholars, furthermore, outline the general trends of the slave trade, identifying the high point of the trade during the Saadian dynasty, between the fifteenth and sixteenth centuries. This time, just after the Moroccan kingdom conquered Timbuktu and the Songhay Empire, saw the full opening of these trans-Saharan trade routes, many of which led to the region around Marrakech. Simultaneously, the Portuguese were benefiting from seabound trade routes that centered on the port city of Mogador, which later became Essaouira. This historical moment, with two cities serving as foci of the sea and land slave trades, provides a source of this locally oriented African authenticity, one that can be claimed through lineage, even skin color.

Though audience engagement is increasingly necessary to publicize or prove authenticity, some type of African lineage provides a boost to a claim. Yet, the place of the gnawa within Morocco has shifted, opening up new avenues. The African-ness of the ritual marginalized the practice and the community for much of the population's history in Morocco, but the same point of difference has since become a marker for Morocco's postindependence diversity. This change is not wholesale, as many—if not most—still eye the gnawa with suspicion, but the African-ness of the music and ritual is central to many performances, especially those that are a part of national and international projects. Even so, a conception of gnawa identity based on African lineage is not the only understanding of who the gnawa are; it just happens to be the most prominent. Many within the community, especially those who work outside of the state festival and international tourism scene, understand gnawa practice to be a local manifestation of Islamic practice. Some liken it to Sufism, though noting important differences, while others categorize it as one of many local Sufi practices, emphasizing the similarity of the gnawa ceremony to other forms of Moroccan religious practice.

Much of the wealth of anthropological scholarship on Islamic practice in Morocco attempts to either describe and analyze a specific form of practice (as in Crapanzano's work with the *hamadsha* Sufi brotherhood in 1973) or draw general conclusions about overarching characteristics across the country's various communities. The prominence of saints (Geertz 1971) or the pilgrimages to their tombs (Eickelman 1976) become markers for explicitly Moroccan variations of Islamic practice in these older ethnographic accounts. Recently, however, more attention has been paid to public forms of behavior, the performance of individual or communal forms of religious practice. While many of these new ethnographic approaches focus on other regions of the Islamic world (for example, Mahmood [2005] and Hirschkind [2006] in Egypt), the idea of performed values, both religious and otherwise, have appeared in the Moroccan context (see Kapchan [1996] and Slyomovics [2005], for example). Within music and religion more directly, Waugh's (2005) descriptions of performance practices across a variety of Sufi groups locates embodied actions within the larger realm of religious experience. Whether using measures of piety like traveling to Mecca on pilgrimage (the *hajj*), praying daily, or abstaining from drinking or smoking, for example, or a similarity to local manifestations of Sufism such as saint veneration, gathering at a "lodge" (*zawiya*), chanting (*dhikr*), and ecstatic experience (*al-hal*), examples abound from across the gnawa community that make explicit the links between the ritual and more popular forms of religious activity. Or, perhaps more accurately, counterexamples defy attempts to bound off gnawa practice as un-Islamic, foreign, or exclusive to the immoral, drinkers, smokers, or sex and drug addicts.

I argue that the advent of popular music aesthetics and the observable shift in listening practices that highlights gnawa as entertainment has led to this third source of authenticity: the ability to engage an audience, most often demonstrated through commercial success or shows of virtuosity. This is exemplified by the respect accorded to Hamid al-Qasri. Qasri, who, until recently, was the gnawa musician in residence at the palace in Rabat, made a career for himself through television and other new media. As a musician, he aimed for a clear studio sound by using nylon instead of gut strings, amplification, and well-rehearsed ensembles to achieve tight performances. He has worked closely with jazz musicians on a huge variety of fusion projects. Some in the community of performers degrade his style and performance abilities, claiming that his wordplay and movement between unrelated songs demonstrate his lack of ritual knowledge. Other ritual leaders commend his virtuosic negotiation of contemporary aesthetic tastes.

Initially, I attempted to conceive of this ability to entertain as a second layer of performance practice, something differentiating between sacred and commercial or secular activity, but I came to realize that these ideas do not create a useful continuum. There is commercial activity present in the rituals of the most revered elders who eschew musical change. Simultaneously, the success of ritual, as measured by the instigation of healing trance, seems to be dependent not on a specific style of performance but on a performer's ability to connect with his audience. Trances can be vigorous in those rituals led by young musicians who learned from CDs, and I have witnessed possessions breaking out in the middle of large audiences at festivals that were so "commercial" that large banners advertising cell phone networks hung on each side of the stage. Some adepts are so sensitive to the music that they can fall into trance when they hear gnawa music played in television advertisements or on the news. Instead of focusing on the performer's intentions or his efforts to earn an income, I find it more fruitful to consider his approach to his audience. This places control over the experience in the hands of the listener or trancer. This is important, as it is the listener who supports favorite performers financially through hire or gifts and by recommending them to friends.

Now, the road to notoriety and respect can proceed through pious activity as a Muslim; performance that effectively represents an African heritage; or superstardom, virtuosity, and a legion of fans. These three very different self-identifications must, in reality, interact as an individual performer notes his strengths and embarks on a career as a professional gnawa musician. The first may concentrate on rituals and Islamic festivities, whereas the second can orient toward performance opportunities deemed "folkloric." The third, in turn, may lean toward work with fusion bands, on television, and collaboration with other genres' artists. Yet in reality, the same musician might choose to straddle elements of each of these strategies, drawing on each source by navigating the industry's opportunities: changing the autobiographical focus, dress, repertoire, or singing styles depending on the audience. Although authenticity is very much a negotiated performance of self, in this case a new mode of "claiming" is very much at play.

Authenticity as a singular and well-defined force within the community of musicians, producers, participants, fans, and ritual clients does not exist. Instead, the specter of authenticity is constantly hovering over performance. Its opacity, how authentic a performance is, is up for debate. If the answer is "not very" if the performer, context, audience, or musical content somehow fails to pass muster--the result can be catastrophic. In one ritual, a failure to fully "work the spirits" meant that Sidi Mimun, one of the most powerful spirits, jumped from a black cow into a m'allem. He turned vehemently angry and inconsolable and remained so for the rest of the evening. At another ritual I attended, the failure of a young m'allem to fully appease Sidi Hamu forced the client's family into hiring another group of musicians to redo the ritual later in the week, at a significant financial cost. These events are not cheap, and success is not guaranteed. Authenticity can become a sign of ability, a measure of authority within a ritual, or a signifier of a performer's control over and leadership of the ceremony. In this sense, authenticity is a practical matter, something proven. But the relationship between ritual success and anticipated future success is discursive, dependent on the opinions and beliefs of those who do the hiring, the listening, and the trancing. This authenticity is, therefore, more of a set of potential authenticities. African-ness, piety, and an ability to engage an audience made up of bodies and spirits coalesce in some way to give authority, necessarily deemed authentic by those in the room (including the unseen spirits), to the music and musicians. Where an inauthentic performance fails, an authentic one heals.

Performing Islam(s)

Martin Stokes writes that music "constructs trajectories rather than boundaries across space" (1994, 4). In the chapters that follow, I highlight how people use music to reify boundaries while simultaneously building trajectories across them. This research emphasizes the specific strategies of musicians, audiences, religious authorities, and the government, both successful and otherwise, to define themselves and their competition through musical practice and other sounded debate. I demonstrate how music and performance practice sit alongside verbal discourses to identify, create, and critique claims of identity. These claims are not only those of the individual performer aggrandizing his authenticity. Musical performance is also central to discourses regarding the gnawa population's piety, just as it is to wider conversations on what Islam is and should be, and what it should look and sound like, in Morocco. While I focus on the economic pressures of the music industry, I do not deny that these questions carry out long lives within the conversations held in cafés across Morocco's landscape. They poke at ideals of national or religious identity, getting especially tangled when those two begin to conflate, as they so often do. Discourses, both verbal and musical, live their lives in public or semi-public spaces in Morocco.

As Davide Panagia describes, the noise of the utterance, so central to the soundscape, is lost, undocumented. As a result, the sounds that constitute everyday life disappear, leading to the primacy of texted history. Since "the culture of popular classes is largely oral," historians are forced into writing the history of literate elites. His concern that "this approach seems undemocratic" sits along-side his assertion that democracy itself is "noisy" (Panagia 2009, 51). Arguments, debates, commercial markets, everyday experience as it passes, these aspects of life are noisy, defined, in some ways, by their sounds. These assertive debates cir-cle some of the country's most important issues and inundate the aural landscape of the most significant public spaces. As I go on to describe, the negotiation of boundaries (or drawing of trajectories) constitutes an important aspect of gnawa music and Islam more generally.

With the fairly recent increase in "sounded" histories (Corbin 1998; Ong 2000; Sterne 2002) and anthropologies (Porcello et al. 2010; Samuels et al. 2010; Weiner 2009), a growing portion of these texts address the Islamic world (see Gaffney 1994; Lee 1999; Hirschkind 2006 among others). The connections be-tween aurality (or orality) and Islam are striking. The stylistic and referential power of the recitation of the Qur'an shows throughout ethnomusicological scholarship (see Danielson 1987; Nelson 2001; Rasmussen 2010) and the import-ance of communal listening is central to works on music, ritual, and preach-ing (Gaffney 1994; Shannon 2003; Waugh 2005). Furthermore, one could argue a theological basis for an aural reading of history in Islamic societies from the institutionalized privileging of the aural over the visual.

While generalizations of a society's sensory priorities are easily scrutinized (see Sterne [2002, 17], regarding Ong [2000]), there are aspects of Islamic belief and practice that warrant such considerations. Educational systems based in rec-itation and memorization (Eickelman 1995), for example, imply a privileged sense of hearing or listening. As does the prevalence of the *hafez*, a Muslim who memo-rizes the Qur'an in its entirety by making use of poetic and aural elements of the text. Moreover, the contentious relationship between Islam (especially in its conservative reformist varieties) and religious iconography suggests a theological discomfort with visual representation. Perhaps most powerful, however, is the direct connection to the divine that aurality, or hearing, can give the Sufi adept. *Sama'* (listening) is one of the most important communal practices within many Sufi brotherhoods, holding a powerful and transformative potency. Through lis-tening, the adept might achieve *fna'*, or the "extinction" of the self, into the divine (Racy 2003; Waugh 2005). Just as Ong suggests in reference to Christianity, Islam closely associates the sonic with divinity.

Musical practices exist within these social and theological contexts. As Deb-orah Kapchan describes, "actively engaging in the Sufi liturgy allows the individ-ual to emerge in community" (2009, 21). Music and musical ritual, listening and embodiment, these are the aural and physical practices that create *suhba*, "friend-ship" or "community," even when the brotherhood (or sisterhood) is in a foreign land. Stokes reminds us that ethnicities "can never be understood outside of wider power relations in which they are embedded" (1994, 7). In Morocco, especially in the urban areas that constitute the basis of my research, these power relations involve religious fragmentation just as often as they establish ethnicity. The larger power relationships that Stokes references, however, span the boundaries between individual organizations. The interactions between groups can lead to social collaboration, but it often also results in competition and heated theological debate.

These debates, which invoke music in important ways, exist between religious practices deemed both within and outside of the "mainstream." Throughout these chapters, I describe gnawa ritual as being marginalized or otherwise contested. The practices that exist within the ritual involve interactions with spirits who exist fully within the Muslim worldview yet simultaneously sit outside of the institutionalized and top-down manifestations of Islam that most of the population conceives of as appropriate: the Islam of the state that is led by the king who is, according to the constitution, the "Commander of the Faithful" (see Waterbury 1970; Munson 1993). While professing to be Muslim, however, many in Morocco do not carry out the required or recommended practices that fully demonstrate piety, not only those who profess allegiance to or interest in specific communities and organizations. Just as many Christians in the United States do not attend weekly church services, many faithful Moroccan Muslims do not visit the mosque or pray on their own five times daily. This is despite the fact that certain activities, such as fasting during the holy month of Ramadan, are widely practiced thanks in part to informal conscription—social pressure from an overwhelming Muslim majority population. Further, restaurants like McDonalds that stay open during the daylight hours of Ramadan will forbid the sale of food to Muslims (or those who may appear to be Moroccan) due to legal ramifications of helping a Muslim break the fast. The practice of mainstream Islam can be a very public activity, even for those who do not participate in their professed faith privately or even for those who do not believe.

Various forms of Sufism or activities such as gnawa ritual participation are public acts of religious practice situated outside of this mainstream conception of Islam. I use the phrase *conception of* distinctly because the idea of a mainstream Islam does not match the practice of all who identify as normative Muslims, whatever that might mean in the country today. Further, a measure of majority Islam, religion as it is practiced by the most Moroccans, might very well show something far removed from the expectations of the top-down Islamic standards that are formally and informally sanctioned by state religious institutions. Therefore, when I refer to mainstream, institutional, or popular Islamic practice, I speak of this idea—the concept of what most Moroccan Muslims feel that they *should* do, though fewer actually *are* doing it—and not to the actual measurable religious practice of the population as a whole. The place of music within these public discourses in creating and reinforcing binaries between mainstream and marginalized forms of Islamic practice should not be underestimated.

Although global influences on religious practice (that is, fundamentalism, international Sufi networks) and musical activity (through the world music industry or tourism circuits, for example) are important for the continual development of the Moroccan music industry, festivals, and nationalist goals, most gnawa music comes from local artists and is consumed locally. Moroccan artists who perform at festivals or whose CDs are for sale at market stalls have rarely achieved the international reputations of groups like the two Master Musicians of Jajouka ensembles (see Schuyler 2000). The majority who make their livings through performances within Morocco and to Moroccans may be the most responsible for the aesthetic changes that I discuss in the following chapters. They are also the most susceptible to critique from their audiences and peers, as they commodify religious performance practices for local audiences who recognize the significance of relationships between new and older traditions and who understand the connotations at play.

Local concerns gain steam when the debates enter the realm of Islamic theology. As long recognized by past researchers, Islam in Morocco is a complex of local practices, making anthropological research into belief quite difficult (see Crawford and Newcomb 2013; see also foundational examples like Geertz 1971; Eickelman 1976; Rabinow 1977). Perspectives on the proper methods and traditions for demonstrating faith are born out of vigorous discourse and debates (Asad 1996; el-Zein 1977) that often include the appropriateness of specific music (and ritual) practice. Fueled by the intimate connections between "music" and dhikr, and the performativity of both, ritual is easily "translated" (Kapchan 2008) for noninitiated domestic and international listeners. Public discourse about groups like the *tijaniyya*, *'issawa*, hamadsha, and gnawa present examples of the ways in which these debates define brotherhoods and their constituent religious practices as appropriate or inappropriate, Muslim or not Muslim, and Sufi or not Sufi, often with little regard for each groups' opinions regarding its own ontology.

As Barth describes, polyethnic (or in this case, poly-religious) interaction forces each group to recognize each other's codes of conduct as different from its own (1970, 16). This contact between groups then leads to "the very foundations on which embracing social systems are built" (10), making interaction the basis by which populations define themselves in terms of each other. These debates surrounding musical and ritual practice, then, are a driving force behind the creation of boundaries. At the same time, these commodified musical forms, whether popular or ritual, incorporate elements associated with various groups, contesting those same boundaries at the behest of a performer's creativity or an audience member's request. In this way, religiously oriented musical practices in Morocco, as demonstrated by the gnawa ritual, both affirm a distinction between populations and transgress the very boundaries that those distinctions imply.

Public musical performance is, therefore, an important realm in which artists and authorities (political, religious, and commercial) create and transform identities. Donna Buchanan, following James Clifford, asserts that culture is "temporal, contested, and emergent." Her writing highlights individuals who are "always engaged in many activities and interpersonal relationships simultaneously"

(Buchanan 2006, xvii). These include social relationships (religious or ethnic communities), relationships with their own beliefs and religious perspectives (negotiating sacred and secular), their past (reconstructing tradition, nostalgia), and the world around them (interacting with national and global economic and political systems). The individuals contributing to emergent culture are those who "musick," to draw on Christopher Small's (1999) broad understanding of the term. Clients, clients' families, neighbors, non-gnawa musicians, producers, and fans all had clear and distinct perspectives on who the gnawa are and what they do. Some are supportive, others devoted. Many are dismissive, even antagonistic. Their opinions are based on a mix of experience and ideology, but the experiences and ideologies are as diverse as the individuals themselves. Furthermore, not only did the non-gnawa Moroccans I spoke to have vastly different levels of familiarity with the gnawa ritual, but gnawa leaders themselves rarely expressed identical ontologies and histories of their own community, questioning whether it can even be conceived of as a unified whole. The music, ritual, and belief structures all proved malleable, shifting or bending to new performance contexts and pressures. The narrative of this book follows the sound—the music—of the negotiation of authenticity, demand, and opportunity.

This book is organized in two large sections. The first, which continues through chapter 4, examines gnawa history and contemporary practice through various narratives of authenticity. Chapters 2 and 3 address the performative maintenance of African heritage and Islamic piety among gnawa practitioners. The marginalization resulting from a history in slavery has been important for both the insular nature of the ritual and the more recent outward expressions of inclusion and diversity across Morocco. Gnawa practices are potent and sacred, with power coming from somewhere unseen, hidden in the trees of the forest or the waters of the ocean. By critically examining this narrative, I open space for the alternatives permeating the community. Like much of Moroccan society, the vast majority the gnawa performers and listeners self-identify as Muslims. Piety is important to them, as is reconciling their interests in the "gnawa sciences" with their faith. By recognizing the possessing spirits as local or regional saints, and by identifying the goal of ritual as remembrance (dhikr) instead of spirit possession, this narrative speaks of ritual change, modern disruption, and irreverent spectacle. Chapter 4 outlines the pressures on young gnawa musicians embarking on a career in contemporary Morocco. The influences of the popular music industry provide new options for those looking to learn and advance. New ways of learning the gnawa repertoire, along with changing audience musical tastes, are bringing profound innovation to ceremonies and stages. Audience members hire young performers based not on their heritage or piety, their history or education, but because of how they sound and how they entertain their listeners in concerts (or on trains!). Their ability to move bodies implies a skill with moving spirits.

Chapter 5 operates as a pivot, a short interlude. In it, I look to the post-independence period through contemporary times with an emphasis on the role of gnawa music within popular culture. Early stars like Houcine Slaoui, Nass al-Ghiwane, and Jil Jilala of the 1950s through '70s created Morocco's first national popular music sound, one that included gnawa musical elements at its core and left an indelible influence on contemporary audience tastes. Simultaneously, my time spent performing with *malhun* and hamadsha ensembles gave me insights into the tremendous marketing power of including gnawa music within these and other non-gnawa genres. This circulation of musical influence opens doors for performers, but ritual performance practice also has to adapt as ceremonial musicians grapple with the demands of new clients and audiences, not to mention the spirits themselves.

The second section of this book focuses on how musicians and audiences navigate these changing influences, pressures, and tastes. Chapter 6 shows musicians' efforts at negotiating and appeasing their various audiences: clients in need of healing, family and friends looking for an evening of entertainment, and spirits building relationships with possessed bodies. Drawing on ethnographic research from Fez, Meknes, and the pilgrimage site of Sidi Ali, I show how gnawa musicians blend the boundaries between ritual and entertainment through musical innovation. Often at the behest of audiences, they perform a far more recent version of the ritual repertoire, adapt dance music rhythms into the ceremony's music, and highlight the presence of Aisha, a spirit adopted by the gnawa from the hamadsha spiritual tradition. The resulting dramatic ritual innovations are driven by this nexus of listener taste and performer creativity. They show performers reaching out to changing audiences and redefining authentic performance practice within the ritual.

Chapter 7 returns to the ritual ceremony, where gnawa musicians encounter their clients and audiences in new ways. As listeners and clients demand more spectacle and virtuosity, a new performance practice has taken hold. This type of playing, called *marsawiyya*, grows out of an adaptation of Moroccan popular music ideals and gnawa ritual needs. It quickly found favor across the country, largely overtaking regional variants. As it coincided with a rise in recording practices that fostered the development of a set of "hits," marsawiyya pushed many older songs out of use and instigated debates about appropriate musical and ritual repertoire across the community. In chapter 8, attention shifts to a wider lens of the country's festivalized heritage industry, where the gnawa exist as a dynamic symbol of national pride and inclusiveness, religious tolerance, peace, and diversity. The changes to performance practice that result from this increase in attention leave many in the gnawa community nostalgic for the previous generation's aesthetic and ideological tastes, for the values of a very different gnawa history and heritage. Elders like Mulay al-Tahir of Tamesluht, Aziz wuld Ba Blan of Fez, and 'Abd al-Latif Makhzumi of Marrakech reify older styles despite dwindling interest from audiences. Each engages the heritage industry differently. They question the "spectacle" of contemporary gnawa performances—in ritual and on stage—and instead give voice to an alternative, more local, version. By listening and performing gnawa music nostalgically, these practitioners strategically critique the broad definitions of "gnawa," "Sufism," and "Moroccan Islam" circulated by state heritage festivals.

These chapters describe discursively performed constructions of authenticity in gnawa music. By following contemporary performance practice, they move beyond previous attempts to situate the population within Morocco's complex Islamic ritual structures. The economic and social realities of these gnawa performers show individuals struggling to develop their talents, find meaningful work, live their lives according to their diverse understandings of appropriate piety, reverently honor their ancestors, honor saints and spirits, have fun, and heal others. Each performs *tgnawit*, his or her "gnawa-ness," accordingly. This marker of authenticity both comes from the community—as conferred by elders—and is created from the personal beliefs, histories, and goals of the individual. As it is increasingly untangled from traditional systems of learning, as seen with many in the newest generation of ritual leaders, the performance of authenticity embodies the present alongside the past, bringing gnawa musical and ritual power to new audiences on their own terms.

Notes

1. The Maghreb refers to northwest Africa and includes Morocco, Algeria, and Tunisia. Some scholars also include Mauritania and Libya. Most gnawa performers and ritual participants now self-identify as Moroccan, but there remains a sense of authenticity and pride connected to those performers who have darker skin or can otherwise connect their family histories to these regions to the south.

2. See Chimamanda Ngozi Adichie, "The Danger of a Single Story," TEDGlobal, July 2009, https://www.ted.com/talks/chimamanda_adichie_the_danger_of_a_single_story.

3. The musician who leads the ritual, called a mʻallem, is almost always a man. Some examples exist of women playing the hajhuj and leading ensembles in commercial settings, but they are the rare exception to the norm. One group of women assembled by ʻAbd al-Rahim Amrani of Fez performs on national television somewhat regularly, demonstrating that there is room for female voices within the genre. Their exceptionality as women, epitomized by their title of Bnat Gnawa (Gnawa Girls), is notable in performance and the exception to the rule. Roles that are generally fulfilled by women include the seer (*shuwwafa*), who diagnoses potential clients, and the muqaddima, who usually prepares and presides over ritual events for clients, hires musicians, directs the cooking and presentation of food to audience members, and cares for trancing bodies during the ritual. Because of this consistency, I refer to the mʻallem as a male, using "he" or "his," and the muqaddima as a female, using "she" or "her," throughout these pages. A majority of those who go into trance are women, and a study of their experiences as trancing bodies would be quite fruitful. As a man in this community, I did not have sufficient opportunity and access into those conversations to draw strong conclusions. For a one approach to this question, see Feriali (2009).

2 Defending Ritual Authority

*T*HE SMELL OF *rolled cigarettes mixed with* kif, *a type of ground cannabis, wafted through the outdoor air during a break in the action. The* gnawa *ensemble was squirreled away outside of a home in the Boujloud neighborhood of Fez. I remember the event well, as it was my first ritual ceremony. M'allem 'Abd al-Rzaq had invited me shortly after I began taking lessons with him. I was uncomfortable and hyperaware, worried that my recorder would disrupt the proceedings, worried too that my presence would be unwelcome. At this point, in 2007, I had never met this family or even been down this alley, let alone in the family's home for a sacred healing ritual. From the middle of the night until well after the sun rose the next morning, however, I was welcomed into the community. Two or three young men huddled me away during these breaks to, as far as I can tell, practice their English. Others warned me about what was going on: be careful, they would say. "Don't confuse this with Islam; it's just a thing we do here," they would later imply. In other moments, I would try to engage the musicians, but they were tougher. At this early stage, I did not know them. Plus, my* darija skills *(Morocco's local variant of spoken Arabic) were insufficient for catching the deep colloquialisms tossed about between long friends.*

The event was not 'Abd al-Rzaq's but was led by another local m'allem *whom I had previously met. His name was Gaga, and according to 'Abd al-Rzaq, he knew this family well. When the family hired a* muqaddima, *a woman to prepare the healing ceremony, they requested Gaga, despite her recommendations otherwise. As a backup in case of potential problems, the muqaddima asked that my teacher be present as well, and he took over during some of the more difficult and idiosyncratic musical segments of the long night. Over ten or so hours, we heard music for entertainment followed by pieces aligned with white spirits, blue ones, red ones, and so on through the local pantheon. Some continued for a while as men and women from around the room went into trances, possessed by these supernatural figures. Though they technically "fell" (tah) into trance, most simply stood and made their way over to the incense burner that sat in front of the musicians. One, however, was more surprisingly violent. He was in a folding chair in the back of the room, sitting next to me. It was three or four o'clock in the morning, and he had fallen asleep on the chair in front of him. Moroccan-style couches circled the space, hugging the walls, as in most of the region's living rooms. These chairs were for neighbors and friends who came to witness and participate in the evening. Usually they were fairly empty, as many young men who came and went spent most of their time outside,* smoking on the stoop and family and friends lounged on the couches. I, myself, was struggling to stay awake at the late hour, and seeing a young man sleeping next to me, perhaps eighteen years old and cozy in his hooded sweater, was not helping. The music rolled on as one woman, possessed, was swaying from side to side, bent at the hip in front of the musicians. As I watched my drowsy neighbor, feeling guilty for my jealousy, he too began to sway ever so subtly in his seat. Suddenly, his legs kicked out, throwing the chair that he was resting on across the room as he landed flat on his belly, hitting the tile floor hard. I sat in disbelief, trying to get out of the way as those around me grabbed him by the arms and dragged him over to the incense. They wafted it into his face for a few moments until he stood, also bent at the waist and with his hands clasped behind his back, still swaying. This, I was told, was the first time he was called to possession by a spirit. In the future, it should be gentler.

Hours later, the evening ended suddenly. The mood lightened over the course of the final segment as the sun rose. The musicians stopped, chanted their last blessings, and began to pack. The open living room was quickly full of small tables. Family members brought out bowls of chickpea soup (hummus) and children began to play, laughing. As if to show me that this was not over, though, the musicians brought a goat into the room, blessed it, and, with a "bismillah," cut its throat. The sacrifice was for the host, who sat in a chair in the middle of the room while we ate our breakfast soup. Musicians surrounded the woman and tapped her head, shoulders, and knees with the bloodied knife, requesting the blessings of her possessing spirit for the year to come. The goat's body was whisked away, taken to be stripped of its skin and butchered. Young girls with squeegees pushed the blood into the room's corner drain, cleaning the tile floor. The laughing and playing continued, the ensemble was paid, and we left.

I have always had a hard time figuring out what someone means in Morocco when talking about the gnawa. It is an identifier that gets used in so many ways to refer to this ambiguous community of performers and listeners, healers and patients. Sometimes the word references a history, invoking slavery, marginalization, and a subsequent rise in popularity. Other times it appears to cite those who provide a service, a localized music therapy. It can identify the musicians. Or it can encapsulate everyone involved: listeners, clients, family lines, performers, assistants, fans, and so on. Certain people used the word gnawa to refer, quietly and reverently, to the elders of their neighborhoods, the ones who had some sort of questionable power over the spirits that come and go, occasionally popping into and disrupting peoples' lives. Many talked about the gnawa as irreverent hucksters, charlatans who use fear to extract money from those who have insufficient faith in Allah's benevolence. In truth, the gnawa can be any or all of these things.

The gnawa community is large and growing rapidly. While older masters in their sixties, seventies, and eighties pass away, their music captures the imagination of new generations. Young boys commonly join the ensembles of older performers, helping out in any way that they can. Some take lessons, like a violin student might, while others sit alongside ensembles during rituals, beating out the rhythmic patterns on their knees and mouthing the words to the songs. Others look up videos of famous performers on YouTube or Facebook and get together with friends to learn how to mimic their favorites. When the time comes each summer for the Essaouira world music festival, one that features the music of the gnawa in collaboration with many American, European, and sub-Saharan African guests, groups of friends crowd onto buses and ride for hours. One bus trip that I took from Essaouira to Fez after the festival took sixteen hours, thanks to frequent engine problems. Because it was vastly oversold, many of the gnawa fans who had enjoyed the weekend's festival crammed onto the floor, filling the long central aisle and sitting cross-legged for the duration. Others hung out of the door for some fresh air as we wound through the mountain roads. These young fans are drawn to the music and dedicated to the gnawa, however they define the term. Some love the groovy ritual sounds that inspire their own possessing spirits, building a relationship or answering a calling. Some simply want to be stars, to learn to play the music and follow in the footsteps of the musicians that they see on satellite television and on CD inserts that cover the walls of music shops around the corner from their homes.

Even so, there remains a certain nostalgia for an earlier era despite the unquestionable power that fame, youth, and new media exert on contemporary religious life in Morocco. The past lives on, refracted through contemporary lenses that too often render it static, an unchanging precursor to the present. The descriptions of the tradition from interviews with *m'allemin* and listeners alike that inform the narratives that follow do this very thing; they pit a fixed past, whether remembered or imagined, against a problematic contemporary reality (see chap. 8). Gnawa history is an oral history, much of which is lost.[1] Whether a lamentation for something gone or a banner of continuity, tradition continues to inform gnawa music and the conflicting wealth of attitudes toward it. Even the most innovative performances feature iconic instruments or familiar melodic shapes. There is a respect for what came before that permeates this music. There is also, however, suspicion. The marginalization of previous centuries still boils to the fore when I discuss my work with non-gnawa Moroccans, even some who are sitting in the room watching a spouse fall into trance. This music is loved; it is a beacon of healing power, of communal identity. It is feared, powerful and mysterious. And it is hated, especially by those who see it pulling Muslim believers away from their faith and toward local superstition. Gnawa music sits at the center of the fight for Morocco's identity, its piety, and its social history. As such, these rituals and others that animate Sufism across the country serve many masters. Practitioners, fans, politicians, scholars, journalists, entrepreneurs, festival founders, and others pull these sounds into a wide variety of contexts and draw unexpected meanings from their performances. At the same time, some try to pull back. They attempt to reclaim the music and ritual in order to discipline these meanings.

This chapter and the next address the performative maintenance of identity and authenticity among gnawa practitioners. The marginalization resulting from a history in slavery has been important for both the insular nature of the ritual and the more recent outward expressions of inclusion and diversity across Morocco. I outline the gnawa ritual and analyze the role that practitioners and spirits play in developing two overlapping narratives of authenticity. Performance decisions from musicians and the discussions of journalists and scholars tell a narrative of history imbued with slavery, focusing on the mysterious strength of the gnawa over the spiritual realm, their power to incite possession and healing. Gnawa practices are potent and sacred, with power coming from somewhere unseen, hidden in the trees of the forest or the waters of the ocean. Furthermore, critically examining this common description of the gnawa and their ritual opens space for other competing versions that permeate the community.

The Gnawa Ritual

Gnawa rituals and beliefs center on the *lila* or *derdba*, two names for an all-night trance-based spirit possession ceremony. The event and its music engage the senses to incite possession trance in both paying clients and the invited family or friends who make up an audience of spectators. Colorful cloths and incense identify each group of spirits and invite and empower them to take full control of those who need healing. Most frequently, the healing is physical or emotional. In my experiences, ritual therapy centered on clients who suffered from respiratory or mental issues, though witnesses described instances of vanishing goiters and one client showed me an X-ray of her suddenly fused broken leg. This powerful manipulation of and relationship with *jnun* (spirits) and deceased Muslim saints, as well as the ability to cause clients to lose consciousness and enter trance, places the gnawa largely outside of mainstream Islam. This is despite their participation in state-sanctioned festivals and other projects celebrating the diversity of Islamic practice throughout Morocco. Hicham Aidi (2014) notes these projects as the most recent writer to explore the Essaouira Festival of World Music's political and social efforts toward inclusivity within an era of globalized Islam. Meanwhile, the gnawa population's history, embedded as it is with a sense of marginalization because of its past ties to slavery (see el Hamel 2013), remains significant despite its rising cache within Morocco's popular culture.

The impact of the gnawa's racial and spiritual outsider status has had a paradoxical effect on their place within contemporary Morocco. As Spadola (2014), Kapchan (2007), and others note, the gnawa are held up as a symbol of diversity within "Moroccan Islam," yet they provoke the ire of many Muslims with whom I spoke. While this may be a sign of Saudi Arabian religious and political influence, the sentiment extends beyond the white-robed and bearded men typically associated with that particular form of conservatism. At virtually every gnawa ritual that I attended during two years of fieldwork, at least one member of the audience, usually a man, would confide to me that this ritual practice must not be understood as true Islam, or even as Islam at all. In November 2010, one man explained to me how "this is Moroccan culture, but not Islam." He was caring for a woman who tranced throughout the evening event, who was requesting and receiving the blessings of the sacrifice to her spirit. He participated and believed in gnawa practice and power but did not want it confused with his religion. Often, the men paying for the rituals I attended did so only at the request of an ill wife and, even then, only after exhausting all other potential healing outlets, both conventional and traditional.

The sound and ritual content of gnawa practices provide source material for innovation within the popular music industry in Morocco, especially since independence. The music features semi-improvised sung phrases from the group's leader, called a m'allem (pl. m'allemin), punctuated by responses from the rest of the ensemble, the *drari*. The m'allem directs the ritual and chooses when and how to interact with possessing spirits. As he sings each song, he plays instrumental passages that rhythmically engage the overtaken trancer. The melodies of the *hajhuj* are generally oriented around a small number of pentatonic sets within the instrument's octave range, though some borrowed songs make use of other melodic influences.[2] The instrument is constructed much like an *ngoni* or banjo: a leather membrane stretched over a rectangular wooden body providing a resonator for three strings.[3] The gut strings, two of which extend the full length of the instrument while a shorter third string runs between them, are connected to the wooden neck with leather loops used for tuning. While striking the strings with his fingers using a technique similar to that of the down stroke used by "claw hammer" old-time banjo players, the m'allem accents certain notes by percussively hitting the skin membrane.

The rest of the ensemble claps and plays the *qaraqib*, large castanets made from two pieces of iron fastened at the bottom with a strip of leather. Most groups use between two and seven of these drari, sometimes called *qarqabi*, creating a loud blanket of rhythmic momentum as the songs elide and tempi increase. The word drari implies "those who are dependent," as in children. In the case of the members of a gnawa troupe, its use references the dependency between these ensemble members and the m'allem from whom they learn the art of gnawa performance and ritual. They also dance during the entertainment portion (*fraja*) and opening blessings of the ceremony. They may perform specialized trances, acting out motions appropriate to one or more of the possessing spirits as the night progresses. The content of these dances can include cutting one's arm, drinking boiling water, or covering oneself with dripping candle wax for Sidi Mimun, a particularly violent sub-Saharan spirit; eating raw eggs or meat for the *ghabawiyyin*, a set of spirits from the forest; or holding a Qur'an, using prayer beads, and chanting verses for Sidi Ibrahim. Following many of these specialized trances, the entranced dancer may accept monetary donations in exchange for the possessing spirit's *baraka* (supernatural blessing).[4] Drari can hold different roles within the ensemble and some eventually become m'allemin (see chap. 4). Throughout the event, they sing answers to the m'allem's verses and belt out the longer refrains.

The gnawa are a population of Moroccans who claim literal and spiritual lineage from the country's past slaves.[5] Between 1492, when the Iberian Peninsula returned to Catholic hands, and 1591, when the Moroccan empire claimed Timbuktu, the Kingdom of Morocco's slave trade shifted dramatically to the south, completing its control of trans-Saharan trade routes and fully opening the door for sub-Saharan slavery to replace lost trade for slaves from Europe. The new populations that came to Morocco from across the desert brought religious beliefs with them and, over time, fused them with new Islamic faith into a syncretic cosmology. Many of the newly arrived slaves were already Muslim, having converted before the arrival of the Moroccans. While this led to legal gymnastics as religious scholars struggled to justify the enslavement of fellow Muslims, something forbidden in the Qur'an (see el Hamel 2008, 247–48), it also resulted in the juxtapositions of spirits and saints and of rituals and practices from a wide range of geographic and spiritual influences. These fusions of Islamic and, in some cases, non-Islamic practices gave rise to the identity of the gnawa, a population that represents this history of encounter, marginalization, and ritual power across Morocco.

The lila ceremony sits firmly at the center of the tradition. The name means "night" and refers to a possession ritual that typically lasts from 10:00 p.m. until shortly after sunrise. There are other versions that are shorter or longer, including an 'ashiyya (lit. evening, pl. 'ashiyyat) that begins in the early evening and ends in the middle of the night. Many older gnawa participants remember ceremonies that extended multiple days, nostalgically reflecting on the loss of depth that they see plaguing contemporary practice.[6]

The event opens with performed musical entertainment, the fraja, or an outdoor procession called the 'ada. The order of these two segments differs across the country. In the area around Fez and Meknes, where I did much of my research, the 'ada loudly declaims the beginning of a ceremony. In Essaouira, Marrakech, and elsewhere, the ensemble finishes the fraja before getting up and going outside to process, using the 'ada to mark the opening of the possession segment, the main ceremonial context. Once the event moves outside for the 'ada, friends and family surround the ensemble and the person who needs healing. The m'allem and a trusted member of the drari beat out rhythms on two or three *tbal*, large drums slung over their shoulders. One or two drari beat out consistent accompanimental rhythmic patterns on the larger of these instruments. The m'allem, in turn, improvises rhythms and places accents to signal and interact with the rest of the dancing drari using the smallest tbal. He slowly speeds up the tempo, adding drama and excitement to the event. Ululations from women who fill the streets punctuate the sound of the tbal, the qaraqib, and the ensemble's hollered chants, which increase as the crowd grows. The 'ada can be a powerful spiritual moment; the client, who remains the focus of the event because of some spirit-caused malady, might fall to the dirt in the beginnings of a trance. When the music stops, the crowd yells its blessings—"Prayers and peace be upon the Messenger of God . . ."—and continues through the common invocation:

Al-sla wa al-salam 'ala rasul Allah
La jah illa jah sidna Muhammad
Allah ma' al-jah al-'ali

Prayers and peace be upon the Messenger of Allah
There is no other path than that of our Prophet
God is with [those who choose] *the righteous path*

A member of the ensemble may circle the crowd, offering dates and milk. At least one person, a musician or someone from the family, takes up a large candle and leads the group back into the household, having announced the ceremony to the neighborhood and welcomed the spirits. After the procession, the group prepares the ritual space, the *rahba*, for the trances that will follow. The vast majority of these events occur in households. During a *mussem* (pl. *muwasim*), a pilgrimage, ensembles or families may rent a space: an apartment, the basement of a hotel, or a garage will do. Otherwise it might be the central room of the family home. This space, with its tiled floor and walls and perhaps an open ceiling if it is a *dar* or *riyad* (two types of traditional homes in Morocco's old *medina* quarters), resonates with the sound of the qaraqib. The first songs bless the room and prepare those sitting around the room for what is to come. In Fez, the fraja follows, with the drari dancing intricate steps and formations, stomping patterns with their bare feet to accent the musical phrases from the hajhuj. The audience members sit, backs against the wall, and fill every corner of the space. Any couches adorning the borders of the room are full, with people squished in shoulder to shoulder. Adjacent rooms are likely also packed pretty tightly, perhaps one of which has been claimed by husbands and brothers who smoke kif and cigarettes while watching the dances. At this point, no one is trancing, though all are fully occupied. They are engaged in the musicians' movements or otherwise milling around preparing, distributing, or consuming tea and cookies.

Once the 'ada has announced the event to the neighborhood and the spirits have been invited, the *mluk* portion of the event begins. It contains eight parts, each dedicated to a specific spirit or set of spirits. These spirits, called mluk, come from a mixture of Islamic figures, historical saints, and jnun, a category of beings—like angels and humans—who appear throughout the Qur'an.[7] Most that appear in gnawa rituals are believed to be of African descent, figures that arrived alongside the slaves, brought from their shared past. Each of the eight sets of spirits is associated with a color, manifested in the bright cloths used to drape those who are in trance; an incense that feeds these spirits and saints; and a unique musical repertory. The relationships forged through possession with spirits are mutually beneficial and serve to mend or reinforce the link between possessing spirits or saints (often called mluk, literally "owners") and *maskun* (roughly, possessee).[8] Through music and trance, mluk are invited to fully overtake the maskun, appearing through trance (*jadba*) for the purpose of healing illness or providing a divine or supernatural blessing, baraka. Adepts are required to host a lila, complete with an accompanying animal sacrifice that happens before or after the event, once each year in order to maintain the relationship with the mluk. A failure to do so carries the threat of repercussions that most frequently manifest as harm to one's health, finances, family, or employment. This process of religious fusion is not unique to Morocco or the gnawa. Syncretic practices that are similar, but Afro-Catholic instead of Afro-Islamic, pervade Brazil, Cuba, and Haiti, for example, and similarly capture national imaginations in those countries (see Matory 2005, Largey 2006, Hagedorn 2001). The inclusion of jnun and acts of possession draw criticism from many Moroccans that the gnawa are not true Muslim believers and keep the gnawa outside mainstream conceptions of appropriate Islamic practice.

The Mluk during the Lila

The personalities of the mluk appear in two ways during a lila ceremony. First, each is known for his or her general character. The *shurfa'*, a name derived from *sharif*, are descendants of the Prophet Muhammad. They are noble, wear white, and are the first to appear in ceremonies in Fez. Many of the mluk also have specific behaviors and ritual practices. *Al-kuhl* spirits (led by Sidi Mimun) wear black and are considered to be both powerful and dangerous. When possessed, their adepts may use a knife, cutting repeatedly at their forearms. Gaga, a m'allem in Fez who is "owned" by one of these "black spirits," held his arm in front of me to show the many deep scars running across it from his wrist to his elbow. Lalla Malika loves to dance, so her portion of the lila has an uplifting party atmosphere. This is one of the only points where those who are not possessed join in, dancing alongside those who are deep in trance. Other figures are similarly known by the characteristics and behaviors of their adepts. Recognizing and fostering the presence of a spirit are some of the foremost responsibilities of the ritual leaders, the m'allem and the muqaddima. Their success in facilitating possession is necessary for the proper unfolding of the ceremony. Aside from hiring the mʻallem, the muqaddima directs the course of the ceremony alongside the ritual musicians. This role is most frequently, but not exclusively, carried out by an older woman who is generally the liaison between the host and the musicians. She maintains control over the entirety of the ceremony, including the preparation and distribution of food and the care of those who are maskun. She cares for and directs the usage of most ritual paraphernalia—the colored cloths, candles, sacrifice, and incense—over the course of the evening.

Each spirit's color shows in the clothing worn by individuals who hope or intend to become possessed during the ceremony. Although a woman who has a long relationship with Sidi Hamu may plan ahead and wear a bright-red *jallaba*, for example, the muqaddima comes prepared with a large bag of colored scarves that match each spirit. As individuals succumb to the spirits, they may stand and walk toward the musicians and incense or violently spasm to the floor. If they fall, the muqaddima and her assistants—or concerned family members sitting nearby—drag the limp body to the incense. The spirit feeds on the cloud of smoke floating up from the burner and, as the body rises again, the muqaddima will tie the appropriate colored scarf around the waist or cover the now dancing body with a brightly colored jallaba from the bag. Men or women in trance bend at the waist, sometimes with hands clasped behind their backs, and rock their heads up and down, swaying from side to side. The motion sends long hair flying as it gains ferocity and the arms loosen and flail. As trancing spirits take hold of the body, however, the wild motion syncs into a pattern. The body and the music come together to bridle the vigor of the moment. Songs elide and the music speeds up. The mʻallem focuses on the moving body in front of him. He cuts off the singing but nods to his drari, telling them to play more loudly, to clap even more sound from the qaraqib. The volume of the iron and the hajhuj makes the sound visceral, like a rock concert where you can feel your chest pound with the beat. The senses are overwhelmed in the moment, with the smells of incense and bodies stuffed into the enclosed space, food cooking in an attached kitchen, and smoke from cigarettes filling the air. In an especially intense moment, the mʻallem may stop the qaraqib and continue alone. The sudden change of musical texture exposes the virtuosic semi-improvisation on the hajhuj as the worn ears of listeners and spirits alike focus their attention. Then, catharsis arrives as the trancing body interrupts the pattern, swaying momentarily. The muqaddima or another assistant—who has been standing nearby, just in case—helps the person to a nearby seat as he or she surfaces from the experience.

In the past, according to elders, each person attending a ceremony may have a spirit, but such a relationship was not a requirement for being there. Those who were not maskun could (and can) still fully participate musically through clapping and chanting. They also have the option of assisting in simple tasks, such as the distribution of food or chairs or tending to the entrance to keep out unruly youth, those who have been drinking, or other potential unwelcome guests. Those who have a relationship with the spirits maintain similar roles until the music begins for their mluk and they fall into the trance state. In contemporary practice, a host of a lila event may have anywhere from one to all of the spirits. Traditionally, individuals would maintain one such relationship, but in most events that I have seen, the host would leave the room after each trance, returning with a new jallaba that was colored for the next set of spirits. She (many hosts and afflicted are women) would then enter into a new trance as the cycle continued. I was told by a number of m'allemin that this practice of trancing for each spirit is a recent trend.

Table 2.1 outlines the collection of spirits and their order through the progression of the lila ceremony in Fez. This is a skeletal overview since, as my experiences with many different m'allemin demonstrated, the content and order of the ceremony are not strict. There is a vast difference between how the progression of events deals with the male spirits and the female ones. With both sets, it is not always clear as to the existence of one definitive spirit or a group of supernatural beings that fall into a category. Therefore, Sidi Musa might be the Moses who appears in the Qur'an, parting the Red Sea to free the Hebrew slaves from the Egyptians. He may also be the spirit of a Moroccan saint who lived near the water, whose shrine sits on the Atlantic coast outside of the city of Salé, near Rabat. Or, according to yet other interpretations of the gnawa ritual pantheon, these "blue spirits" are supernatural beings with a special relationship to water who claim some relationship to, dependence on, or lineage from one of these two figures. The identities of these mluk are not set. Rather, they provide a venue for debate regarding gnawa theology, history, and relationship to Islam and Moroccan Sufism.

The appearance of the male spirits is strictly ordered. The specific order, however, varies from one region to another across the country. This can be seen by the various descriptions of the ritual ceremony that appear in scholarship completed in cities throughout Morocco (see Fuson 2009, 116, for an outline of Marrakech's ritual). The chain of songs, colors, and scents adjusts according to the coming and going of the segments' associated mluk. This order can become especially important for those who reside in or identify with specific cities. For example, m'allemin in Fez note that they begin with the 'ada procession. This encloses the entirety of the ceremony as part of the ritual instead of conceptualizing the fraja as a sort of prelude. Therefore, they sanctify the event as a whole, allowing them to claim a greater spiritual authenticity that lines up with their city, one that is commonly argued to be the cradle of religious life in Morocco. Marrakech's practitioners instead highlight the virtuosic music and dance of the fraja and its narrations of slavery in a way that posits the city more firmly, through performance, as the authentic geographic center of this sub-Saharan African tradition.

The female spirits (*al-nisa'*), unlike the male, are not strictly ordered. Furthermore, the inclusion of specific female spirits is not completely necessary.

Table 2.1. Chart of mluk names, sections, and general characteristics as explained by M'allem Abd al-Rzaq and as they generally appear in Fez.

Mluk	Color	Description and Prominent Figures
Al-Hawsawiyyin		*These first seven sets are primarily male*
Shurfa'	white	Noble, of holy lineage; Abd al-Qadr Jilani
Al-Kuhl	black	Powerful, often self-mutilating; Sidi Mimun; Ghumami
Sidi Musa	blue	Use of water during possession, including a dance while one of the drari balances a full bowl of water on his head; may refer to either a saint enshrined in Salé or the Moses who parted the Red Sea
Sidi Hamu	red	Butcher; red drink passed around the room and consumed by those in attendance
Buhala	multicolored	Wears a patchwork jallaba known as a *darbala*; considered to be "crazy" (*hamaq*) or possessed (*majnun*)
Mulay Ibrahim	green	Holy; trancing adept often holds the Qur'an or prayer beads and recites verses from the holy book; refers to either a local saint from near Marrakech or the Abraham who was willing to sacrifice his son Isaac
Ghabawiyyin	brown	Unknown spirits from the forest; slower, more powerful and secretive than most of the others; trancing adepts may hold candles close to their faces and clothing
Al-Nisa'		*The final spirits are primarily female and much more interchangeable than those listed above. The four most common in Fez's ceremonies are below.*
Lalla Malika	purple	Loves to dance, wealthy; the only point in the ritual where nontrancing members of the audience rise and dance along with those who are possessed
Lalla Rqiyya	brown	Not commonly included outside of Fez
Lalla Mira	yellow	Appears in ritual across the country
Lalla Aisha	black	The most powerful of the female spirits; includes music adapted from the hamadsha; lights are often turned off for the trance

Aside from Aisha, who to my knowledge now appears consistently throughout the country, the set of female spirits that appears in any given ritual is the result of an informal local negotiation. Certain cities have relationships with specific female figures: Fez's lilat often include Lalla Arabiyya, who has a shrine dedicated to her memory in the old city. A host might have a relationship with a specific spirit that he or she can request ahead of time. Or certain participants may simply enjoy the music associated with one of the women and may request their inclusion in the ceremony. The order of these spirits is somewhat inconsistent, but the four in Table 2.1 appear as listed in most ceremonies in Fez.

Claiming and Defending Tgnawit

The ritual and commercial success of a contemporary gnawa m'allem depends on his possession of an ambiguous trait, *tgnawit*. The word most directly translates to "gnawa-ness." Timothy Fuson notes the linguistic similarity between tgnawit and, as an example, *tnajjarit* (carpentry). Where carpentry comes from the root "carpenter," tgnawit derives from "gnawi," thus insinuating the artistic and technical craft of the practitioner (2009, 17–18). Following this etymology, as a master carpenter builds a strong and trustworthy wooden structure, the musician in possession of tgnawit is able to successfully enact, maintain, and navigate a powerful ritual ceremony. He who claims tgnawit must have proven his legitimacy through a demonstration of requisite spiritual knowledge, technical ability, and artistry. Descriptions abound within the community of ritual juries, events where the local masters gathered to judge a potential new m'allem. Abdelhafid Chlyeh (1998) quotes one such trainee, Abdelatif, at length as he recounts his own anxiety with the approach of just such an event.[9] Georges Lapassade, discussing Essaouira, explains that a new m'allem can assert his expertise through a "thèse pratique de gnaoua" (1976, 202). M'allem Aziz wuld Ba Blan of Fez described the local system to me in a conversation one evening in a way that sounded similar to the professional hierarchies of Sufi brotherhoods like Fez's *'issawa* and *hamadsha* troupes. He remembered a local *blan* or *blani*, figures who had authority over other m'allemin in the city. This leader, along with a cohort of other elders, held sway over the decision to approve or reject a potential new m'allem's claim of mastery after observing him in a ritual demonstration. By controlling the decision-making process and the power to grant or reject claims to tgnawit, elders maintained the authority over the sound of the ritual and its priorities. Embedded within the ceremony and music were references to communal history and identity, as well as Muslim values. This system effectively balanced local religious practice and a heritage of otherness.

A variety of contemporary pressures, many of which are economic, have whittled away at this centralized authority. Most importantly, the juried exhibition of learned musical skill and spiritual knowledge that Abdelatif and Aziz remember so vividly no longer exists. The bestowal of tgnawit on prospective m'allemin has ceased to be a systematic act carried out by the community. Claiming authority and authenticity as a ritual leader now happens in a sort of Wild West atmosphere, conjuring images of medicine shows. Performers are deemed effective by the community insofar as they demonstrate their effectiveness, but different audiences and leaders value instrumental technique, vocal power, control of the spirits, the ability to enact trance, the simple knowledge of the musical repertoire, or other elements of "gnawa-ness" more than others. This leads to a great deal of confusion for potential clients, especially those who are unfamiliar with the local community. Perhaps they moved or learned only recently that a family member's ailment is from a spiritual encounter that requires the therapeutic treatment of a gnawa ritual. How do you choose who should organize and lead your family's ceremony?

Despite the loss of a centralized "graduation" from apprenticeship to professional life, tgnawit continues to exist as a discursively applied honor. If the respected m'allemin of a city or region know and approve of the skills of a younger performer, it will be a boon for his professional opportunities. Recommendations mean something and carry weight across the country. In this way, social networks remain important. Performances at pilgrimage sites, like the ones in Sidi Ali that inform later chapters, provide chances for a younger performer to be seen and heard by many of these elder musicians from around the country. Increasingly, there is another side to this discursive version of tgnawit. It is not only the community of well-regarded gnawa musicians who can influence the careers of new m'allemin. A second overlapping network of listeners make their own recommendations to potential clients. These listeners have a wide range of experience with the gnawa: some may be nonmusician family members or close friends who participate within the gnawa community. They may work hard to maintain its traditions. Others, however, listen to the latest recordings from those musicians who record widely within the music industry, basing their aesthetic tastes and opinions on a small handful of YouTube recordings and television performances. As commercial recordings and performance opportunities continue to bring new audiences into the ceremonies, the performance practices and ritual techniques that these clients are looking for become influential. M'allemin who adjust for these new aesthetic trends will find more work among this growing client base and, without a centralized system of maintaining a musical repertoire and ritual progression, stylistic change will spread.

Where tgnawit was once exclusively demonstrated and maintained by a few central figures within any given region, it is now subject to wide interpretation. This has led to emphatic debates about the spectacle of possession, the relationship between gnawa music and Islam, the appropriateness of hybrid performances in commercial settings, the legitimacy of new musical styles in ritual, and the effectiveness of learning the "gnawa sciences" (*'ulum al-gnawiyya*) without the close relationship to a master that comes from being an apprentice. These concerns, driven by the changes in the structure of the community, thread the chapters that follow. Claiming, proving, and maintaining one's own tgnawit, one's ritual authority, is a primary factor in the success of a musician's career. The demonstration of it takes as many forms as there are audience tastes. Some musicians prioritize their lineage, even their dark skin tones, to show authenticity through a closeness to the history of slavery and sub-Saharan Africa. Others emphasize their piety, questioning fellow musicians who do not pray or proudly sharing photos from their pilgrimage to Mecca.[10] As the chapters that follow show, these two markers of gnawa identity have been joined, even supplanted in some cases, by a new element of tgnawit: the ability to engage listeners in ritual and adapt to their aesthetic needs and wants. Clients and others who are in the room during a ceremony listen widely, and they want musicians to reflect their own tastes. Some yearn for the austere performances of renowned elders who work hard to maintain an old sound, an aura of tradition. Others hear gnawa music in pop songs on the radio and watch as famed studio musicians perform on satellite television. They need the crisp virtuosity of this sound to engage with or fall into the music. The heaviness of an older style would fail them and, in turn, their possessing spirit. With different markets come new performance styles and a diversification of what gnawa music sounds like.

This brings a certain fluidity to the meaning of tgnawit. There is no clear technical and widely understood definition. What qualifies as authentic or authoritative practice within a ceremony differs widely as musical tastes and ritual preferences vary among clients, audiences, and even spirits. One of the most common criticisms of contemporary ritual practice that I heard during conversations with m'allemin was that many rituals are carried out by musicians who have no tgnawit at all. If you lack it, you can still market yourself and find work. This declamation serves a dual purpose. First, it gives a meaning to tgnawit itself, even if that meaning is vague. When a member of the community references an absence of ability or knowledge in a m'allem, she is pointing to an element of legitimacy that is missing. Perhaps the m'allem was self-taught, avoiding the apprenticeship system, or left his master too early. The fact that the m'allem found a client demonstrates the tricky nature of determining tgnawit. At least one family decided that he possessed it and gave him the important responsibility of caring for the therapeutic healing of a loved one. Criticisms of other m'allemin on the basis of the possession of tgnawit have a second purpose, one born of competition. As the debates that percolate through the community nuance the meaning of ritual authority and authenticity, they also impact the reputations of the figures being discussed. Those who can demand authority on the topic raise their own status while those who act independently of extant systems or outside of expectations must overcome the criticisms levied against them. In this way, tgnawit exists "in the eye of the beholder," so to speak.

I hesitate to claim that ritual legitimacy parallels the way that a politician builds a voter base for a local election, courting important figures within the area and convincing people that she would be good for a potential job. Two major points supersede this reading. First, while being a gnawa practitioner has become a potential occupation over the past decades, much to the dismay of some, it is still also a calling. The job, if one can call it that, involves religious obligations. A m'allem, or any other member of the community of ritual practitioners, is taking on this work to maintain a relationship with one or more spirits. The pay can be lucrative for the biggest stars, but for most, the work is hard and the hours long. The dreams are not always for fame and fortune: gnawa m'allemin across the country use their income to feed their families and help out the drari who fill their ensembles. Second, tgnawit is something demonstrated. While the debates inform potential clients as they make decisions about who should lead their needed ritual, the discursive pressures succumb to performed realities. If a young m'allem takes a job—perhaps charging less or working for free to help convince a client to give him a chance—and the ceremony is wildly successful, his tgnawit grows. The respect, the demonstrated legitimacy, may only spread through the neighborhood, but leading a ritual full of powerful trance and effective healing can lead to a slightly wider circle of potential clients. Perhaps unfairly, however, news of demonstrated failure spreads much more quickly and opens that performer to criticism. Tgnawit must be presented, argued for, and defended by a m'allem and his supporters. It appears prominently and frequently throughout casual discussions, which occasionally become heated, about performers, performative decisions, the history of the gnawa, and the religious implications of being gnawi. These debates about tgnawit form an arena of discourse in which m'allemin and knowledgeable gnawa lovers (*muhibbin*) craft the meanings of their self-identification and practices.

The next chapter focuses on two general conceptions of tgnawit. One invokes an African ahistorical reading of the music and ritual while the other places legitimacy firmly within Islamic practice in Morocco, linking the gnawa to local Sufism. These two conceptions of gnawa history and religious identity demonstrate very different ideas of authenticity and authority. Most m'allemin consider the gnawa identity as some combination of these two potential sources, yet all of those with whom I spoke explicitly highlighted one or the other in their own self-identification, setting themselves somewhere on an imagined continuum between them. In actual ritual activity, individual m'allemin draw from both sources—African heritage and Islamic piety—to emphasize their own effective tgnawit. They do so in varying ways for different audiences, always aware of who is listening and what the performance's purpose is. In this way, the m'allem and his ensemble orient themselves strategically within the professional pressures of a life as a musician, an idea that I return to in later chapters. M'allemin intentionally demonstrate their identities and credentials through the musical performance, layering elements of their history, faith, and dedication to the "gnawa sciences" to create the most broad, deep, and effective version of their own legitimacy that they can reasonably defend.

Because the possession of, and ability to publicly demonstrate, tgnawit is essential to professional success as gnawa practitioner, m'allemin emphasize experiences that demonstrate their possession of one source or the other. This theme returns in chapters 5, 6, and 7, as performers increasingly utilize a third source of potential ritual authority: the ability to effectively engage an audience, both those participating in ritual for healing reasons and those who are listening for their own entertainment. As listeners' and potential clients' tastes shift and they increasingly wish to hear ritual music that more closely incorporates the aesthetics of popular music, they look for performers who borrow songs and performance styles from Morocco's wider musical soundscape. In this way, musical virtuosity and commercial success increasingly contribute to listeners' values regarding performers, leading to a redefinition of tgnawit that allows virtuosity and success to stand as valid performable sources of authentic ritual performance practice. In turn, as I describe later, the musical content of the ritual shifts to account for changing listener expectations. To best understand how these different orientations of tgnawit operate in the ceremony, I move to a discussion of the segments of the lila ceremony itself.

Notes

1. Because my work was primarily ethnographic in nature, I did not attend to a history or historiography of the gnawa. That remains a largely unaddressed area, though an arduous one, that would benefit from scholarly attention.

2. The origins of these three names are debatable. *Ginbri*, *gimbri*, or *guembri* is common in the literature about the gnawa, but because there are other instruments that share this term, I will use hajhuj here. It is the term most common in Fez, where I did much of my fieldwork.

3. The ngoni is an instrument from West Africa, most commonly associated with the *griot* traditions of praise singing based there. See Charry (1996) for details on the organological relationships between these instruments throughout northwest and west Africa.

4. Baraka is typically considered "divine" blessing, but the unclear nature and motives of the spirits from the gnawa pantheon, and the marginalization that results from their participation in the ritual, gives me reason to use "supernatural" here instead. The baraka received from Sufi ceremonies, pilgrimages to tombs and shrines, the king of Morocco, or other proximity to holy figures maps out identically to the baraka found in gnawa ceremonies, though the gnawa's perceived sub-Saharan origins and other religious, social, and economic factors give fodder to critics who deride their baraka as ominous, evil, or witchcraft. See Eickelman (1976) and Crapanzano (1981) for more on the logic of baraka in Moroccan spirituality.

5. The following description of the gnawa represents the most commonly narrated history, by both m'allemin and popular sources, such as the journalism that precedes the annual Essaouira festival.

6. Randy Weston, an American jazz piano player, also remembers a longer ceremony. In his autobiography, he recounts a memory of his first lila experience, one that took place over multiple nights in 1969 (Weston and Jenkins 2010, 175).

7. For example: Qur'an 15:27, 114:6, and Surat 72, titled "al-Jinn."

8. The term *maskun* derives from the Arabic verb "to live" or "to reside." It is used to identify an occupied residence, as in an apartment that has a tenant. A vacant apartment would be "not maskun" (*mamaskunsh*) just as is a person who does not have a relationship

with a gnawa spirit. The use of "residence" as a central conception of the relationship between spirit and human strengthens the long-term implications of gnawa spirit possession.

9. The quoted history makes up the entirety of the chapter titled "Abdelatif."

10. The pilgrimage to Mecca, called the *hajj*, is one of the pillars of Islam but is not required of all Muslims. It is something to be worked toward. Some gnawa musicians, like Aziz wuld Ba Blan of Fez, have made this pilgrimage.

3 African Routes and Sufi Roots

Al-sla wa al-salam ʿala rasul allah . . .
Blessings and peace be upon the Messenger of Allah . . .

THE MEMBERS OF Mʿallem ʿAbd al-Kabir Marshan's ensemble were standing in a wide circle. We were in the basement of an empty hotel in Mulay Abdullah, a small town in the mountains outside of Marrakech. It was midday; the sun was still shining even though rain threatened to come through the open center of the building. A young boy, a member of the group, held the horns of one of the three goats that waited alongside the far blue wall.

The previous day, I had gone to Marrakech's Djmaʿ al-Fnaʾ, the large market square that hosts herbalists, snake charmers, trained monkeys, and salesmen of all types throughout the day. Though gnawa *musicians doing acrobatics for domestic and international tourists alike continue to use this space to gather clients, they now mostly pose with tourists for photos. I wanted to know who these street musicians were and whether they were associated with* mʿallemin *or considered rogue charlatans, as they often are in Fez. This is how I met Rashid. After convincing him that, no, I did not need my photo taken, he quickly invited me to join his troupe on a trip to the nearby town for a ceremony. I accepted and met the group the next morning. We spent the vast majority of the long day waiting, sitting on a comfortable balcony, drinking tea and smoking. Rashid lounged across some cushions, while other group members sat in plastic chairs, chatting and sleeping. Some members occasionally checked in with everyone else, mostly helping with the afternoon project—stringing a tarp over the open ceiling. I assumed that this was for some ritual purpose until later, when it rained and I realized that certain ritual needs—like staying dry—were far more basic.*

Mʿallem ʿAbd al-Kabir and his son Hicham had called his group, the clients, and the clients' guests to the hotel's first floor. Small candles were burning on a plate in the center of the room, surrounded by rose water bottles with holes punched in the caps. The men began chanting invocations as they pulled the first ram to the middle and rolled it onto its back. Next to me, one of the guests, a relative visiting from France, was recording a video on her camera. I also had my video camera going. They held the animal's legs and swept a large knife across its neck, just as I had seen when I had assisted with the ʿAid al-Kabir celebrations that end the month of Ramadan a few times before and since. Letting go, the goat stood and started to walk across the room before getting woozy from the loss of blood. It staggered to one side and fell against a post before it spasmed and passed away, blood pooling on the floor. M'allem 'Abd al-Kabir walked through the room shaking a rose water bottle, spraying it at the circle of people and the animal on the floor. The boy pulled the second animal to the center, and Hicham began the process again.

A woman, the muqaddima, *recited a litany of blessings over the three animals, punctuated by "amin" (amen) from the group. The ensemble members wore their "street" clothes, some with rolled up pants and barefoot so as to keep their shoes clean, as they worked with the animals. Those in the circle held their hands out, palms up, joining the invocations. The boy toed one of the goats, which was still kicking slowly. Hicham walked into my video frame holding a 200 dirham note in his hand, leading a new blessing that was followed by another litany chanted by the group. An older woman, sitting on a box on the side of the room, outstretched her arms to receive the blessing. Another in a series of sung chants, each different from the last, interrupted the recitation.*

The m'allem returned with a chicken, asking the young boy to bring the incense burner closer. He held the flapping chicken above it and then down on the floor, where he sacrificed it and splashed the bird with rose water. The flapping continued through another chant, this one accompanied by rhythmic clapping. The repeating "amin" from the group grew stronger. The French guest gave another 200 dirhams, prompting another chant. The older woman asked for more energy and clapping, and the group obliged, returning to the invocation with more vigor. In Mulay Abdullah, a pilgrimage site for many in the gnawa community around Marrakech, M'allem 'Abd al-Kabir Marshan and his ensemble sacrificed three goats and a chicken in the basement of a small hotel to open the ritual evening that was to follow. This dbiha, *this sacrifice, was a gift from the client to her spirits, and it was a large gift at that.*

M'allem 'Abd al-Kabir, in a later interview back in Marrakech, placed himself within a firmly sub-Saharan African tradition through his childhood wet nurse, a dark-skinned black woman from West Africa. His early career began as a popular music singer, a performer of taqtuqa, *a local dance style. Some of his DVDs were on sale in the CD stalls around the market square. But the draw of gnawa history, ceremony, and music, and the transfer of* tgnawit *that came from his wet nurse, pulled him toward the ritual tradition. Just as the blood of the sacrifice empowered the ceremony, it was milk that nourished him and brought him into a lineage of slavery and spiritual authority. His son, an excellent m'allem in his own right and a stand-in for his father during the long overnight ceremonies, solidifies the lineage, extending the connection through a new generation. The line to sub-Saharan Africa—to a genealogical tgnawit—goes through both blood and milk.*

Performing an African identity

This chapter addresses the distance between discursive accounts of Muslim and African versions of tgnawit and demonstrates how each is performed. Musicians from across the terrain of tgnawit draw on both within their ritual work, and each negotiates his individualized position between them by incorporating performance practices, professional values, religious sensibilities, and aesthetic tastes in unique ways. My intent here is to pull apart the debates and pragmatic forces that influence these performative decisions. Contrasting sources of tgnawit authenticity inform individual iterations of gnawa performance. I argue that highlighting one's own source of tgnawit is an act of self-identification that invokes personal history, religious ideology, and aesthetic taste. By pointing at the differences between these two senses of tgnawit, I do not mean to imply that they are mutually exclusive. It is, however, common for certain groups to prioritize one or the other. For instance, a group that aims to orient and project itself as especially African will often accentuate its virtuosity in performing the professional predefined dances and acrobatics that constitute certain ritual segments, especially those that tell the story of the gnawa's history of slavery.

The gnawa repertoire includes a number of references to the past, both as slavery and as Islamic spirituality. Lyrical content has especially become a focal point of scholarship as it provides a distinct source of direct referential discourse on the past. By explicitly noting transcribed lyrics and analyzing them with an eye for places, peoples, and languages from sub-Saharan Africa, scholars construct a defense for the common narrative of gnawa that heightens the place of slavery. Chouki El Hamel (2008), a historian, does this most directly by going so far as to compare gnawa lyrics to those of the blues in America. He identifies moments in songs that, like the blues, maintain a collective memory. They create a repository that directly connects a marginalized past to a performed present. This strategy of aligning the gnawa alongside African American musical traditions appears throughout journalistic scholarship as well (see Kirchgassner 2007 for one sample). It is a compelling way to orient the gnawa for foreign audiences that are unfamiliar with the histories of Morocco, sub-Saharan Africa, or Islam.

These comparisons with African American musical history are not without merit, as the gnawa repertoire continually calls up an imagined memory of an ancestral home. For example, El Hamel notes that there are a number of songs, dances, and chants that "are claimed and used by the *gnawa* as the means to access the spiritual realm" (2008, 244). He references the lyrics of "Lalla Yamma" (Lady Mother), which sing the names of specific ethnicities, citing them as part of a gnawa lineage, as a "Lady Mother." There are calls for the Fulani (of Niger), the Bambarawi (Bambara, of Mali), the Sudani (generic term for the Sudan or Sahel, the region spanning from modern-day Sudan to Mauritania), and the Hawsawi (the Hausa, also of Niger).[1] Specific calls to these four regions, language groups, or ethnicities occur throughout the opening segment of the gnawa ceremony. The seven major groups of spirits are even categorized together by many artists as "al-hawsawiyyin," those from Hausaland.[2] Their histories, though, are imprecise, as is the geographic knowledge of the mʿallemin who use the terms. The uses of Fulani, Bambara, Sudani, and Hausa all emphasize an understanding of the diverse histories from which the gnawa supposedly came, but they also illuminate the storied aspects of such a performed discourse. Taken together, references to these four groups suggest the sub-Saharan origins of the gnawa and their spirits, but they are imprecise and even interchangeable symbols of an unknown past dislodged from the specific geographic location of their referents. This obscurity mirrors the generalized nature of the gnawa history narrative more broadly. Where recent generations' accounts of ritual change point to individuals who influenced it, the longer arc of the community's history is embedded within the metaphors of song lyrics and dance movements. The expanding ambiguity of a term like *Bambara*, which may reference a West African deity, a religious belief system, an ethnolinguistic group, a small geographic region, or even the larger region of the Sahel, is one example of the difficulty of pinpointing a history. Each definition bubbles up into various discussions about the gnawa and their ritual history, pointing to the discursive power of these uncertainties. They can be used to reinforce narratives of authenticity just as they can contradict others, making this space and the metaphors that enact them within ritual powerful tools for building and maintaining one's authority and authenticity.

Stories that connect the gnawa to their ambiguous past abound, retold again and again in order to firmly buttress this trans-Saharan link. For instance, M'allem 'Abd al-Rzaq told me of a trip he had taken to Mali for a festival. When he performed "Vangara Vangara," the Bambara speakers in the audience understood the lyrics. This is one of the songs that contain words whose specific meanings are unknown to the gnawa—they exist as artifacts from this past. The texts are said to come from sub-Saharan Africa, brought to Morocco with the forced migrations, and identify explicit points of historic connection to the "motherland." Some of these mysterious words sing of unknown places or individuals; others are simply interjections. "Vangara" is a close approximation of "Bambara," linking the two words phonetically, and while 'Abd al-Rzaq could not recount to me the exact lyrics that were understood (or what his sub-Saharan listeners said they meant), the importance of his story was that, first, audiences understood them and, second, in his interpretation, these lyrics demonstrate this link to sub-Saharan communities. Many such tales exist, and performers pass them around frequently, almost as if to reaffirm their history. While these linguistic vestiges and ethnic group names appear throughout the gnawa repertoire, they are particularly concentrated in the *fraja* portion of the ritual event. These lyric references to sub-Saharan Africa, and by association, to the history of trans-Saharan slavery, pepper one particular suite: the "Awlad Bambara" (Children of Bambara). Again, Bambara is taken generically as either the entire Sahel region or the spiritual deity prominent in West Africa, and the gnawa, as the children of Bambara, are members of a lineage that links directly back there.

It is here that the gnawa most directly perform their history as sub-Saharan Africans. Not only do lyrics contain these explicit images of migration, yearning to return (El Hamel 2008, 247–48), and inequality (Fuson 2009, 281), but dances also enact the same experiences throughout the fraja. As this portion of the event provides an opportunity for the performers to emphasize their training, it features acrobatics, difficult synchronization of rhythmic clapping or foot stomping, and demonstrative choreography. The acrobatics include spins, jumps, and ducking in pairs or groups, all aligned with the music coming from the *hajhuj*. *Drari* perform their history of forced work in the fields or military servitude as they mime agricultural gestures or carry imagined guns. Upon questioning, no m'allem was able to identify a point in time when these danced motions appeared in the fraja, nor did anyone articulate a history of this segment's codification. This is unlike the portion of the ceremony that follows; the music that animates the *mluk* possessions has changed both recently and rapidly according to shifting audience demands, as described in the chapters that follow.

Many within and outside of the contemporary gnawa community highlight this continued relationship between the ritual and slavery. A dark skin color and questionable spiritual associations pushed the gnawa into the margins of Moroccan social life. The world music industry and music festivals now bring a great deal of attention to the sounds and content of gnawa rituals, but they remain problematic for many within the country. Even those who attend rituals are not always particularly happy about being there. For conservative Muslims, gnawa rituals become a therapy of last resort, something to be undertaken only after all other options—local or Western—have been utterly exhausted. Yet the connection to marginalization and slavery is weaker now than it was as Moroccans from all walks enter into the community. While genetic history and a dark skin color are not the only markers of tgnawit, they remain powerful symbols of authenticity. Connecting oneself to sub-Saharan Africa or the experience of slavery remains common, especially in the age of the music business, festival tourism, and the journalism and scholarship that remarks on both. Deborah Kapchan writes:

> Today not all Gnawa have a history in slavery (due to apprenticeships by non-Gnawa), yet this part of their past remains prominent in representations by scholars (Pâques 1991), music producers, and only sometimes by the Gnawa themselves. Foregrounding the history of Gnawa slavery links them to the larger African diaspora. . . . Of course one is never actually liberated of or by the spirits in Gnawa ceremonies, as the spirits are permanent inhabitants of their hosts. In the spiraling of *tgnawit* into the world music market, however, trance is represented more as a medium of liberation than a symbol of possession. (2007, 23)

This perceived liberation that is so often linked to the notion of trance by outsiders counters actual gnawa practice. Since the relationship between the individual and the mluk is one that extends throughout life, liberation is, in a sense, an inappropriate metaphor for gnawa trance. This is despite the sense of relief among participants who remove the weight of a displeased mluk (Feriali 2009, 87). It falls closer, however, to a sense of cooperation. As Kapchan argues here, the liberation-via-trance that appears in world music representations of the gnawa is aligned with slavery and the African diaspora, tying the ritual's music to the larger world of internationally distributed commercial musical products, a line of inquiry that her research follows closely. What Kapchan also notes is the importance of the trance, or at least the idea of trance, in public performance contexts.

Different segments of the ceremony, different aural components of the sound of the event, different texts, behaviors, and practices all direct the attention of the musicians, audiences, participants, detractors, and scholars toward the representation of "Africa." The continent is made present, enacted through the arts and healing practices, even embedded into these sounded practices. The performance is of a remembered Africa, what Richard Jankowsky refers to as "the idea of Africa" (2010, 199; see also Ebron 2002). In his book on the *stambeli* of Tunisia, a population that shares a number of characteristics with the gnawa, Jankowsky identifies specific elements of ceremony, language, music, and theology that connect those in Tunisia to possible historical ancestors, groups in sub-Saharan Africa (mostly in the Sahel region) who partake in similar activities today. He orients the stambeli as "African" by linking them with past and present relatives, creating a sort of family tree based on ritual practices and linguistic relationships (see also Pâques 1964). Few solidify these networks of performed culture through the clear and precise review of recent ethnographic literature that Jankowsky provides. The vast majority of his observations apply to both groups, the gnawa and the stambeli, and a replication of his analysis is not my aim here. What is more intriguing, and deserves attention within Morocco and the relevant international world music economic systems, is the performance or presentation of the idea of Africa, African history, African religion, and the slave trade.

I wish to underscore here the many ways in which the presentation of Africa in gnawa performance relates to the self-identification of the gnawa as Sufi Muslim. I follow the common criticisms drawn against the gnawa from external domestic sources and the processes by which some gnawa themselves strategically distance their music from Islam. There is a wealth of scholarship on the commercialization and commercial representation of the gnawa and similar groups when beset by global interests (see Kapchan 2007; Sum 2010), and potential global opportunities are certainly powerful influences on any musician's self-representation. Here, though, I hope to outline domestic concerns. While I reference commercial "temptations" like money and fame, I see these forces as local—pressures and potentials that have an impact on individual artists' lives. Instead of looking outward, I hope to emphasize the locality of these decisions, these representations, and the ways in which the opportunities presented to a few musicians might have an effect on, and are interpreted by, other members of the domestic community.

Similarly, the presentation of "African-ness" is useful when one wishes to emphasize or impose an "otherness" on the gnawa. This can be an intentional strategy, in international festivals for non-Muslim audiences or even in presentations for middle-class Moroccan youth, for example. It can also be part of an effort to further marginalize the gnawa, as many Moroccans attempt to clarify their own position as "mainstream" Muslims by saying things like "that isn't real Islam." In both senses, this imagined Africa plays a central role in defining and redefining both the gnawa and Islam more generally. The gnawa's place within some concept of mainstream Islam in Morocco is largely aligned with the nation's own African-ness. Foregrounding the gnawa in various contexts can serve a wide range of aims: for example, it can celebrate the diversity inherent in Islamic practice or it can demonstrate the extent to which unbelievers are twisting the religion itself. This question becomes a proxy for outside influence within Islamic practice, with the idea of Africa taking the role of either innovator or corruptor. The issue also turns inward, as gnawa musicians themselves reflect on the changes coming into their own rituals. As the music that animates the ceremony rises in popularity, thanks to the industry's superstars and music festival performances, the identity of the gnawa shifts. Questions of heritage abound as the community of performers, casual fans, and conservative Muslims across the country work to define and live their faith piously, whatever that might mean to them.

Piety: Being a Gnawa Muslim

While in Marrakech and Tamesluht in the spring of 2011, I had my first opportunity to speak with ritual leaders, m'allemin, who were between seventy and eighty years old. They argued that the gnawa were Sufi, categorically placing them within the larger realm of Islam. They equated the possession that happens during a ceremony to *dhikr*, remembrances of Allah and local saints, a term explicitly connected to Sufi ritual practices. According to their descriptions of the way the tradition should operate, a m'allem would perform *lilat* one or two times each year. This is in contrast to the present gnawa tradition that I observed, where each adept is expected to host a lila annually, meaning that a m'allem may play two or three such rituals in a busy week. Moreover, in the past m'allemin were not economically tied to the performance of rituals. They only accepted gifts, as an exchange for *baraka*, and had other jobs; for example, Mulay al-Tahir, blind and long since retired, is still known throughout town as "the fisher." In fact, when I was told to find and speak to him, I was not given his name as Mulay al-Tahir al-Gnawi (the gnawa) but instead as Mulay al-Tahir al-Hayat (the fisherman). While his vocational title is an anomaly today, Mulay al-Tahir and others continue to describe the m'allemin of previous generations in terms of their day jobs and not their association with musical or ritual activity.

Annual or semiannual gnawa gatherings featured music described as slower and simpler than that of today's events. A m'allem would perform with two or three drari accompanying the hajhuj. The sound was less virtuosic, the dance less acrobatic. Listeners would reach *al-hal*, a terminology that implies the higher state of experience and consciousness and, like dhikr, is associated with Sufi ceremonies. Furthermore, the spirits of today were all once living saints, historical figures, and real people. Sidi Mimun, the violent black spirit who caused those whom he possessed to drink boiling water or cut themselves with a knife, was a pharmacist who gave medications to the poor. Sidi Musa was not the Moses found in the Qur'an or Bible but a local holy man. Songs directed to these figures did not have the goal of inciting possession. They supplicated these saints, asking them to pray for the living and provide the baraka that Allah had bestowed on them. Like many Sufi saints, Sidi Mimun has a number of tombs across the country. Bodies are buried in each, but pilgrims do not know exactly which one contains the real body. Similarly, M'allem 'Abd al-Rzaq once took me on a walk around Fez and showed me the venerated burial sites of Sidi Hamu, Lalla Rqiyya, Sidi Mimun, Lalla Mira, and other figures who possess adepts throughout the gnawa ceremony. Each was well marked and can be a powerful space for ritual activity when clients require intervention that goes beyond the sacrifice of the home ceremony. Although the question of whether these tombs contain the actual body of the saints is interesting, what is important here is the fact that those who come to these sites conceive of saints like Sidi Mimun as historical figures who once lived and have now passed. This is quite different from interpretations of these figures as spirits who come from sub-Saharan Africa or elsewhere and have never been living historical figures. The perceptual change, these m'allemin relayed to me, grew out of economics. By including the specific and often violent trances mentioned above, which these elders deride as "magic" (*shaghma*), the musicians could create a spectacle and request donations. By entertaining the audiences, performers could ensure themselves more work and create an occupation from their ritual knowledge and technical ability. What you see now, they said, bore little resemblance to who the gnawa were.

I entered into many of these conversations by asking about the addition of new elements to what was considered to be a closed ritual ceremony. "Who added these new songs, and when?" I would ask. On some occasions, m'allemin or gnawa lovers could pinpoint specific individuals and dates that I could confirm through other interviews. Not surprisingly, many from these older generations knew the musical and ritual histories better than younger artists. Even so, the most interesting difference between these two narratives—gnawa as Sufi or gnawa as African—lies not in their disputed or proven details, but in their use of tense. The Sufi reading of the gnawa concentrates on who they were, in the defined and experienced past. Conversely, the African emphasis focuses on who they are and always have been since their arrival from sub-Saharan Africa. The sense of past extends all the way back to the unknowable. History, according to this narrative of gnawa identity, does not engage the passing of time. As a result, the "African" perspective is of a gnawa practice that is and has been constant, even static, while the "Sufi" one cites something different from what you now see and hear. It is not clear how these narratives worked in time preceding the memory of today's elders. Even the most nuanced approaches to gnawa history that I heard stopped at the memories of grandparents. Those who speak about the gnawa as having been different from who they are today are themselves too young to remember the conversations and debates of their own elders. Instead, these figures are memorialized and described as pillars of authority and knowledge, not engaged fighters for the identity of a community. This is likely due to the enclosed nature of the ritual and marginalized status of the people who participated in it. With less reason to represent themselves, the gnawa are left with a weak and unwritten historical record. It is animated in music and dance, but only in broad narrative strokes with few specifics. It is also likely that, because the gnawa saw themselves as Muslims, an Islamic narrative of identity and an African one coincided. For some, they still do, but these components of one's narrative of authenticity now provide strategic opportunities and can be balanced alongside or against each other within the marketplace.

While I have spent a total of about two and a half years in Morocco between 2007 and 2013 working with the gnawa, for a host of reasons I have not spent the majority of that time in the south, considered to be the geographic center of the tradition. Instead, I have lived mainly in Fez, a city in the northern mountains that prides itself as the country's "spiritual cradle." As an important center for Islamic learning, Fez is seen as the home of Sufism while Marrakech and Essaouira, a coastal hub of the slave trade about two hours west of Marrakech, claim the gnawa. Over the past two decades this dichotomy has been effectively reinforced by the Fez Festival of World Sacred Music's emphasis on Sufi performances and the Essaouira Festival of World Music's dedication to the gnawa and related fusion activities. Yet there are active gnawa communities in each of the country's major cities as well as within many less urban regions. Most of these have some sense of local identity expressed musically and through the way the performers and adepts speak about their practices, the melodies and rhythms of songs, the inclusion or omission of certain saints and spirits, or the order of the ritual event itself.

These differences are intentional and performers often describe them as effective representations of the region. To revisit an example mentioned earlier, many gnawa in Fez begin ceremonies with the '*ada* (the procession from the street into the household, also called a *dakhla*) before opening the space by performing music for entertainment and the professional gnawa dancers (the "Awlad

Bambara" and "Nashat" suites, collectively part of the fraja). This is the opposite of the Marrakech *tariq* (literally, path or trek). M'allemin in Fez cast the difference in spiritual terms. By opening with the entertainment (fraja) and then walking outside, the *mrakshi* (those from Marrakech) separate that portion from the rest of the lila, highlighting its entertainment value and segregating it from the ritual. The goal of the fraja in Marrakech and Tamesluht is to allow the drari, those who play the *qaraqib*, to sing responses and perform specialized trances to demonstrate their abilities as professionals. By carrying out extended synchronized and acrobatic dances, they show the audience that they are competent in the gnawa tradition and raise the expectations and confidence for and in the ritual that will follow.

Those from Fez use this "entertainment" segment to accomplish ritual goals more directly by keeping it within the boundaries of the entrance and the rest of the event. The fraja sanctifies the space and introduces the mluk possession phase. Having already completed the ritual's processional entrance, the entirety of the performance that follows, from this point until the following morning, serves the purpose of welcoming spirits, fostering the conditions for trance to occur, and facilitating the improvement of the relationships between mluk and those whom they possess, their *maskun*. The fraja phase gives the musicians and dancers the opportunity to perform these synchronized and acrobatic dances for the spirits, demonstrating their desire to welcome the mluk into the space, the evening, and the bodies of soon-to-be trancers. According to 'Abd al-Rzaq, the difference is important since Fez is a "more spiritual city" than Marrakech and, frankly, that's how things are done here.

As a researcher working with the gnawa in Fez, I became specifically involved in a number of minority variants. Many of the country's most popular gnawa musicians grew up in Marrakech, Essaouira, or Tamesluht, a town about twenty-five kilometers outside central Marrakech.[3] Those who did not grow up in these regions often visited them, spending years as apprentices for older master musicians in order to learn their performance styles and techniques. The attention given to the performance practices, ritual process, and musical styles from Marrakech, elevated these southern variants, making them the dominant gnawa voice. This dominance also created a sense of strict authority and pride around the region's practices. Because of the prominence of the Marrakech tradition, when foreign artists or scholars search for the gnawa, an obvious starting point is the city's famed Djma' al-Fna', the central market square that features costumed gnawa musicians playing the qaraqib for domestic and foreign tourists alike. The long history of this market, and the gnawa's prominent aural place in it has made Marrakech the central source of information about the gnawa for those ranging from casual Moroccan listeners to prominent scholars. In 1998, with the advent of the Essaouira Festival of World Music and its intentional focus on the gnawa, the beach town of Essaouira—which already had its own deep history of local practice (see Lapassade 1976)—joined Marrakech as a hub for gnawa information and authority.

This authority, however, is discursively created. Essaouira and Marrakech were sites of major slave markets.[4] The history that explicitly links these two cities to sub-Saharan Africa through routes of transit provides the region with a strong sense of authoritative authenticity based on its link to a past African lineage. Building on these historical links, the region's prominence is enhanced by the perceived centrality of the African performance practices that exist in these southern cities. Many artists and *muhibbin* conceive of these practices as historically bound, unchanging, and demonstrative of an authenticity based within historical consistency. Thus, expectations of authenticity and authority, coming together, endow artists from the region with a natural (even genetic) tgnawit for many within the larger gnawa community. The sounds from this area, however, are not devoid of change, and there are those m'allemin and muhibbin who question specific performers. Local forms from across the country, including those of Fez, are only one such point of variation within gnawa performance practice. More centrally, even, is the continuum of possibilities implied by a discursively created tgnawit. The southern-centric accounts that highlight the gnawa's African origins often overwhelm other aspects of the tradition that place authenticity and authority (and therefore, tgnawit) within Sufi and larger Islamic spheres. The performative markers of Islamic or Sufi readings of tgnawit are also present within the Essaouira-Marrakech region, but they are more rarely emphasized in this part of the country than they are in places like Fez. This geographic difference is one example of how the prioritization of histories contribute to varied conceptions of both authority and authenticity, of tgnawit. Fez's folding of the fraja into the sacred parts of the ceremony by placing it after the opening 'ada shows one way in which the geographic elements of tgnawit are performed, or at least how the local performance practice is understood within a larger discussion of tgnawit. There are many other ways in which Muslim-ness/Sufi-ness or African-ness can be emphasized as well.

Muslims, Mluk, and M'allemin

The gnawa practice (and perform) their religious beliefs within a "looser Muslim framework" (Feriali 2009, 41). Their worldview sits firmly within the bounds of Islam. Names, places, language, holy figures, histories, stories, prayers, songs, family ties, legal issues, interpersonal relationships, dress, medicine—the everyday life of a gnawa m'allem or adept is informed by perspectives that could be deemed "Islamic culture." Everyday life in Morocco, with the gnawa, is littered with piety. It is a public piety, one that is performed but not necessarily consciously so. Of course there are those who actively adjust their behaviors, countering those of society around them, in an effort to change, or reform, perceived incongruence between the will of Allah and the faults or misunderstandings of man. There are intentional symbols that adorn the body of a man striving for a holy life, outward signs of internal submission to Allah. Arguments abound about whether the bruise on a man's forehead results from years of devout prayer, the pressing of the forehead to the tile floor five times each day for an entire lifetime. The doubter, instead, will insist that such a bruise was self-inflicted. This becomes an absolute symbol of the most cynical kind of performed piety: a man's desire to be seen as holy by his neighbors incites him to wound his own forehead solely for the sake of appearances. The truth, however, is resigned to Allah: "Allah yi'arif" (God knows a man's heart).

Islam, as it is practiced in Morocco, is a very public religion. But as such, it is taken as a given. Small pieties orient daily life, leading the most innocuous of activities through a ritualized performance of religiosity. Some may be conscious, some unconscious. Much of the everyday performance of religious affiliation is so taken for granted it goes unnoticed. In contrast, difference is obvious, noticeable, and questionable. Difference in practice might imply disagreement, contradiction, or even aggressive attack. With religious practice, and especially the public manifestation of it, points of difference become topics of public discourse. Their import quickly overcomes the whole, magnifying what could otherwise be minor departures.

Morocco, historically, has been a fascination of anthropologists. As a site where the popular forms of Islamic faith and practice come to differ wildly from the mainstream tenets of the religion, the study of "Moroccan Islam" has given insight into the ways in which people and communities negotiate the disconnect between traditional and modern religion, transnational and local belief, religious power structures, and a host of other local, regional, national, and international issues. When writing about the gnawa, many scholars emphasize difference: they are a diaspora, from someplace else; they are black, racially not Arab or Berber; their religious practices are African, not Muslim. I argue that the focus on difference has obscured an important element of gnawa self-identification. Simultaneously, the stress on the African histories behind the ritual practices has elevated one aspect of tgnawit at the expense of another, the Muslim piety of the gnawa, which is as important—if not more so—to many potential clients. Audiences search for different sets of criteria when selecting performers for concerts or rituals, and the musicians recognize this as they actively craft the types of tgnawit that they claim within their personal and professional lives.

I assert that Islamic piety is central to the gnawa ritual, just as it is central to public life in Morocco, and should be understood accordingly[5]: they are self-identified Muslims (some even carry Sufi affiliations in addition to their relationships to the gnawa); they practice their faith in much the same way as most Moroccan Muslims, complete with pilgrimages, the veneration of local saints, and the exchange of baraka; they operate, both professionally and otherwise, firmly within the complex networks of Sufism, even when they make no claim to being Sufi. Also, like so many Moroccans who vehemently consider themselves Muslims, many do not pray often or at all, many drink or use drugs, and individuals may have little interest in the trappings of their faith. While I have no statistical evidence to claim specific proportions, I also have no reason to agree with the oft-stated suspicions leveled against the gnawa: that they are amoral or somehow less pious as a group than the population as a whole.[6] The vignette that opened this book, in which the sound of the gnawa bowed before the sound of the *adhan*, highlights the complexities of the relationship between the two sets of practices. The submissiveness of the gnawa in that apartment to institutionalized Islam, represented aurally as it was by the sound of the call to prayer coming through an open window, identifies the importance of both the separation of these two sets of beliefs (those of the gnawa and of Islam) as well as their important interaction within everyday life. These narratives of tgnawit, religious piety, and personal identity similarly demonstrate specific attempts, extreme examples of infinite possible alternatives, to negotiate this relationship within contemporary personal and social life.

Some gnawa participants completely separate these ritual practices from the realm of Islam, noting that one can be non-Muslim and gnawa. In one sense, albeit an oversimplified one, this is not dissimilar to American communities that self-identify as Sufi and participate in musical, dance, and meditation practices borrowed from a conglomeration of various Middle Eastern paths. Practice (music, dance, chant, and meditation) subsumes belief as the defining component of "Sufism," and an idea of sacred that is bounded firmly within a religious, historical, and social contexts is replaced with an idea of the sacred that is flexible, personal, and open for interpretation. For many gnawa, the ritual practice carries similar connotations. There are stories of American tourists who become gnawa (see Schaefer 2009) and musicians who participate and achieve the title of gnawi (some of whom eventually convert to Islam). Because of this research, I often carried a hajhuj around the old city, earning the title "Dris al-Gnawi," an approximation of my first name and the feigned honorific.[7] Yet, if the gnawa identity derives from Sufism, from a set of religious and spiritual experiences that are bounded within Islamic belief and historical context, the meaning of being gnawa changes dramatically. Personal gnawa identity therefore depends closely on these ideas of narrative, yet they are highly personal, negotiable, and debatable.

As an approach to these negotiations between narratives and ideals, so-called Moroccan Islam does have validity as an analytical category. Eickelman (1976), Geertz (1971), Rabinow (1977), Crapanzano (1981), Gellner (1983), and other past scholars note certain shared practices between many Moroccans in the activities—the quotidian rituals—that shape public and private life. With increased urbanization, new educational systems, the ever-present mass media, the advent of advanced personal telecommunications, the use of the internet, and a host of other facilitators of communication within and across previous local, regional, and national boundaries, however, practices have, of course, shifted. Popular culture, changing power structures, and fluid social norms drastically impact the look of daily life. Tradition, unsurprisingly, takes on new meanings. It, in so many forms, comes under attack from all directions. Conversely, new defenders from throughout society, some more unexpected than others, take up its cause. "Tradition defended is never entirely traditional," writes Munson (1993, 78). The Islamic narrative of gnawa identity outlined above is one such defense of so-called tradition.

Many gnawa practitioners promote the Islamic elements of the practice despite the wider perception of the population as African, as "other." M'allemin interact with specific Islamic practices to embed their performance with a vividly Muslim character, making it easy to disagree with claims that one can be gnawa without being Muslim; they reaffirm an intimate connection between a global religion and a local practice. There are those from various levels of Moroccan society that distinctly separate the gnawa from Islam, decrying their practices as illicit and Satanic. There are others who divide the practice from Islam in an attempt to maintain its acceptability: if it is a healing practice, not worship, then it simply exists in another sphere and does not conflict with Islam. Most self-identified gnawa practitioners whom I met, however, see the lila as worship because of the Islamic content that permeates the ritual. My aim here is to outline some of the prominent points of evidence used by those who read tgnawit through a lens of Islamic authenticity. In doing so, I extract certain debates surrounding the theology and ritual as examples of discourses that I heard during the conversations that comprised my fieldwork.

At the center of debates surrounding the place of Islam within gnawa practice (and, conversely, the place of the gnawa within Islam) are the mluk. Relationships with these spiritual figures, or sets of spiritual figures, are at once the focal point of the ritual and the target of external criticism. Debates revolve around two general perspectives. First, the common assertion from non-gnawa Muslims, especially those of the educated middle class with backgrounds in reformist movements, was that these spirits were *jnun*. Mentioned in the Qur'an, a *jinn* is a spirit of dubious intent, either a worshipper of Allah or Satan. By elevating these spirits, making them the subjects of worship, the gnawa were investing their beliefs with polytheism, and because these spirits were not dependably good, gnawa maskun were allowing themselves to be possessed by the followers of Satan. Those mluk who derive identities from African ancestry and force their human possessions to drink boiling water, cut themselves with knives, or run hot wax across their bodies give ample evidence to the idea that the gnawa's ritual work incorporates Satanic worship. Scholars, especially Moroccans, who study the gnawa tradition, use loaded terms such as "demonology" (Feriali 2009) or make resounding statements like "All *jnun* are from Satan" (Adil Walili, personal communication, 2011).[8] While these perspectives also inform my understanding of discourses surrounding the gnawa, they flatten some scholarly pursuits by firmly staking out a theological opinion as to the ontology of spiritual actors, an ontology that is not only unknown but also well beyond our human ability to understand and defend. I believe that, in declaring the mluk to be demons or saints as a starting point for research, I would miss the dynamic social, theological, and musical nuances that create and define gnawa identity, as well as the negotiations that inform claims to tgnawit. Furthermore, those critics who deride the gnawa as illicit, especially those who subscribe to Islamic reformism, question a number of Morocco's other experiential practices as well. Communities like the ʿissawa and hamadsha frequently hear similar critiques: past activities like eating scorpions or "head slashing" that are no longer common surround assumptions about who they are and what they do.

From the perspective of mʿallemin and those who are maskun, the mluk are beings who desire the concrete relationships enacted through the lila ritual. Both ideas of the mluk revolve around the spiritual possession of the body, the supernatural ability to overtake and rule one's physical actions and mental consciousness. These perspectives, however, allow for the associated spirits to be either good or bad—or rather, to act for the benefit or harm of the possessed individual. Thus, the purpose of the event, and the focal point of the gnawa's interactions with the spiritual realm, consists of maintaining and enhancing these relationships. For the gnawa, the mluk's behaviors operate independently of larger forces of good and evil, though certain spirits' personalities are either intrinsically or discursively linked to prophetic lineage or menacing intimidation. Just because the spirit is of a holy lineage does not mean that it acts exclusively out of benevolence. It is worth noting that whether these personality traits are intrinsically part of these spirits' character depends on who and what these figures are, something that gets more theological than what I can reasonably address.

Finally, an actual taxonomy of who and what these spirits are would be quite difficult, as there is no consistent standard. For some, there are eleven spirits; for others, there are eleven groups of spirits. The number eleven, seven male and four female, is not consistent either. The female spirits (or groups of spirits) vary by region or even between individual rituals as described above. (Lalla Arbiyya appears in many rituals in Fez, yet she rarely joins a ritual or maintains a relationship with people elsewhere in the country.) Names and identities are similarly imprecise, as demonstrated by Feriali's (2009) survey questions—which were similar to my own—regarding the identity (or identities) of Lalla Aisha. When I approached different mʿallemin or other practitioners to ask if Aisha Qandisha, Aisha Sudaniyya, and Aisha Hamdushiyya were the same spirit, I received a variety of answers. Those three names also apply to three specific songs popular within the Aisha portion of the lila. It was never clear, or better put, was never consistent if the three songs spoke to three spirits or the three songs spoke to different characteristics of the same spirit. Lalla Aisha poses a number of further interesting considerations that I return to in later chapters.

While many of these spirits—if not all, according to some—are believed to be jnun, certain practitioners hold that there is a distinction between jnun and *awliya* (sing. *wali*). While the jnun are the disembodied spirits that appear in the Qur'an, awliya were living saints. Many of those who lived or died in Morocco have shrines or tombs across the country. A wali, one who was close to God, differs from a *nabi*, a prophet. Prophets, who also appear in the Qur'an, cease after Muhammad, who was the seal of the prophets. They provide the religious community with the words and messages of God. Awliya were holy men and women who lived virtuous lives. Their stories and paths through society are diverse. Cornell's (1998) *Realm of the Saint* outlines thematic consistencies while recognizing that some awliya were powerful, rich, and educated urbanites and others were poor, rural, and reclusive healers. Most crossed through overarching categories and navigated their own ways through the pressures of contemporaneous societies in efforts to embody the virtues laid out by their faith.

Forms of Tgnawit

The strategically defined authenticities that many m'allemin identify and use to locate their own practices lend authority to the performer and validity to the practices within larger spheres of societal networks, leading to the construction and performance of tgnawit. The elements of history, theology, and performance practice that contribute to the variety of conceptions of tgnawit are changing with time, and especially with the experiences that inform the ways in which performers and audiences engage with music in the postindependence industrial circulations of music and ideas in Morocco.

The African contribution to tgnawit continues to grow from a strong sense of tradition based in Marrakech and Essaouira. These two cities' histories as major slave markets embed a history of slavery (and therefore, of diaspora and African lineage) into the music, ritual, and religious identity. Because contemporaneous slave owners successfully broke familial and social ties between slaves, direct links between modern gnawa m'allemin and their ancestry are often created, imagined, or extrapolated from very specific identifiable histories. M'allem 'Abd al-Kabir Marshan's upbringing, described above, is one example of how a physical transfer of blood or milk allow for a claim a tgnawit based on a sub-Saharan authenticity. Thus, a sub-Saharan lineage-based conception of tgnawit is not restricted to those of a racialized physical phenotype or familial descent from slavery. Aziz wuld Ba Blan, an older and respected m'allem in Fez who carries a day job at the royal palace, is known in the community as Aziz Blackman, borrowing from English. He is one of few in Fez who performs an older style of gnawa music. His age and knowledge of a specific repertoire, along with his dark skin color, lend him both authenticity and authority. His tgnawit is derived from a combination of lineage, personal history, and experience.

The moment when the Meknes ceremony came to a pause as the call to prayer drifted through the window highlights the primacy of an Islamic identity for the gnawa. When there is overlap, these men and women prioritize their Muslim faith. The relationship between gnawa and Islamic practice is complicated and varies drastically between participants, but the vast majority of practitioners and audiences self-identify foremost as Muslims. There appear to be two prominent perspectives taken by most listeners and practitioners. The first is that gnawa practice, while not explicitly Muslim, involves participants who are Muslim. It continues, therefore, that certain Islamic elements make their way into the music and ritual because of these shared experiences and beliefs between (almost) all involved. Often, those who locate gnawa identity as a sub-Saharan practice imported over history cite this relationship between practice and faith.

The second, however, places the gnawa alongside other Sufi groups and iden-tify the practices of the ritual as specific performances of the Muslim faith. While this trajectory makes the ritual practice more exclusive—non-Muslims are there-fore nonbelievers—it remains welcoming to outsiders. I have been invited into a number of rituals, observing them as a visiting outsider. In this way, I sit along-side (literally and figuratively) a number of non-gnawa Muslims who are there to enjoy the music and observe the ritual progression as interested participants, but not as maskun. Further, I have been invited as a performer, sitting next to the group, clapping and singing the choral responses. If I were to spend more time, I am told, I would be welcome to join the group in a more defined role that would include the dress, picking up the qaraqib, and singing throughout the ceremony. My relationship with the performers, that of an insider, orients my relationship with the ritual participants, that of an outsider. Even as a non-Muslim, however, I am welcome in a number of intimate ways. The same applies for friends of the hosts or performers, or neighbors. There is a space within the ritual setting that allows for Muslim non-gnawa, non-Muslims, and full believers to sit together and appreciate the experience through each's own lens.

In the following chapters, I outline some of the many performative strat-egies used by m'allemin to fully engage both sources of tgnawit alongside a novel marker of ritual authority and authenticity: commercial success that incorpor-ates virtuosity and innovation. The influx of popular music aesthetics changes the relationship between ritual musicians and their clients, just as new forms of media are quickly shifting the nature of learning. The music industry's influ-ence is bringing gnawa music into the popular consciousness across the coun-try in new ways, and these developments in popular culture, in turn, affect the relationship between listeners, adepts, and performers in ritual settings. It also opens new opportunities for those who strive to find a place within the gnawa community, including young performers working both within and outside of historically normative expectations.

Notes

1. The Sahel refers to the region south of North Africa but still north of West or Central Africa. The term generally connotes countries that are within the Sahara, including parts of Mauritania, Mali, Niger, Chad, and the Sudan. Mali and Niger are the most often cited areas by gnawa musicians when they discuss their ancestries or the origins of the spirits that appear in the ritual.

2. While most artists with whom I worked collected the male spirits together as al-hawsawiyyin, a notable minority instead split the *ghabawiyyin* spirits (of the forest) into two sections and called one of those sections al-hawsawiyyin.

3. The sense of authority that encircles Marrakech's gnawa practice revolves around the city's history as a marketplace for slaves arriving from the trans-Sahara caravan routes. Essaouira, however, was a prominent port for the sea routes of the slave trade as a Portuguese port city (then called Mogador).

4. The city of Essaouira is also home of the *zawiya* of Sidna Bilal, one of the few open lodges dedicated to the gnawa. See Chlyeh (1998) for a larger discussion on the history of the zawiya.

5. This idea of sameness is similar to Kofi Agawu's (2003) argument that African music must be studied on a plane of equivalence, with the same techniques, strategies, and goals as those used for the analysis of Western music. While there are, of course, differences and difference itself is interesting and useful to the researcher (see Erlmann's [2004] response to Agawu), by taking difference as a starting point, we limit our possible conclusions.

6. While living in the poor areas of Fez, especially Fez Jdid, I noticed that many of the gnawa performers who were younger participated in the same sorts of practices as their social and economic peers. The same was the case for adult performers, both m'allemin and other ensemble members. Those gnawa practitioners who went to the mosque regularly generally did not use drugs or drink. Those who did not regularly attend were more likely to engage in illicit activities. Mosque attendance or frequency of prayer, among other things, might provide far more effective demarcations of illicit behavior than gnawa participation does, but these are questions that are outside the larger scope of my research. It appeared to me that those who were from other social and economic backgrounds aligned gnawa partici-pation with poverty and poor education. As such, the assumptions leveled against the poor and uneducated were often extrapolated to include the gnawa as well. Because many gnawa musicians are poor and less educated than the middle or upper classes, many criticisms were generally accurate, though possibly for socioeconomic reasons more so than anything spe-cific to the gnawa themselves.

7. See Schaefer (2009) for a discussion of his own similar experiences while completing fieldwork. He associates the identity of being gnawa with consumerism, as it is by wearing shirts and carrying a "Gnaoua" bag that he identified (and was identified) with the gnawa community.

8. Adil Walili is involved with the gnawa, though he does not see himself (or many other within the gnawa community) as Satin-worshippers. Instead, he had a complicated personal relationship with the gnawa, one that evaded a clear definition during our long and winding conversations in Marrakech.

4 Making a Living as a Contemporary Ritual Musician

*I*N DECEMBER 2012, *Yassine and I were sitting together in first class on a train between Fez and Meknes. We were traveling with ʿAbd al-Rahim Amrani, a hamadsha leader who invited Yassine to perform as a part of a theater work, a musical drama, telling the story of Lalla Aisha. Yassine is roughly my age, in his twenties at the time, and performs gnawa music in concerts, in fusion bands, and in rituals when he can secure the work. He wears glasses, has long black hair, and has a knack for reading a room. He is almost always the center of attention, a consummate performer.*

Yassine is a self-proclaimed gnawa mʿallem. *He learned and continues to learn from whoever will teach him, even people who, like Amrani, are not gnawi, but he carries himself as an expert. Not only has he mastered the standard repertoire, but he also knows elements of the older* fassiyya *style, regional styles from elsewhere in the country, and the mysterious* sebtiyyin, *the ritual for Jewish spirits that is said to have been common before the Jewish community's departure from Morocco's urban centers. His knowledge is* mukhallet, *mixed up. To some, this is a detriment, but he skillfully turns it into the most opportunistic of strengths.*

Yassine was not used to the first-class cars of the train. We usually had to push through the length of the crowded, faded-orange passages between second-class cars to find a spot, but this was a short trip, we had instruments and equipment, and so it was worth the peace of mind that comes with knowing where your seat would be. Second class is loud, with groups of boys huddled around cell phones, laughing about a Facebook video, or men and women yelling over each other. First class is the opposite. Seats are plush; it's darker, quieter, and usually almost empty. Yassine and I were speaking, conspicuously loudly for first class, when he pulled his hajhuj *out to demonstrate something. I, being hyper-self-aware of the class transgressions aligned with public and personal space in an enclosed elite context such as first class—and frankly always hyper-self-aware of my social transgressions and frequent misunderstandings of public and private space in Morocco more generally—feared admonishment or glares from the other passengers. Yassine had no such concerns. He began playing and singing at full voice, filling the train car. This was a performer who has made a young career out of stepping outside of acceptability. His respect for elders and intense desire to learn contradict his lack of patience or interest in limiting himself to one teacher. His extreme confidence and optimism don't help him "follow the rules." But he lives and works at a time when the rules are breaking down.*

After a few minutes, a man from elsewhere on the car came and sat across from Yassine and me. My friend was filling me in on some details of Sidi Musa's music, but he quickly diverted his attention and sang to the new listener. The guy was smiling and clapping along during this break on his long train ride to Rabat. He and Yassine started talking, and the man asked Yassine about his experience: whether he knows and plays ceremonies, where he has traveled—questions of that sort. By the time we arrived in Meknes, Yassine had tentatively arranged to perform a ceremony for the man's family in Rabat, the Moroccan capital city. Rabat has its own deep community of gnawa performers, some of whom are famous throughout the country. But this man was drawn to Yassine; perhaps he had no local connections to draw from. The intimate and informal first-class performance won my friend some work and with it would come the prestige of getting hired to satisfy a distant, and likely upper-class, family's ritual needs. Not only did he "win" the gig on his own terms, but he did so in a fashion that was completely outside the normal "way things are done."

Gnawa superstars in contemporary Morocco achieve the highest levels of success, appearing on major television features and performing on the country's brightest stages. They record pristine studio versions of the tradition's ceremonial music and play these tunes on world tours with jazz and reggae artists. Their fame within the popular music industries make them influential markers of innovative approaches to this musical tradition and innumerable young musicians follow their lead. Attempting to replicate the stardom of Hamid al-Qasri or Majid Bekkas, for example, aspiring young musicians buy or build their own instruments and start practicing immediately. Some align themselves with master musicians and rise through a system based on traditional apprenticeship, performing in rituals and assisting their teacher for years, if not decades. Others, however, choose to learn the hits and stake out a path more familiar to popular musicians. They perform in the streets and on stages, working to expand their audience. These two routes toward a sustainable career intertwine, as each musician struggles to balance commercial priorities alongside the needs of the ritual.

In this chapter, I argue that the modes of learning and advancing through a career as a gnawa musician are dramatically changing. The options available to a young musician belie contradictory priorities, yet the nuanced performer's skills allow him to bridge the gap between them. This chapter focuses on how young artists navigate two common goals: becoming a celebrated popular musician known for virtuosity and fame (a *fnan*, or artist) and earning renown as a m'allem. As previously seen, these are hardly mutually exclusive goals, though they illuminate different priorities for young learners. I outline the stages of the apprenticeship system and the routes of advancement toward ritual specialization, with special attention paid to the economic and social incentives for either continuing in the process or choosing to plateau at different points of their education. I then describe the increasingly popular alternatives to learning and achieving fame, along with the struggles toward self-legitimization that these new modes of learning lead to. The chapter closes by returning to this one young gnawa musician in Fez who aspires to fame within both commercial and ritual settings. Yassine uses his innovative skills and wit to successfully lead a fusion band in concerts across the city and entertain both audiences and possessing spirits (*mluk*) within rituals. His story and performances illuminate the place of creativity within the diverse contemporary gnawa community.

These changes expose the third narrative of authenticity described in previous chapters. Instead of drawing on lineage or piety, who you are or what you do, there is an opening for those who can identify trends and meet clients and audiences where their tastes currently sit. This type of authentic performance requires new skills that are more closely aligned to the popular music industry than traditional ritual, but some level of mastery remains necessary if a performer is to avoid ritual failure and the embarrassment that can come with it. In this way, contemporary authenticity, at least from the perspective of performers like Yassine and his ensemble, is directly linked to a sense of market success, commercial achievement, and stage presence. Many m'allemin struggle with the social, historical, ideological, and economic pressures of professionalism that currently occupy the gnawa community. (To restate an important caveat, this tripartite model of authenticity, *tgnawit*, is just that: a conceptual model based on descriptions I encountered during fieldwork. The reality is one of nuance and negotiation. Furthermore, there are likely to be many other important characteristics that go into an individual understanding of authenticity that simply did not come up during my conversations.)

These musicians and ritual leaders are coming from a training that defies easy labeling as formal or informal. 'Abd al-Rzaq of Fez talks about having traveled the country playing in the streets while learning from various m'allemin for more than ten years of his life. His training finalized with Muhammad Bujma in Fez, whom he continued to perform with until the teacher's death in 2012. His skills and style are heavily influenced, however, by the numerous other teachers who worked closely with him while he apprenticed and traveled so widely. This is how he and others develop a unique personal style and approach to the ritual and repertoire. The questions fall on innovation within a style, or the degree of flexibility afforded to a performer before he transgresses the boundaries surrounding ritual appropriateness (see chap. 8 of this volume; Bellaviti 2015). Clients hire performers, and the glut of competition created from the music's popular success makes it that much more important to stand out from the crowd.

Younger performers, especially those who are learning the gnawa music and ritual right now, come with a different set of expectations and experiences. The effort required to navigate the popular and sacred—to adapt and manipulate performances to fit the needs and wants of audiences—are not quite so troublesome.

The current generation of musicians follows a different logic within their innovative moves. The metaphorical logic of the sharing economy or of crowd sourcing is apt, as compared to the hierarchical educational systems oriented around apprenticeship. This is not wholly new: 'Abd al-Rzaq's travels demonstrate a networked approach to learning. Changing technologies, organizational networks, performative values, and audience tastes have contributed, though, to a dramatic expansion of these efforts as performers increasingly look to new inspirations as they work their way through a quickly changing sense of professionalism.

Cynthia Becker notes the consistency with which gnawa practitioners have been aware of and operating within the national and international marketplace since at least the beginning of the twentieth century, citing a 1904 report that some gnawa were traveling the country to monetize their curative powers (2014, 122). Georges Lapassade thanks Essaouira's 'Abd al-Rahman Kirouche, better known as Paco in the band Nass al-Ghiwane, for his role in creating a cultural movement around gnawa music and trance (1976, 209–10). By 1977, Abdelatif (presumably M'allem 'Abd al-Latif Makhzumi of Marrakech, from the same interview described in chapter 6 in this volume) "decided to no longer conduct ritual ceremonies because the times had changed," citing the then new generation's failure to respect tradition (Chlyeh 1998, 67). In this sense, what Yassine accomplishes on the train, and what other young performers are doing every day, is not new. Yet the institutions of apprenticeship and lineages that endowed practitioners with authority and authenticity, with tgnawit, are opening up thanks to disruptive technologies and the increased entanglements of the local and global music industries. Where there were previously few ways to prove oneself as capable, now there are as many routes as there are audiences. Each audience—whether trancing in a ritual or dancing before a stage—wants to hear what it wants to hear, creating opportunities for those shrewd performers who can engage their listeners and clients, who can satisfy their demands.

Economic Pressures on Ritual Performance

As we have seen in chapter 2, the gnawa community's sense of identity has its roots in Morocco's history of slavery. Viviana Pâques (1964) links gnawa history and culture to its West African antecedents, and Chouki El Hamel (2013) finalizes his book on slavery with a discussion of the contemporary gnawa community's relationship to its past forced migration. Yet gnawa identity as it exists in Morocco now is far more difficult to pin down. Lapassade relays a conversation in which a ritual musician declared that only the ensemble's leader was gnawi. His status came in part from his lineage and ancestral history of slavery. Yet, he goes on to describe how the masters of Essaouira train twenty-five- to thirty-year-olds who are not of the same ancestry but must demonstrate their "thèse pratique de gnaoua," as described in chapter 2, to become masters themselves (1976, 202). The professional identity widens further as many clients consider themselves gnawa, especially those who regularly host and attend ritual ceremonies. In a 2006 interview, Loy Elrich, then artistic director of the Essaouira Festival of World Music, declared to me, "There is not a gnawa population! . . . It's not depending on where you came from or what your name is or your color. . . . Everybody can be gnawa." The adjective *gnawa* is therefore a contentious one. Most who claim it for themselves are avid listeners, clients, or performers. They come from all walks and social classes, though many are urban poor or otherwise marginalized. All recognize the importance of slavery to gnawa ritual and music, but far fewer are themselves of an ancestry that directly links to the experience of enslavement and forced migration.

Especially since independence—and thanks in part to the changes in media, technology, and the postcolonial project of identity construction—the gnawa have slowly come from the margins of society to stand as symbols of Morocco's diversity. Along with race (see Grame 1970), this marginalization was largely due to the central syncretic ritual possession ceremony, the *lila*, and demonstrates the intrigue of the relationship between gnawa practitioners and the frightening world of possessing spirits. The ceremony is for healing, but the allowed presence of friends, family, and neighbors has created an additional element of entertainment. Bertrand Hell highlights this rise in popularity and notes that it is not a new phenomenon. He cites a description of white Muslims wishing to attend black Muslim ritual events in 1808 (2002, 55). More recent changes, however, take a different turn thanks to media attention, recordings, festival performances, and the general popularity of this group within contemporary society.

A troupe of musicians animates both the lila ritual and the similar but shorter—and therefore cheaper—'ashiyya.[1] Flanking the m'allem as he sings and plays the hajhuj is a group of *drari*, ensemble members of varying experience and expertise playing the *qaraqib*. The drari play various roles depending on their professional status or level of apprenticeship. The primary stages of progression, which I return to below, are *juqay*, *koyo*, and *hariqsa*. Some are early in their education and serve as assistants, like the juqay. Others have developed specific skills like the dancing koyo, singing hariqsa, and the *khalifa*, who can "sub in" for the m'allem and play hajhuj when necessary. Advancement through these stages can be a result of a vocational calling or a demand of possessing spirits, or it can come from an eagerness to increase professional viability and economic opportunity within this changing musical-ritual landscape inhabited by the gnawa in contemporary Morocco.

In the introduction to his edited volume, *L'universe des gnaoua*, Abdelhafid Chlyeh opened a new goal for studies of the gnawa. By gathering musical analysis, studies of dance, histories, and other topics, he noted: "Finally, one could investigate the evolution of traditional *gnawa* activities as the master musicians, notably those who are part of the younger generation, are increasingly attracted by the world of spectacle" (1999, 10). Many works follow this question of change. Hell observes how the repertoire heard in public settings has expanded greatly since he began his work with the gnawa (2002, 346). Prominent m'allemin are far more likely to play portions of the most sacred songs for uninitiated audiences. Deborah Kapchan (2007) followed as a gnawa troupe adapted its performance abroad, struggling to align its own sounds and ritual to the needs and tastes of international audiences. And, interestingly, Tamara Turner's (2012) work with 'Abd al-Latif Makhzumi of Marrakech brings into focus much of the backlash against these changes, this attraction to spectacle.

While the ritual event remains a "search for successive spiritual states" (Hell 2002, 162), the performance itself is similarly changing in many ways, two of which I focus on here. First, there is pressure for the m'allem and his troupe to accommodate the tastes of those present in the room. The "dialogue" between performers and trancing bodies tracks the presence of the possessing spirit through a rhythmic and melodic engagement. As audiences and clients in ritual ceremonies listen to more gnawa music through media and festival performances, I would argue that this mutual engagement increasingly requires music that appeals to, or at least falls within the experiences of, audiences. Uninitiated listeners and initiated clients alike often have favorite performers and performance styles. They may love the virtuosity or speed of one or the "heaviness" of another and hire local performers for their lilat (nights) and 'ashiyyat (evenings) accordingly (see chap. 7). Similarly, there are certain "hits" associated with different spirits that clients, or perhaps their possessing spirits when they are midtrance, request over and over. The navigation of this tension between the tastes of audiences and the effectiveness of ritual work plays into a musician's successes within different parts of the gnawa community. While some clients are looking for those who can perform as virtuosos and get audiences moving, others prioritize adherence to different local and national conceptions of gnawa tradition. This leads to vast diversity within the community of performers, and with this diversity comes competition, debate, and criticism. While some performers earn the respect of the community as a whole, most struggle to attain widespread recognition despite large followings from their specific clients and listeners. Chapter 8 outlines some ways in which elder artists make use of new performative opportunities to push back against changing tastes, didactically presenting their vision of what the ritual should look and sound like.

The second pressure on rituals that proves important for this discussion is economic. The aforementioned 'ashiyya is a shortened version of an overnight lila ceremony that moves quickly through the stages of the event. The musicians play songs for all of the spirits but simply choose fewer for each set. Clients and others who are present in the ceremony have the opportunity to appease their possessing spirits and maintain those relationships, but the event may last from 7:00 p.m. to 1:00 a.m. instead of 10:00 p.m. to 6:00 a.m. This alleviates a few concerns. First, the cost is lower. The group of musicians is cheaper and occasionally smaller. The standard practice for the lila is to have an open event for family, friends, and neighbors that includes tea, cookies, and occasional large meals. Breakfast is served at the conclusion, once daylight arrives. The shorter duration of an 'ashiyya requires fewer meals and gets people home in time to sleep before the next workday. Second, the lila can necessitate local government approvals that circumvent urban noise ordinances in some areas. By ending earlier, the family avoids the hassle of dealing with authorities.

Beyond these economic concerns, major shifts are opening cracks for a new generation's participation within the professional life of gnawa ritual and musicianship. People come to the gnawa through a variety of avenues and for diverse reasons. Hell notes three levels of experience, which he calls "circles of support" (2002, 48–57), The first includes those who have fully accepted their call to initiation. This election is sourced from one of three modes of accessing the gnawa community that define some of these potential relationships that bring people to the tradition. One can become a gnawa through direct lineage, which is well known due to the most famous of gnawa families in Marrakech and Essaouira. Baqbu of Marrakech (see Hell 2002, 50) and the Ghania family in Essaouira (see Sum 2011) are good examples. A second way is through wet-nursing—as was seen with 'Abd al-Kabir Marshan—where milk carries "the powers of blood." Hell continues with a third method by which a child can inherit a gnawa identity: redemption. If a gnawa ritual successfully assists a family who is sterile or plagued with reproductive struggles, the resulting child will be "anchored in the world of humans" but maintains an "affiliation" with the spirits. Though lineage remains a powerful element of fostering a gnawa identity in some cases, it can also serve as a hindrance. Not only do many families question the validity and acceptability of these ritual activities, but also those who are active practitioners often discourage their children from following in their footsteps. This was the case with most of the established musicians whom I worked with in Fez, where lineages are not as strong as they are in the renowned southern cities like Marrakech, Tamesluht, and Essaouira that are known for their intergenerational gnawa communities.

This pairs with economic realities of poverty and opportunity to bring about a dramatic change in the initiation process. As there are increasingly few family lineages of gnawa practitioners, especially ritual leaders who attain the status of m'allem, those who love the music and are attracted to the ritual event rely on their talents as singers, dancers, and instrumentalists to find an alternative source of income. Some enter into the traditional apprenticeship system described later in this chapter while others follow the logic of the contemporary music industry. They learn the repertoire from alternative sources like CD recordings or YouTube clips and undertake careers as performers. This has been the case with Yassine and his Gnawa Lions, young musicians who navigate stages and rituals using this novel logic. The vocation of gnawa ritual leadership is changing, though it is doing so inconsistently. Although these younger artists find ways to attract new audiences, traditionalists see them as inexperienced and misguided at best or, at worst, sacrilegious competition. The calling to the vocation can now be musical and does not require the same initiation or election that it once did. Authenticity can develop from audience demands and paying gigs instead of growing out of intimate relationships with powerful spirits that are successfully maintained for years. Further, just as families shift the hours of the ritual, they also show a willingness to hire less experienced m'allemin to cut costs. This opens the door to young performers. As long as "nontraditional" students of tradition like Yassine continue to find clients and audiences, the debates between what a ritual practitioner is and should be will intensify.

While it is easy to categorize artists as working within either ritual or commercial spheres—and indeed, much criticism leveled between competing artists utilizes this binary dichotomy—economics require that most gnawa troupes engage in some type of commercial activity alongside ritual contexts. Most of these artists compete for a limited number of employment opportunities. Some concentrate on strengthening their reputation as ritual leaders, in turn strategically securing more lucrative middle- and upper-class lila performances. Others attempt to grow their name recognition through recordings and festival performances, often eschewing ritual performance opportunities for larger public gatherings. Yet even those who primarily enjoy fame through these public contexts must continue to lead occasional rituals in order to maintain a sense of spiritual legitimacy. M'allem Hamid al-Qasri, one of the most popular gnawa artist in Morocco due in part to the vast catalog of studio recordings and jazz fusion projects to his credit, epitomizes this situation. When asked about al-Qasri as a gnawa ritual practitioner, most other m'allemin respond with indignation. He records in the studio and no longer runs rituals, they often claim. Yet, when speaking with al-Qasri himself in 2011, I learned that this was not the case. He invited me, twice, to rituals that he was hosting in wealthy suburbs of Rabat, Morocco's capital.[2]

A performer who is not known for his gnawa ritual leadership is often called a fnan. M'allem, therefore, is reserved for those who are deemed to truly know and understand the "gnawa sciences" (*'ulum al-gnawiyya*). Yet, as I go on to describe, traditional paths to earning this title are giving way to a wider, or watered-down, meaning as performers appoint themselves m'allem, a status that might be reinforced by fans or press regardless of training or experience. The word appears across trades in Morocco as a signifier of expertise: an ironworker or tailor might be a m'allem. The bestowal of the honorific is a measure of virtuosity, vocal technique and projection, or ritual knowledge. The characteristics by which a noninitiate journalist or fan might identify expertise—and therefore m'allem-hood—are broad, causing frustration and confusion among those who adhere to the apprenticeship system of learning and advancement. Hamid al-Qasri was often referred to as fnan in conversations I had with other m'allemin, emphasizing the widespread belief that he is only a commercial performer and not a practitioner of the gnawa ritual. As such, the economic and ritual lives of a gnawa artist intersect a great deal.

Even those artists who avoid commercial performances for the non-gnawa public engage in the economic sphere, as gnawa music and ritual are possible sources of income, potentially able to supply a sufficient living wage. 'Abd al-Rzaq achieved the level of economic stability that allows him to effectively provide for his family between his gnawa work and his day job guarding and managing a workshop. They have a house in the old city of Fez, and he maintains an office in Blida, one of the older quarters, not far from a musical instrument shop owned by his past teacher, Si Muhammad Bujma. As the m'allem, 'Abd al-Rzaq receives clients directly in his office to negotiate the terms of a future ritual. He then hires the appropriate number of his most trusted drari. He controls the rations of payment to each performer after the completion of the event, allowing him to reward those who performed well or completed extra tasks throughout the ritual.[3] Others push toward bigger goals of commercial stardom and festival stages like the young Yassine. Many choose to stay within their neighborhoods, becoming an integral part of their local gnawa communities as knowledgeable but amateur ritual leaders.

A successful ensemble member, a drari, can monetize his skill as a vocalist or an instrumentalist and negotiate his way through the local scene. When asked about why some gnawa artists do not express the interest in making the shift from drari (as an apprentice) to m'allem, 'Abd al-Rzaq explained the risks inherent in making such a step. As a drari, a gnawa musician is essentially a freelance performer. Many hone close relationships with one or two specific m'allemin, ensuring that they are the first to be called for any performance. Others spend much of their time and energy "circling" (*duwwar*) the streets, essentially busking for both Moroccan and foreign tourist audiences sitting in cafés. As a professional drari gains experience with different m'allemin, learning the nuances of their personal tastes, styles, and pacing, he is able to both demand larger shares of the income, though this does not approach the share kept by the m'allem, and find more consistent employment by working with many different m'allemin. For these reasons, many drari decide that making the leap to the next level is not the right choice. They maximize their skills as ensemble members and find opportunities to thrive within the community by performing with one or more m'allemin across the country. The most experienced drari hold great esteem and can lend an air of authority to even the greenest young m'allem. The role of the drari is therefore an important one with diverse performative and economic opportunities.

Learning and Advancing as Drari

The process by which someone becomes a gnawa m'allem has changed dramatically over the past generation. This is likely a continued change from previous generations, as well, but the stark contemporary developments are what dominate the conversation of older m'allemin. The description of the younger generation is not unlike similar conversations about youth held throughout the world, and they contain large doses of nostalgia alongside a range of other emotions. Here I outline the standard levels of escalation available to a dedicated drari as he advances through his career. Some drari climb through these steps in an effort to achieve the distinction of being a m'allem, something traditionally granted by a teacher. Others find a point along this process to stop, a place that fits their skill sets or spiritual calling well. Drari who do not have the ambition to advance or lack skill as a singer or instrumentalist may specialize as a permanent figure in one of these other roles. Advancing to the level of a featured vocalist, a hariqsa, to take advantage of vocal skill and knowledge of specific complex songs, for example, will likely lead to an increase in performance opportunities and pay with a variety of m'allemin.

The advancement through these roles relates to a variety of factors, including age, skill, spiritual calling, and ambition. As I go on to describe, the youngest members of the ensemble, perhaps adolescents who are newly interested in gnawa music, spirits, and community, often occupy the first stage (juqay). With time, these young learners develop their skills as singers, then on the qaraqib, and finally on the hajhuj. To the frustration of their teachers, youth often circumvent this progression by acquiring a hajhuj on their own and learning songs and styles from prominent recording artists. They do so using CDs, circulated digital recordings on cell phones or other media, and YouTube or similar online platforms. As adolescents continue on a training that can extend into old age, they may become known for their vocal, instrumental, or dance abilities. Some of these stages, especially that of a dancer (koyo) depend on a relationship with specific spirits or groups of spirits. The dance accompanying the blue spirits, focused on that of Sidi Musa for example, features the dancer to perform semi-acrobatic ground moves while balancing a bowl of water on his head. While the dancers always have a relationship with that particular set of spirits, in my experience, they are also always strong dancers in general. Zakari from Marrakech, whose dance opened chapter 1, spent his teens learning to break-dance before bringing that skill set into the gnawa ceremony as a featured koyo.

The relationship between the activities of the ceremony and those goals and skills that relate to the world outside is fluid and dynamic. Just as Zakari's dances relate to his pop culture abilities, others master the vocal or instrumental parts of songs not only because of their relationship with the sprits that receive those songs but also to prove themselves as able performers for their m'allem, the possessing spirits, the audience, any cell phones that may be recording, and even any ethnographers like myself who might be in the room. This, therefore, is not a hard and fast progression of advancement. It is a template, something that serves as an ideal for teachers as they watch their apprentices grow. Frequently, however, these stages provide a path not taken by younger performers who aim for careers as gnawa practitioners on their own terms, both within rituals and on stages.

A new learner begins as a juqay, essentially a personal assistant to the m'allem. At this point, he has decided to enter into the process of learning tgnawit, the art and science of the gnawa, and chosen a teacher. A good juqay will carry out a range of the nonmusical tasks for his teacher both on a regular daily basis and during ritual evenings. He will hang around, generally attempting to learn and understand the livelihood while being introduced to the community. During spare moments, he will have the opportunity to ask questions. Common tasks for a juqay include running minor errands, bringing coffee or tea throughout the day, and carrying the hajhuj or other instruments. When deemed trustworthy, these tasks extend to the realm of caring for the ritual paraphernalia (incense, rose water, dates, milk, and so on) and holding a goat or other large animal still during the *dbiha*, the sacrificial killing that denotes a proper ritual.

The content of lessons is not consistent. Many older m'allemin tell me about how they would hear the way their teacher performed a song, sit all night attempting to remember it, and run home to try to figure the nuances out after a performance was over. This has changed dramatically, especially with the advent of recording functionality in even the most inexpensive cell phones. It is not uncommon to see a group of drari or youth on the street huddled around a cell phone, listening to a ritual performance from the evening before. At this point, the assistant is unpaid or poorly paid, usually does not play an instrument during the events, and may dance during the *fraja* (entertainment opening) segments that require the entire group. He will concentrate on memorizing the responses of the songs and may mimic the rhythms of the qaraqib by patting his hands on his knees.

Most frequently, young members of the group hold this role, even children as young as ten. The boundaries are flexible. During a lila in Mulay Ibrahim, outside of Marrakech in 2011, M'allem 'Abd al-Kabir Marshan's troupe featured an adolescent juqay whose acrobatics wowed the audience. He served as an intern of sorts, doing all of the errands expected of his status, like holding the goats during the sacrifice described previously, but his virtuosity as a dancer showed his auspicious potential as a koyo. He was active during the opening segments of the event but mostly only sat alongside the other drari once the possessions began. From this vantage point, he could continue his education by memorizing choral responses and beating out qaraqib patterns. Over time, if given the opportunity and calling, he will likely move more fully into the next phase of his apprenticeship.

The remaining roles are primarily defined by specific types of musical participation in the ritual event. The koyo plays one of the two *tbal* (or sometimes three) during the opening and closing of the ritual. The *tbal* is the large marching drum, slung over the shoulder during the procession into the home and opening entertainment segments of the ceremony. Some regions' m'allemin reintroduce the tbal at the end of the mluk sections, closing the event. The koyo plays a consistent dotted-eighth/sixteenth note pattern on the smaller of the two tbal, called the *fradi*. The m'allem plays a second, larger instrument called the *zwaqi*, the decoration. He uses a series of stock and improvised rhythmic figures to communicate with the dancing members of the group. As the m'allem speeds up subtly over time, the koyo's main task is keeping his accompaniment pattern locked into that changing tempo.

While this is the standard job of the koyo as described to me, I also hear the word used to compliment the featured dancers during the fraja. The performance is judged by this koyo's ability to both lock into the rhythmic and melodic intricacies and his virtuosity in both standard motions and improvised inspiration. The example of Zakari described in chapter 1 demonstrates the importance of ability within the dance. By incorporating moves from his break-dancing days into his entranced dance, during which he balances a bowl of water on his head, he effectively brings his own experience into communion with his possessing spirit's ritual needs. He and others explained to me that the balancing of the bowl, like the ability to cut oneself with a knife or the resistance to burning candles that highlight trances in other segments of the ritual, proves the possession. These feats of balance and endurance of pain are only possible for the embodying spirit; they are superhuman. Yet the spirit taking over Zakari took advantage of his young and athletic body to perform a spectacle of spins and rolls during that 2010 event in Meknes.

A very different koyo was a part of 'Abd al-Wahid Stitu's troupe at a lila in the 2013 pilgrimage festival (*mussem*) in Sidi Ali. The troupe was a group of elder m'allemin who came together for the week's events. These were old friends from different parts of the country, and there was a certain festivity surrounding the evening. One elder m'allem from Asilah acted as koyo and danced during many of the ritual segments, for many of the possessing spirits. His moves were restrained, reverent, and far from the acrobatics of the young Zakari, yet his stature within the community and expertise in aligning his dance with Stitu's hajhuj playing garnered him similarly enthusiastic responses from those present. After an especially well-received dance, the koyo may turn and begin reciting blessings on those around him in exchanged for monetary gifts. These blessings and gifts punctuate the end of a ritual segment. Thus, a good koyo can inspire larger gifts from the ritual audience, making his an important economic contribution to the ensemble.

The hariqsa's role is that of a vocal assistant to the m'allem. While the juqay, koyo, and khalifa (substitute hajhuj player, described later) could carry out their jobs while knowing only the choral responses of each song, a hariqsa steps in when the m'allem's voice needs a break. He, therefore, must know a number of verses for the song and be able to sing loudly, clearly, and confidently. Most often, a hariqsa's opportunity to take over is planned in advance for a point in the ceremony when the m'allem will need a short rest. For this reason, a hariqsa may not need to know the entire repertoire, but his use is certainly greater if he has a comprehensive grasp of it, as he could take over on the fly if necessary.

Usually, there will be one member of a group who serves as hariqsa. This person has many opportunities during his turn as the main vocalist to demonstrate his high level of knowledge and understanding of tgnawit. Sometimes, though, a drari is able to achieve the state of hariqsa solely through his vocal clarity and power. This is especially the case for those who are in groups led by a m'allem whose voice is not particularly strong. Interestingly, many uses of a hariqsa that I have witnessed came during the most well-known songs in the repertoire, especially those that required a slightly different vocal timbre, higher range, understanding of scalar patterns not standard to gnawa performance, or heightened endurance.[4] For example, 'Abd al-Rzaq once served as hariqsa and khalifa for his brother in a performance and took over during the more difficult songs, notably "Aisha Hamdushiyya." The use of drari in supporting roles can backfire, however, or be a crutch. In 2012, a young m'allem in his thirties invited me to a lila where two of his skilled drari served the role of hariqsa. They assisted the leader after his voice wore out from the struggle to sing over the rest of the ensemble at about 3:00 a.m. In this case, the frequent use of a hariqsa opened the young performer up to criticism that he did not have the requisite vocal strength to properly lead a ritual ceremony. His inexperience with more complicated repertoire and his fatigue during the long event proved costly for the clients. Fearing that the spirits were unsatisfied, they hired another m'allem to complete a second lila a few nights later.

The last major role that I discuss here is that of the khalifa. This is a member of the ensemble who has the skill to take the hajhuj and play. The instrument is a very physical one and quickly wears out the hand, especially the right index finger. A look at a m'allem's hand shows the abuse that the rough instrument causes. Despite the use of henna and other techniques to strengthen the skin, cuts, bleeding, ripped fingernails, and other injuries might require a m'allem to stop in the middle of a song. On occasion, however, the khalifa's role is preplanned, allowing the m'allem to take a moment of respite from the expected fatigue. In contemporary practice, with shorter rituals and the frequent use of amplification, the khalifa is less common. Like with the hariqsa, a m'allem can strategically use the khalifa to augment the ritual experience for clients, as Gaga used 'Abd al-Rzaq during the first ritual that I attended in 2006. He was able to take some short breaks while also showing his status as the leader of an ensemble that featured an established local m'allem, something rare within the community.

This track of advancement through tasks, dance, singing, and playing shows a specific hierarchy of skills. It does not imply that one is more valued than the other as a skill, since every group must be made up of those who specialize in each, but it does demonstrate that, for the drari, rhythmic understanding and lyrical knowledge are more important than virtuosity on the hajhuj. Not all groups use a khalifa, yet every ensemble needs good dancers, tbal players, and vocalists.

The final arrival comes when the learner is deemed to be a m'allem. At this point, the student ceases to be a drari and goes out on his own, assembling his own ensemble of drari and looking for work. This process might take thirty years or more to complete and many drari, especially those who become a well-known koyo, khalifa, or hariqsa, maintain a productive career without ever making this last move. Once the drari becomes a m'allem, it becomes inappropriate for him to enter into another m'allem's group as a drari except under specific circumstances, vastly limiting his economic opportunities. Instead of trying to become a trusted drari for m'allemin, he must directly attempt to secure work for himself and his group by building a wider reputation among the community. This final move may be the result of a calling, spirits demanding this next step from an adept, but increasingly it is born of the ambition of the musician and ritual leader. Striving to become a m'allem requires the mastery of instrumental technique, a vast repertoire, singing ability and the vocal strength to project over an ensemble, and an intimate understanding of the "gnawa sciences." This ritual knowledge is especially equivocal as the ways in which musicians make this last step is changing dramatically.

Creativity and Change in the Educational System

Historically, the teacher granted the status of m'allem. Students who learn the repertoire and ascend through these steps often move around, usually visiting other cities, in search of a more complete understanding. Most current m'allemin are able to list a variety of cities from across Morocco in which they spent time working with different teachers. Some older m'allemin claim to have taught a host of contemporary stars. I frequently hear statements like "[So and so] sat right here and learned from me," (often followed by a negative judgment about how this now well-known performer did not stay long enough and, therefore, has a deficient understanding of tgnawit). The also common "[So and so] will tell you that he taught every m'allem in Morocco if you ask him" quickly counters this sentiment.

The bestowal of status and achievement has changed dramatically according to those of previous generations. According to 'Abd al-Rzaq and others in Fez, when a drari wanted to prove himself, he would assemble a lila and play it in its entirety. He would invite all of the prominent m'allemin of the city, who would sit in the back and watch, judging. This performance, not unlike a juried recital or dissertation defense, would end in a discussion between the "judges" and a decision to grant the new status to the drari or to require him to continue his studies and practice until future notice. Some have told me of citywide leaders who acted as final arbiters and made these decisions, something closer in line to contemporary practice in the hamadsha and ʿissawa brotherhoods.[5] Teachers celebrate those drari who go through this process and achieve their rank via this apprenticeship system by praising them in conversation and even tacking their photos to the walls of their homes, as was the case with Mʿallem Hamid, an established gnawi who lives in the Fez Jdid neighborhood adjacent to the Fez medina, who frequently turned toward a picture of his student Hicham that hung above his low couches. Hicham's move to Belgium following his studies did not disturb his mʿallem. Instead of interpreting it as a grab for fame and money in Europe, a criticism he levied against other young gnawi who travel extensively, he saw his student as doing a service. The Moroccan diaspora in Belgium, he explained, would need someone of Hicham's character and ability. Those drari who do not complete the training and testing, and instead choose to self-identify as mʿallemin, receive the scorn of those same elders. While some older professional drari articulate similar biases, many do not. This may be due to the fact that a less skilled or experienced mʿallem might still pay them to join his ensemble. In fact, some performers who self-identify as mʿallemin go out of their way to hire prominent drari in an effort to bolster the respect given to their group. One gnawa musician that I often ran into during lila ceremonies around Fez was Hamid Sharif. He appeared in the drari of many younger mʿallemin and served as an authority figure for those whom he performed with. They looked to his presence as a sign of the ensemble's value to potential clients, and his willingness to be a leader for these young groups, even though he was not the mʿallem, helped him to get a great deal of work and influence in the community.

The frustrations expressed by most current mʿallemin, though, is that young students want to learn the hajhuj right away. Because there are no consistent "lessons" to be had in most cases, the younger members turn to CDs and other recordings. Once they learn a few tracks, as the story goes, they call themselves mʿallemin and go find work. The insult that older mʿallemin articulate comes from how younger players focus on the musical content instead of the ritual and lyric knowledge. Their repertoire does not go beyond the most famous songs, meaning that when they are asked to extend a specific portion of the ceremony by a possessed client, they may run out of songs and replay the ones that they have just performed.

Many aspiring students of the most recent generation garner their knowledge from very different sources.[6] First, instead of traveling extensively, they collect recordings, fostering the ability to identify and replicate the performance and vocal style of the country's most recorded mʿallemin. Those who are not well connected turn to street performance, learning on their own and taking advantage of this informal stage to demonstrate both mastery and creativity. The role of listening and musical memory is vastly different, as learners now have the ability to pause, rewind, and revisit their aural sources using widely available recording technology (including cell phones). Learners who remain outside of the standard semiformal educational system described in the previous sections, however, lack a mechanism by which they can prove their ritual knowledge. While the descriptions of "juried" lila performances may be more nostalgia than past standard practice, apprentices still had the opportunity to impress their teachers and others whom they met through their teachers' connections. Instead, YouTube and public performances assist these contemporary students of the gnawa sciences as they aspire to renown.

While in Marrakech one evening, I experienced a salient example of this novel process of musical and ritual transmission. As I was walking with a friend and knowledgeable gnawa participant named Adil Walili, we passed a group of youth on the side of the road. It was the late evening, perhaps even the early morning, yet these young men were energetically engaged in what appeared to be impromptu performances of the most well-known pieces of the gnawa repertoire, they were jamming. They stopped Adil, begging him to join. As we sat, I heard exact replications of some of the most known recordings. They passed the hajhuj around between songs, taking turns as the m'allem. Each knew some of the lyrics, but none continued beyond the first few lines, likely because most recorded songs are shorter than the versions performed in ritual. The musical diversity of their knowledge was limited, but their vocal and instrumental virtuosity was well beyond that of some of the most prominent m'allemin of the older generations. Adil, however, was their informal teacher, their informal m'allem. His knowledge went beyond these recordings, but he only rarely performs with troupes in ritual settings. He looks forward to continuing his training, but in the meantime, he must continue working at a nearby restaurant in order to feed his family.

These young adults trade recordings, share YouTube videos, and generally critique each other as they all work to improve their own performance techniques. Yet they are left outside of a system that still requires a direct relationship for both ritual knowledge and an honorific title of legitimacy. In one sense, their education parallels the crowd sourcing that is so common throughout our modern world's learning, as sites like Wikipedia become collaborative efforts toward an end goal. Their aspirations are therefore rooted in the current world of the gnawa, not a nostalgic memory. They are just as competitive for tourist gigs, some festivals, and recording opportunities, especially in fusion settings, but they are almost completely incapable of winning any ritual clients. They must prove their tgnawit through new means, by winning over the respect of their peers and listeners outside of the ceremony. Those artists that most fully connect with an audience, either in ritual or on stage, will be successful in sharing and monetizing their own version of tgnawit.

Working within this New Authenticity

In the following pages, I return to Yassine, the talented young gnawi who chose to operate in ambiguity outside of the system outlined in the previous sections. Living in Fez, Yassine has spent time with m'allemin from around the region but did not follow through the traditional system of learning. Instead, he sees his gnawa performance as a commercial activity, and he orients his performance practices and economic goals accordingly. He targets youth in nonritual settings and claims to have little interest in carrying out the healing practices associated with the gnawa tradition. Yet he accepts ritual work when opportunities arise, most frequently resulting from his active staged performance schedule. His lila ceremonies can be quite small, as those who need a therapeutic ritual but lack the connections within the gnawa community comprise his most frequent clients. News of his performance of ceremonies provokes the ire and disdain of most other m'allemin in Fez. Their opinions of him range from uninterested to offended, as he is seen as taking work that should rightfully go to the "true" experienced m'allemin. That is, when others have heard of him at all. 'Abd al-Rzaq, for example, was dismissive when I asked what he thought of these younger m'allemin finding work; they do what they want, he told me. Yassine is one of the more successful young gnawi that I met who pursued an alternative career path more akin to that of a professional musician than a ritual leader. Perhaps those who would hire Yassine simply would not be interested in sitting through (or paying for) 'Abd al-Rzaq's version of the ceremony.

When I returned to Morocco in the summer of 2012, I decided to bring my new banjo, an instrument that has been a mainstay in Moroccan music since the 1970s. This is thanks in part to the music of groups like Nass al-Ghiwane, which brought a variety of Moroccan regional traditions together and created what was arguably Morocco's first popular music (see chap. 5). When Nass al-Ghiwane's Alal al-Alili put down his 'ud in favor of the louder and easier-to-tune six-string banjo, he found an instrument that closely approximated the sound of a variety of traditional instruments. I performed with Yassine during a religious music festival in Fez in Ramadan 2012 organized by 'Abd al-Rahim Amrani, the prominent hamadsha leader and local impresario. As is common for Amrani's events, the conclusion of this concert featured a hastily assembled fusion project. Four of us, myself on violin, Yassine on hajhuj, and two percussionists (one on *djembe*, a West African drum uncommon in any tradition featured during the event) accompanied a *malhun* (a genre of popular sung poetry) singer from Meknes. At this point, I knew only a small handful of malhun melodies, so I was forced to rely on my aural skills to follow. Yassine, filling out the roll of a rhythmic bass part, did the same.

Later, I was reintroduced to Yassine by a mutual friend, Omar Channafi. Omar is a young Moroccan photographer and a budding impresario of cultural events in his own right. His frequent activities are well attended and include exhibitions that readily feature musical performances. For one such event, Omar invited a number of musicians from different backgrounds, representing his ideals of this young, affluent community. Through the rehearsals for this event, I toyed with a few ways in which I could join my own tastes and skills on the banjo with Yassine's ideas about gnawa fusion. The resulting performance included freestyle slam poetry in a variety of languages, opening an opportunity to bring in a funk and hip-hop rhythmic sensibility. Alternating between repetitive rhythmic phrases and some underlying claw hammer patterns, I was able to settle into the ambiguous harmonic motion implied by the pentatonic scales used by the gnawa. By the end of the evening, the audience of twenty-somethings and teenagers were on their feet, dancing and singing along. Yassine invited me to continue playing with his own group, the Gnawa Lions, possibly in reference to his own mane of dark hair. In my second time playing with this group, at another of Omar's events, I had to pay far closer attention to this new iteration's drum set player and found a role akin to that of the funk rhythm guitarist.

I point out my own place within the textural fabric of Yassine's group because of the flexibility of creativity he afforded me. He met each of my additions with excitement that made his eagerness in searching for a "fusion" with Western funk and hip-hop explicit. Other members of the most recent version of the Lions were Fouad, a *sh'abi* violinist, and Bin Kiran, a keyboardist, both experienced in Moroccan popular music. They spent these two performances, like I did, searching for ways to fit their personal voices into a collaborative space alongside Yassine's playing and singing. His array of percussionists, two young qaraqib players and a djembe player, sang the choral responses to Yassine's calls, and the sound of the tradition remained at the front of the texture. With each passing performance, however, we found our respective pocket more quickly and the fusing became less ragged. And after each, Yassine was more excited about the next.

Among young gnawa musicians who found success as performers on stages, Yassine was notable in how he parlayed his skill with audiences into ritual performance opportunities. In ritual, he used his experiences from outside of the standard training to his benefit. His performance aimed to entertain his clients while demonstrating the hard-earned knowledge from his intense individual study. One of my lasting impressions comes from an event where Yassine was hired to perform the rare Jewish gnawa ceremony in January 2013 (see Hell 2002, 272–73). The event features a repertoire vastly different from that of the standard ritual, and few m'allemin bother to learn it due to its uncommon usage. Some of the possessing spirits are identical, but there are others (such as Da'ud, or King David) who might be more commonly associated with the Jewish tradition. The event features specific paraphernalia, including candles, occasionally a cross or crucifix (demonstrating some slippage in the understanding of non-Muslim faiths), and often some type of alcohol. In fact, the presence of alcohol is the most common reason cited by m'allemin when explaining to me why they do not carry out this type of ceremony, as it is prohibited within Islam. Others have clandestine photos with Johnny Walker bottles that they pull out to show their knowledge of and experience with this ceremonial repertoire.

During the small event (the ensemble featured only one qaraqib player and only the client's family was present), Yassine fell victim to a common issue with young players: he knew some of this nonstandard repertoire, but he could not keep up with the continued desires of the trancing and dancing clients. They wanted to continue, partially because his performance was inciting trance in his listeners, but also because they were having a great time. The host, a *shuwwafa*, or clairvoyant, who works as a *muqaddima* when hosting other lila ceremonies throughout the year, demonstrated her possession by reading the futures of the women who were present. To maintain the musical inertia through the event, Yassine went back and repeated a few songs. As the afternoon moved on, however, he began to take liberties. Eventually during a performance of "Hammadi," a song that also appears in portions of the standard ritual event, Yassine improvised texts about his own life. The listeners laughed as he wound his way through his musical story. He had departed significantly from the ritual, but his music was still based within it and accomplished its ritual task. Yassine the artist, the fnan, was proving himself a creative and successful m'allem, at least for this small group of trancing listeners.

The Gnawa Lovers

The economic struggles of a professional career as a gnawa musician combine with the range of new technologies available to young learners and listeners to greatly influence the aesthetics of public performance. Modes of learning are dramatically changing thanks to the innovations and aspirations of young artists like Yassine or those youth on the side of that road in Marrakech. They are not only performers but also a prominent group of influential consumers of gnawa recordings. Their ways of learning take new technologies, values, and goals as given. They use their cell phones and YouTube to stay aware of what different artists are doing, to get ideas for their own playing, and to share their innovations with the rest of their young community. They are the *muhibbin*, the lovers of this music.

The young artists use what they hear around them, incorporating the sounds of prominent recorded gnawa musicians and those of popular music to build their audiences. They are playing to others like them, but they are still tied to a traditional system that values ritual knowledge and efficacy. As they step outside of the institution of apprenticeship, they must find alternatives for building their esteem, their authority, and their tgnawit. They do so by knowing and fully engaging their audiences. Some listeners want to be entertained while others judge the performers based on their depth of knowledge. Yassine works hard to talk the talk while walking the walk. He keeps a notebook that he fills with different versions of ritual song texts that he hears in recordings, lila rituals, and staged performances as he travels the country. He is quick to demonstrate Algerian versions of a few songs from the repertoire or other regional variations. He approaches gnawa musical diversity and history like a scholar. But when he takes the stage with his band, he and his Lions get the audience up and dancing by digging into what they want: a funky pop beat. They turn giddy when he slides into a tune typical of a wedding celebration. This is the audience of people whose tastes align with his own; they are his cohort, the muhibbin who love what he does. It is these audiences, not the elders, who effect such dramatic change on the system of learning and advancement in Morocco. Their values bear performers who speak to them, who play the songs that they want to hear, and who do it in modern ways. Often the performers who engage these audiences lack the ritual knowledge of those who apprentice themselves and become drari, and as such, their ceremonies are wont to fail. But they know how to work a crowd. And, as Yassine's examples show, some can certainly entertain the spirits as well.

This move toward entertainment, an inclusive turn that engages ritual audiences more intentionally, resulted from a change in those very listeners present when men and women—family, friends, and neighbors—would fall into trance. Musicians who are quite different from Yassine respond to this pressure by orienting their own identities and performance practices toward their communities, their audiences, and their values. The music of the gnawa ritual now pervades Morocco's popular culture, and not only in reference to the projects and collaborations aimed toward world music markets. The sound permeates the domestic scene as musicians from across the country's wealth of diverse genres scramble to find ways to incorporate the powerful music into their own. Chapter 5 moves toward the history of this popular climb from the margins to the mainstream.

Notes

1. Many scholars of contemporary gnawa practice note, and often lament, the shortening of the ritual as a sign of the "desacralization" of gnawa practice (for an example, see Hell 2002, 351).

2. Despite two invitations that demonstrated al-Qasri's desire to show that he was, in fact, a ritual leader, I was unable to attend either. I look forward to reconnecting with al-Qasri during a future research visit, when I can witness the content of his ritual practice. Promoters will occasionally refer to a night of music as a lila, even though the intention of trance is absent. Even during these events, however, individual *maskun* may become overtaken by their possessing spirits. He was clear with me in stating that his lila ceremonies contained ritual healing.

3. The division of income is fluid and depends on the individual m'allem, the relationship between the m'allem and the drari, and other concerns specific to that instance.

4. Though there are a few scales that are common throughout the gnawa repertoire, possibly because they are idiomatic to the hajhuj, some songs across the lila feature nonstandard melodic content that is borrowed from other Moroccan genres. The most well-known example is "Aisha Hamdushiyya," which comes from the hamadsha ritual and features a pitch content, melodic structure, meter, and texture that is different from most songs that surround it during the ceremony (see chap. 6). Others are borrowed from the *jallaliyyat* tradition, popular music styles, *malhun*, Andalusian modes (*tubuʿ*), and the Arabic classical modes (*maqamat*).

5. Chlyeh (1998, 60–64) quotes Abdelatif at length as he describes his visions, emotions, and his memory of the community that surrounded his own experience as he conducted a ritual for the first time.

6. What I outline here is a form of semiformal education, a system with its own informal institutions. No mʿallemin with whom I worked were able to identify an explicit system with distinct members, even in the broadest sense, yet the idea that something that once was is now faltering was consistent in interviews. The difference appears to be in relation to a changing mode of transmission. While the semiformal system still exists, the individualistic mode of learning the gnawa music and ritual, described in the following sections, is now far more common. The celebration of those learners who remain faithful to the apprenticeship system becomes a way to preserve this system and influence young learners away from relying on CDs for their musical knowledge and the trappings of commercial fame. The efficacy of this strategy in the attitudes of young learners would be an interesting and fruitful avenue of research.

5 New Opportunities

Muhammad Sousi, a malhun singer in Fez, invited me to join his ensemble in 2012. His group welcomed me, and I began to join them in performances, first on violin and then on banjo. Malhun is a popular genre of accompanied sung poetry. It closely resembles classical poetic forms and that similarity gives the malhun a respected place within the country's arts. Moroccans across the country, however, love it without regard to their own background or economic class. The poorest Moroccans are ready to sing long segments of their favorite texts upon request while the wealthiest gather in hotel ballrooms to celebrate malhun as national cultural heritage.

Sousi attempted to teach me melodies ahead of time by rote, but my primary task was finding the white long shirt and baggy pants, red hat, and yellow pointed shoes that would help me to fit in during concerts. I followed the ensemble's melodies in performance, taking advantage of the repetitive nature of the musical content to "fake" my way through gigs. While it was a mentally exhausting task, it taught me to hear patterns within the lines and ornamentations. In fact, the rest of the ensemble was doing something similar as they worked to follow the soloists' twists and turns through specific passages (though they had the luxury of knowing the melody in advance!). I performed with the ensemble in unexpected settings ranging from the stage of the Fez Festival of World Sacred Music to a suburban fashion show. In each instance, I learned a bit more about how the music worked and what it meant to the listeners.

When I arrived at his home in Fez's new city one afternoon, Sousi grandly informed me that he was creating the first malhun song in gnawa style. He knew that I was learning hajhuj and asked me to bring it along. I struggled to follow his ornamentations on the instrument but quickly realized that, first, I did not have the necessary mastery of either the gnawa instrument or malhun's melodic structures to fuse the two and, second, the song was hardly idiomatic to the hajhuj anyhow. Another performer could have found a workable line to play, but it was not happening for me, at least not quickly. We set the idea aside and moved on to other things.

During that summer's Fez Festival of World Sacred Music, Sousi asked me to bring my garb, my violin, and my hajhuj to join his group on the large Bab Boujloud stage. The festival's two main stages could hardly feature more different lineups. The Bab Makina stage hosts paid concerts with mostly international artists. I have seen Senegalese singer Youssou N'Dour, French rapper 'Abd Al Malik, and

American artist Ben Harper performing there. *The Boujloud stage, which takes over the large square just outside the* medina, *is for free concerts and focuses on domestic musicians. The audiences at Boujloud can be young, but many families come out as well. Boys push to the gates right in front of the stage, mothers sit farther back on steps and ledges around the square. People mill while food vendors cut back and forth selling candies and fresh potato chips.*

Sousi wanted to introduce his gnawa-style malhun at some point during the event. Sadly, I had to stash my hajhuj pretty far away and needed some warning before we started the song, not that I knew what to play anyhow. I did not get that warning. Given our rehearsal's success, I was neither too disappointed nor was I surprised at the oversight (which may not have been unintentional). Even without the hajhuj, which would likely be inaudible anyway thanks to the microphone placement, Sousi had set up plenty of nods to a gnawa style. The percussionists in his group pulled out a tbal *and* qaraqib. *The group had a simple and clear chant refrain that responded to Sousi's "calls." The poem's melody was in a borrowed Andalusian mode that echoed the pentatonic gnawa sound. Then, surprising me and much to the delight of the crowd, an older member of the ensemble stood and began to mimic different dance gestures from the early parts of the gnawa ceremony. He spun gingerly and shuffled back and forth across the stage. The ensemble had only learned the specifics of the tune before we went on stage, but it worked. The performance was far from the best of the night, but it was one of the most well received. Cheers followed every gesture as the musicians played to the crowd's enjoyment of this fusion. The melody is now part of Sousi's repertoire, as he aligns it with different religious texts. It always seems to be a crowd favorite and a mark of his ensemble's uniqueness within a crowded field of malhun singers.*

Shifting Aesthetics and Schizophonia

Spiritual sounds and beliefs percolate into popular culture, quickly engaging the soundscape of public life. As the musical components of Morocco's gnawa practitioners conflated a new aesthetic to Islamic values through performance—aurally joining sub-Saharan and Sufi rituals—their sound became a malleable part of the Moroccan popular culture industries. In this chapter, I illuminate how artists within and outside of gnawa tradition utilize the intersection of music and belief to demarcate novel boundaries for publicly articulated Muslim values. As gnawa practices became essential parts of Morocco's national soundtrack, many pragmatic artists incorporated gnawa songs into inspired popular contexts. The ritual changed as well, thanks in part to the shifting aesthetic tastes of audiences and performers. Both processes continue today. In the following pages, I locate ways in which audience demands influence those in the music industry to borrow from the gnawa ritual. The historical and ethnographic contexts of these exchanges demonstrate the interrelationships and overlaps that obfuscate boundaries of sacred and secular in the musical world of these listeners and performers. In doing so, they reinforce a vision of *tgnawit* that comes with virtuosity, commercial success, and an ability to adjust musical and ritual content to effectively match audience expectations and tastes.

Public performances of diverse and previously marginalized sacred ritual practices have widened the bounds of what constitutes proper public Islamic piety in Morocco. This has been the result of an intentional top-down cultural project led by the monarchy since independence in 1956 and grew out of French attempts at negotiating political power during the colonial period. The project has not simply led to a more tolerant population, however, but also given fuel to the rise of conservative reactionaries within the debate about appropriate public (and private) behavior. While larger processes and communities are obviously at play in such debates, here I focus on the gnawa and how their ritual music has entered mainstream popular culture.

Jonathan Shannon (2006) uses the metaphor of improvisation to describe the ways in which practitioners of Syrian *tarab* play with intellectual and economic capital to navigate the local challenges and opportunities of modernity. By improvising modernity, performers and audiences resolve competing understandings of Islam that are prominent across Syria (and, thanks to satellite television and the internet, the wider Islamic world). Their movement through professional life recognizes the importance of the global distribution of material and ideas while demonstrating a nuanced understanding of local decisions. Moroccan performers' worldviews sit firmly within the bounds of Islam, though they similarly improvise their way through the sacred and secular pressures of life as a performer. Names, places, language, holy figures, histories, stories, prayers, songs, and dress, for example, all inform everyday experience through what could be deemed "Islamic culture." Life in Morocco is littered with a performed public piety that can imbue the most innocuous of activities with a ritualized piousness. The gnawa provide one example: as they and other marginal brotherhoods become increasingly conspicuous and celebrated, more diverse artists draw on their music. Fans and detractors alike publicly debate these changing markers of public piety. Heterogeneous communities constantly process ethical tastes against this swirl of aural aesthetic signs, improvising and negotiating their relationships with—and within—modern life.

In dealing with ritual, religious, and folkloric musical performances, I examine the ways in which aesthetics shifted over the past decades, especially since the dominant influence of mass communications and commodification. Ritual groups including the *hamadsha*, gnawa, and 'issawa have long histories of commodifying their own musical practice in market squares, at weddings (Nabti 2006), and at sacred festivals that may or may not be related to each group's individual cosmology. These groups bridged the divide between religious and commercial performance, using their music to advertise their in-home ritual services to potential clients or to otherwise collect money from spectators. The public presence of these groups led to the introduction of their musical styles into the larger soundscape of the nation, in other words, into a growing Moroccan national consciousness. The understanding of this music in Morocco shifted, as a larger uninitiated community had the opportunity to publicly listen to music that otherwise existed only within the confines of religious or ethnic enclaves. The literal trajectories of music in public space traversed otherwise strict boundaries.

The aesthetic changes and innovations generated by these public sounds flowed directly into the creation and consumption of popular music in Morocco. They are also embedded into the meanings and nostalgic references of folkloric presentations across the country (see chap. 8). The commodification of a musical product—be it a previously religious song, instrument, groove, timbre, text, melody, or even an extramusical aspect of performance—changes the aesthetics of the community. Artists have new sounds and structures at their disposal, just as audiences develop new expectations. This process of commodification existed in the colonial-era market squares, and while it continues in similar venues today, its influence grew exponentially with the rise of technology and artists' adaptation to the economic opportunities of the contemporary music industry.

The concept of schizophonia, an idea that is inextricably linked to the soundscape itself (Feld 1994; Schafer 1994), cites the removal of context from musical sounds and ideas. As music is separated from its surroundings through recording, staged performance, or something similar, it is open to manipulation of the type that is instrumental in popular music. Schizophonia, used most frequently in discourses in global music and the music industry, often implies the disappearance of context as musicians use the medium of recording to reduce music from contextualized social practices to flat—though interesting—sounds. From here, they can reuse these sounds toward ends that bear little resemblance to the original musical context: a lullaby can provide exotica in a dance club track, for example. In this way, music and musicians can be easily exploited, especially because they often bear little decision-making power in how their musical creations are later used (see Meintjes 1990; Feld 1996).

While this is very much a part of the popular music industry's reality in Morocco, with gnawa music appearing throughout diverse genres from jazz to hip-hop, I focus here on domestic circulations of musical ideas. Instead of reducing a ritual recording to a "pure" sound, I witnessed transformations in Morocco that commonly allowed for artists to remove and revise ritual weight or meaning from their musical products in an effort to orient their own authenticity in performance. They used recordings and performances to perform their own *type* of context, demonstrating that they were a certain *type* of gnawa artist. In doing so, they recontextualized and reoriented themselves in different settings for different audiences and to different ends day in and day out. The logic of being a freelance musician proved a powerful strategy for navigating the complexities of professional life. As such, across these chapters I have been investigating the ways in which musicians intentionally manipulate local knowledge of contexts, creating new religious and musical statements *from* this background understanding, not *despite* previous aural connotations to ritual and religion. I examine how artists utilize referential meanings in their source materials to support their own needs, especially in reference to curating a narrative of authenticity based on a combination of Muslim piety, African heritage, and commercial success.

These efforts, however, are not exclusive to gnawa *m'allemin* or other practitioners. Musicians from across Morocco's diverse popular and religious genres make use of the rising spiritual and economic power of the gnawa ritual's repertoire and timbre. The notoriety of gnawa music escalated once foreign musicians visiting the country after independence heard and loved it. Moroccan artists took note and, as can be seen now in the huge variety of fusion projects that pepper the airways and festival stages, they found audiences across the country. Youth, especially young men, turn to gnawa music and its collaborative potential with hip-hop, but as I describe in the sections that follow, even the most austere performers of pious religious music have made use of this powerfully pentatonic aesthetic. The schizophonia that both decontextualizes and recontextualizes gnawa music and ritual has brought extraordinary attention to the population's musicians. With that comes opportunity at all levels for performers and listeners alike. It also blurs perceived divides between traditional and popular music—or between sacred and secular—that dramatically affect how the music and ritual operate within this improvised modernity.

Representing Popular Music

The integration of popular aesthetics into gnawa ritual music and the converse, where ritual aesthetics enter the popular imagination, highlight important questions of category and taxonomy. These questions are generally pregnant with extramusical meaning and carry vast ideologies. Hotly contested debates about religious practice, public piety, and youth musical aesthetics weave through even the most benign discussions of gnawa music in Morocco. Musical and ritual identity conflate, especially in the minds of those less familiar with the traditional practice and its contemporary forms. These questions can pull in two directions, sometimes simultaneously. They can take concerns of tradition and innovation, for example, and bring them together, celebrating the old in the guise of the new. Similarly, they can isolate categories and strengthen boundaries between them, just as conservatives railing against what they see as problematic innovation within religious practice separate the gnawa ritual from their view of proper Muslim faith.

In looking at the collaborative efforts with and borrowings from gnawa musicians that permeate so much of the domestic popular culture industry, my focus is on the slippery lines drawn between sacred and popular music. As examples from 'Abd al-Hadi bil-Khayat and Muhammad Sousi demonstrate, gnawa music's influence on popular music is not limited to jazz and hip-hop from artists like Majid Bekkas and Hassan Hakmoun. The most austere performers make use of the music when it suits their needs. While this speaks volumes about the acceptance of gnawa music, it also reflects on the economic pressures levied against all professional musicians in Morocco, regardless of ideological bent. Arguments toward mutual exclusivity, toward firm and clear boundaries between ideas about what music is and does, illuminate the ways in which the production and consumption of these musical styles poke holes through categorical walls. Someone can be both entertained and healed in a ritual, just as certain performances carry layers drawing from an array of influences. Seemingly exclusive categories overlap throughout musical and religious life, and the ever more popular sound of the gnawa proves to be no exception.

In *Representing African Music*, Kofi Agawu notes the difficulty in defining and classifying popular music. His recommendation: "Perhaps we should stop dreaming of an adequate taxonomy and speak simply of varieties of African popular music" (2003, 122). The diversity of musical practice in Morocco, as anywhere, has the power to cripple any attempt to create a tight, comprehensive, and cohesive definition of popular music. As recent scholarship demonstrates, however, the simple distinctions of technological usage fall short as well (Larkin 2008; Lee 1999). As Jonathan Sterne describes, narratives that forget the cultural context of technological innovation "cast technologies themselves as primary agents of historical change: technological deification is the religion behind claims like 'the telephone changed the way we do business'" (2002, 7). While technology is a major part of many forms of popular music, it is not the defining aspect, the thing that makes music "popular." I argue, instead, that it is the ways in which the artists decontextualize their own experiences, intentionally creating something "new" that is intentionally defined as popular, that deems a music as such. Artists and their audiences determine the ontology of their creations.

In the Moroccan context, music that brings together different styles to create something new is most apparent in the hip-hop fusions of groups like Fnaïr that intentionally incorporate samples from across the country's musical landscape into their very modern and slickly produced beats. Even more famous is the music of Nass al-Ghiwane, who combined previous rural forms to create a novel sound in the 1970s. Music entering into a "pop" category could include that of *sh'abi* artists like Hajib or Said Senhaji. Senhaji's songs about Aisha—a spirit from the hamadsha brotherhood's tradition who now appears in the gnawa ritual (see chap. 6)—are excellent examples of religious references that are firmly a part of the popular music circuit.

Words like *popular* and *traditional* are labels, applied by artists, fans, adepts, critics, and scholars alike, that do productive work in describing some aspect of how the music or performance practice exists in the world. They illuminate the roles played by the music, whether it juxtaposes an idea into something new (as popular music can do) or, perhaps, attempts to reify an idealized form of something worth celebrating (something that traditional music can do). Both terms carry a depth of baggage. Much of that baggage intersects and overlaps. They are adjectives that coincide to describe certain performances, such as those on stage at the Essaouira Festival of World Music, where the traditional and popular forms of gnawa performance can be nearly indistinguishable. Or, perhaps better put, performances often carry out both roles at once.

As the coming chapters move through descriptions of "popular music" aesthetics within the gnawa ritual, it is exactly this baggage that I am looking to identify. Few agree exactly on where specific musical traits fall, though many suggest that faster tempi and increased spectacle in ritual performance are clear examples of popular music's influence. Even those who do not point to those traits based in popular music aesthetics, however, note that the music "sounds" more like popular music and that certain practitioners are actively pursuing the ideals of the popular music industry. The specifics of terms like these foreground performer intent and context, but even they move aside as unimportant when faced with the opinions of many listeners. Take one story that was often repeated by young men sitting next to me at rituals; it was about a grandmother who, when gnawa music came on during a television show one night, stood and danced, falling into a deep state of possession. It did not matter what the show was about or what type of gnawa music was playing. When her spirit was called, her spirit came. No matter how "popular" the context—which was on television, after all— the music did what it is supposed to do. The sounds defied the vast distance that they traveled—to a satellite and back—to be anything but "popular": they made an old woman's living room into a space for a mediated healing ritual.

Walter Armbrust writes, "In the end there is no all-purpose definition of popular culture. Trying to arrive at one would be a waste of time. The forms of popular culture should arise from ethnography, not from preconceived packages" (2000, 25). I intend for the flexibility of these terms to open the space within my ethnography for locally relevant definitions of popular culture (and folklore). By privileging process over product, disparate forms of popular culture and music can ease into the rough analytical label. Armbrust continues by stating, "We want to shift our focus away from what it is and toward a focus on what it does" (26). I hope to follow in this path, looking at popular and folkloric performance styles in terms of what they do rather than what I think they might be.

The Gnawa within Morocco's Popular Culture

Morocco's colonial past heavily influenced the development of popular music in the country (Baldassarre 2003). Visiting artists and internationally circulating recordings of popular music led artists like Nass al-Ghiwane and Jil Jilala to create national genres and styles from elements of Amazight, Sufi, and gnawa music. Similarly, artistic activity in Interzone Tangier[1] and the surrounding Rif Mountains highlighted the ways in which Moroccan artists like the Master Musicians of Jajouka could enter into the global circuit via a local context (Schuyler 2000). Morocco's relationship with globalization follows the processes outlined by Jocelyne Guilbault, where globalization is an "opportunity to redefine and promote local identity" (1993, 138). As a significant tourist economy, the Moroccan state and domestic commercial interests continue to promote the country and many of its regions through festivals intended for international audiences. The prices in markets rise during festivals, as do lodging costs. The Moroccan national economy relies in many ways on an ability to promote and market Moroccan cultural identity internationally.

Moroccans and the Moroccan state navigate global migrations of culture (Appadurai 1996) through opaque measures of musical, cultural, and religious authenticity. They do so by embracing the wide array of available tools, some of which appear to be mutually exclusive: hybridity and purity, innovation and nostalgia, or showmanship and reverence. To this end, the gnawa also have a long history of pragmatism both within and outside of the ritual marketplace. Some gnawa musicians have become famous performers while maintaining their respect within the gnawa community. Others, however, are less successful. They are seen as "selling out," losing some element of their tgnawit as they gain prominence. The growth of attention toward the gnawa comes from a host of conflating factors ranging from changes to the ritual aesthetic to the shifting nature of professionalism within the community. Some other groups are following the model that the gnawa discovered, though few individuals—let alone an entire tradition—have seen quite the same level of transformation.

Hybridity flows through the examples that populate the remainder of this chapter. Even those who perform music lifted straight from their ceremonial repertoire, such as M'allem 'Abd al-Latif (see chap. 8), borrow gestures and strategies from the stage when they walk into a small venue or hotel restaurant. For the individuals and ensembles who are far more intentional with their fusions, like Nass al-Ghiwane's Paco, hybridity provides both an approach and an audience. Furthermore, the meanings created in commercial and ritual contexts play differently on various crowds, serving to accentuate an intertextuality that exists within and across performative styles (Kapchan and Turner 1999). The need to prove religious legitimacy while building a client base demonstrates that both contexts remain potent—even while they are changing.

There are two types of hybridity here. In the case of 'Abd al-Qadr's projects that I describe in the section that follows, ritual musicians enter into collaborative efforts. As Deborah Klein writes, not only are these part of the global world music circuit, they also maintain significance as local strategies in "globally connected villages" (2007, 83). In other cases, like Muhammad Sousi's malhun, non-gnawa artists reconfigure their own sound into something hybrid, playing on the same opportunities afforded ritual musicians and enabled (or perhaps inspired) by the growing audience for the previously marginal sound. These are not collaborations per se, but they work within the same pools of intertextuality and hybridity that connect a controversial possession ceremony to popular entertainment.

The aural symbols of Morocco's diversity circulate through a popular culture industry that has changed dramatically since independence. In the 1970s, the Moroccan recording industry became a collection of disconnected regional networks after the institution of new legal business ownership structures (Callen 2006). Musical genres that thrived in one part of the country were virtually unknown elsewhere, systematically reinforcing the fractured aesthetic tastes of the new nation. This same decade, however, saw the rise of a new generation of bands exemplifying changing aesthetic trends: these include Nass al-Ghiwane, Jil Jilala, and Lem Shahab. By combining stylistic attributes from various sacred and secular traditions across the country, they assembled the beginnings of a nationally resonant popular music.

Nass al-Ghiwane in particular became foundational for changes in the perception of gnawa music. 'Abd al-Rahman Kirouche, known as Paco, came from a family of gnawa musicians in the small coastal town of Essaouira. While the band had used gnawa instruments early on, before Paco's arrival, he infused the group with a new focus that dramatically changed its sound. The band began to perform adaptations of ritual gnawa chants and phrases. The low bass sound of his hajhuj playing comes through prominently in songs like "Mahmouna," "Ghir Khoudouni," and "Ya Bani Insane" while gnawa-influenced rhythms animate "El Madi Fate" and others. "Narjak Ana Lamchite," from the band's *Live Olympia 76* album provides a crisp example of the group clearly borrowing from Paco's history and incorporating that sound into its own style of songwriting.

It is hard to overstate the importance of these 1970s-era bands, as they brought gnawa and other regional traditions including malhun, hamadsha, and 'issawa into pop-fusion genres. Furthermore, they conflated this youth-oriented popular music with political activism through the lightly concealed protest that weaves through many songs, including, as an example, "Fin Ghadi Biyya Khouyya" ("Where are you taking us, Brother?," see Dernouny and Zoulef 1980 and Sayed 2011). These groups helped to firmly plant the gnawa as a recognized Moroccan musical practice. While there are similar populations with comparable musical traditions in Algeria and Tunisia, within Morocco, the gnawa are celebrated as a postindependence symbol of the country's Islamic diversity. This has enabled a much wider variety of musical borrowings into the frame of national popular music.

Simultaneously, an intentional top-down cultural project led by the monarchy grew out of French strategies of negotiating political power during the colonial period. Emilio Spadola (2014) outlines the various rationales used by both French colonial powers and postcolonial nationalist elites as they buttressed specific versions of Islam. He describes these efforts as attempts to reinforce local hierarchical practices in countering the rising influence of reformist versions of Islam within Morocco's borders. Alessandra Ciucci (2010) follows a similar arc through 'aita music and the contentious sounds of *shikhat*. In that instance, she writes, Moroccan nationalists "re-valorize" the music by "re-orienting" the performers. The Moroccan "specialists" she describes re-orientalize the music through the "objectification of the *shikhat* that deprives them of their own volition and voice" (82) in an effort to situate them within a normative moral system. In a similar way, debate surrounding the gnawa flows through both popular culture and the political landscape. The musical choices of public artists, not just gnawa musicians, therefore, carry wide implications.

While gnawa music is known internationally through collaborative projects such as those by Randy Weston, Pharaoh Sanders, Jimmy Page and Robert Plant, and the annual participants in the Essaouira Festival of World Music, efforts of the local sort highlighted by Deborah Klein (2007) regarding Yorùbá bàtá drumming can be more pertinent to the everyday lives of most practitioners. The pressures of outside listeners are certainly a part of the story of gnawa performance, even well before independence. Lapassade (1976, 209–10) and Hell (2002, 55) both mention instances where noninitiated listeners came to the gnawa for entertainment occurring as far back as the turn of the last century. Becker describes a historical account of performers traveling across the country to find new listeners in Tangier (2014, 122). Wider circulations and marketplaces are not new considerations for the contemporary performer. Instead, they are firmly part of the gnawa ritual's history, as are the stresses and influences of a local economy that so effectively fuses the priorities of live music as entertainment and ritual activity as healing.

Each group of spirits has songs specific to its constituent members. Melodies and texts define songs, and though they appear within larger sets of music in ritual, they are often recorded or borrowed as individual pieces. Many of these appear in popular settings whole, with or without the appropriate texts. Sometimes, however, artists simply use identifiably gnawa pentatonic scalar patterns or one of the rhythms of the qaraqib (*iqa' gnawiyya*) to allude to the ritual mystique. Though these types of borrowings have been moving through the country's music scene since before independence, it was with Nass al-Ghiwane's attention that the gnawa sound became both extraordinarily popular and politically charged.

While jazz, funk, reggae, and blues fusion have been very successful for gnawa musicians domestically and internationally, the remainder of this chapter focuses on two specific projects that depict the influence of the gnawa on mainstream conservative musical tastes in Morocco. The inclusion of gnawa in these aesthetic spheres demonstrates a significant shift in public expression of Islam in Morocco. Enjoying the sound of the gnawa does not always carry the consequence of placing the listener outside of the bounds of mainstream Islamic piety as it once did. Instead, it allows for breadth of pious performance techniques and aesthetics, many of which inform the strategies that m'allemin use in studios and on stages. This gives fodder to certain conservative audiences for whom these aesthetic and ethic links continue while bringing the debate about public piety into public spaces.

'Abd al-Hadi bil-Khayat: "Ya Buhali"

"Ya Buhali" by 'Abd al-Hadi bil-Khayat, tells the story of unrequited love, as the speaker pleads to Buhali, one of the gnawa spirits.[2] He invokes ritual paraphernalia and begs for assistance from a spirit who ignores his calls despite his intentions and attention. Musically, the song is a departure from bil-Khayat's Middle Eastern–influenced style. As an 'ud[3] player who studied and performed in Cairo for much of his early career, the performer's songs typically bear much more in common, stylistically, with those of Egypt's "golden age." In addition, his poems and musical style appeal to elite audiences, and his listeners are much less likely to fit the young revolutionary stereotypes that are associated with the audiences of gnawa fusion projects. Furthermore, biographical narratives about bil-Khayat's Islamic faith form an important part of his public image. In the 1980s, before this song's release, bil-Khayat completed the pilgrimage to Mecca and quit music. He refocused his life and passion on his Muslim faith and decided to cease performing. At the request of the then-reigning king, Hassan II, he returned to his career, but with a newfound ethical focus. The fact that this song was released after this conversion story demonstrates a changing relationship between the gnawa and more conservative audiences.

In the song, bil-Khayat adapts his sound to invoke the gnawa. He maintains his classical ensemble but adds two string instruments. One, the hajhuj, directly reflects his desire to incorporate the sound of the gnawa. He also brings a *lotar*, a string instrument that aurally cites other Moroccan popular folk music genres active throughout the country. M'allem 'Abd al-Qadr of Rabat, who played the hajhuj in the debut performance, explained to me that they were taught their parts to the song orally by rote over the course of the week preceding the staged performance. This was not a collaborative among creative peers, and even though he, a professional gnawa ritual leader, was present, his aesthetic input was not requested. The hajhuj and lotar accompaniment makes use of a common gnawa pentatonic formula that lacks a third and a rhythmic pattern dividing a compound meter into twos and threes. The hemiola feel of the string introduction (Example 5.1, mm: 4–5) plays with musical ideas that appear in the portion of the ritual that sings to female spirits, figures whose music is likely borrowed from

Example 5.1. "Ya Buhali" instrumental melody during the introduction. Hajhuj and lotar are shown with note stems pointed up; string melody has note stems pointed down.

popular music styles. In this sense, bil-Khayat is borrowing these figures back, reincorporating them into his own music after they have been steeped in a ritual aesthetic. The voice enters, lamenting the spirit's failure to assist in finding love.

> *Ya Buhali, bu darbala, gulti liyya, dir al-niyya*
> *Dirt al-niyya wa raʿi marhum*
> *Bkhur hadi hayta biyya wa dakhanha kuwwa ʾainiyya*
> *Wa ki al-nar al-hayta biyya wa ya Buhali*

O Buhali, wearer of the *darbala* [a patchwork garment identified
    with this spirit],
you told me to act with good intention
I acted with good intention and my vision is gravely lacking
This incense surrounds me and its smoke burns my eyes
And what is this fire that surrounds me, O Buhali?

In the song's text, bil-Khayat utilizes much of the language of or about the gnawa. For example, in recounting to Buhali, he describes his condition by saying, "I saw her there and was burned, not knowing what caused my addiction." More explicitly, the refrain sings of incense, smoke, and fire. He draws an analogy between gnawa ceremonial practice and love, a startling connection for a conservative religious singer whose standard elite and educated audience may disregard gnawa practice as a shameful and distasteful degradation of Islamic belief. Further, this work represents an example of creative and innovative hybridity within popular culture, though it is a highly unequal collaboration. Al-Qadr was not a part of any discussion surrounding the representation of gnawa music or ritual within the song. That it translated ritual content into a narrative of love exoticizes the ceremonial process. The m'allem, however, took part as a paid member of a professional ensemble, fully participating within the norms of the music industry.

Muhammad Sousi's Fez Festival of World Sacred Music Performance

The 2011 Fez Sacred Music Festival performance that opened this chapter provides a second fusion example. Muhammad Sousi's first ever malhun song in the rhythm and style of the gnawa did not include any gnawa musicians and, despite nods toward the ritual tradition, the show that day stayed close to the genre's norms and expectations. Sousi adhered to malhun's aesthetic conservatism while carving out space for his own innovation. Most listeners prefer the previous generation's great singers—Toulali and Bouzoubaa, for example—to today's live performances. The nostalgia surrounding these performers' scratchy recordings, now available almost exclusively as MP3 CDs or YouTube videos, certainly bleeds into popular opinion regarding their stature. Contemporary performances remain consistent with these older styles and the most widely heard poems in today's concert settings are compositions from generations ago. Musical material is recycled; new contexts and new music often feature melodies from old and famous performances. This musical stability extends to the point that, as Muhammad Sousi explained to me, while there are many hundreds of options, only about thirty melodies animate the vast majority of the musical output. Introducing a new melody based on gnawa pitch content and rhythm, therefore, was a stark innovation within the tradition. This is more striking given that malhun, especially in the city of Fez, is linked to Islamic piety in even the most secular of love poems. While instrumental accompaniment and poetic style makes this less explicitly devotional than other genres of recitation like *sama'*,[4] most poems praise Allah and the prophet, often culminating in a rise of excitement that evokes the aural climax of local Sufi ceremonies.

Morocco has seen a resurgence in malhun since the 1970s as part of the same popular music trends described above. Nass al-Ghiwane sang malhun-influenced pieces including "Allah ya Moulana," but Jil Jilala essentially "covered" a variety of poems from the malhun tradition. Members of the current generation of malhun singers continue to innovate, though they do so within the genre's conservative structures. Singers redefine melodies while incorporating novel elements from throughout Morocco's rich musical landscape to orient their sound toward increasingly large mass audiences. They are aware of trends and tastes, just as the poets always have been.[5] Musical innovations, including the importation of rhythms and instruments from religious practices, jazz, and rock, demonstrate intentional efforts to expand audiences.

The closing verse of a malhun poem incorporates a dramatic change in rhythm, melody, texture, and overall energy. The ensemble moves into a new meter, or at least a quicker tempo, and typically shifts into a call-and-response iteration of the poem's *harba*, its refrain, called the *insiraf*. Audience members often stand and begin clapping and singing along, sometimes going so far as to climb onto the stage with the ensemble. To get this sound and atmosphere, the insiraf moves from one of the standard malhun rhythms to something borrowed from ritual or popular music. This final verse can also feature local ritual sounds during Fez's malhun performances. To borrow Jonathan Shannon's term, it's "suficized" (2011, 261). This localizes the sound while differentiating it for

Example 5.2. Melody of "Lutfiyya" in a pentatonic "gnawa style" as sung by Muhammad Sousi.

national audiences. Muhammad Sousi uses this technique on satellite television to make his performances unique, even sacred. They are proudly from Fez, *fassi*. While almost all of his pieces end with an insiraf that is either 'issawa or hamadsha based, he made an especially shrewd move during the Fez Festival of World Sacred Music concert described at the opening of this chapter. His group often includes members from local Sufi troupes, and in this instance he wanted to further widen his ensemble's appeal by incorporating the gnawa.

To create a new setting for an old poem, Sousi invited gnawa percussionists to perform with the ensemble.[6] An elder member of the ensemble enacted some movements featured in the opening portions of the tradition's possession healing ritual. Like many malhun melodies, the performance featured the repetition of a melodic phrase performed heterophonically by the entire group. While this sounds more like malhun than gnawa music, the melodic shape does follow a pentatonic structure similar to that of the other tradition (see example 5.2). Certainly, different members of the audience enjoyed different elements of this hybrid performance. Perhaps most telling, though, when I asked him why he wanted to play a gnawa-style malhun piece for this particular large, open-air crowd, his response was strikingly simple: "Because the people will like it." But what was Sousi providing for his audience? What did listeners like so much about his rousing festival performance? The concert was part of a series that included Moroccan rappers, a famous gnawa musician, and a sh'abi singer of the type heard at weddings across the country. Each night drew a very different crowd, but many were there for every concert, eager to get out, hear some music, and enjoy the social scene around the square.[7] Sousi wanted to appeal to this wider audience of Moroccans of all ages and, in doing so, hoped to expand his own fan base. He alluded to the gnawa, using the percussionists, timbre, and dance, but the poetry remained purely within the malhun tradition. And it worked: the crowd was energized, its members screaming when they heard the qaraqib opening the song.

Ritual Aesthetics

The divisions between distinct religious practices or different groups of listeners are far from clear. As individuals hear and react to new musical ideas, they may incorporate related behaviors and beliefs into their own lives. In turn, these aural changes follow modern society's networked forms of social organization. Musical tastes and public behaviors identify a web of interactive relationships not unlike those formed through Twitter or Facebook. With gnawa music's increasing fame comes greater interest. This widening network of listeners casts itself far from the ritual-centric relationships that are so frequently held up as crucial and central. The nature of listeners' engagement with ritual itself is in flux. Clients may be possessed by a number of spirits—or all of them—instead of just one, for example. As was the case with younger musicians working outside of the system described in chapter 4, clients and other listeners are finding new ways to listen to and be healed by gnawa music. This is not to say that the ritual is diminishing in importance, but its content is changing. Even conservative performers who push back against what they see as a slow degradation of the ritual similarly undertake new models of performance to maintain their own claimed authenticities. The ritual filters popular aesthetics, though the realities of the ever-growing listening community prevent a ceremonial firewall against them.

Questions of authenticity, perhaps in a singular deserving of a capital A, surround these developments. The nature of reverence surrounding sacred experience problematizes innovations. The problematics that arise, though, are as myriad as the number of outspoken debaters. Charles Lindholm describes pluralistic moves in anthropology that "invalidate any assertion of authenticity" (2002, 334), repudiating them as ideological. Instead he argues for an anthropology that seeks a basis for authentic experience. "The sacred is where you find it," he concludes (337). The current state of the gnawa ritual emphasizes this point, as ceremonies themselves are diverse in different ways than they used to be. Whereas geographic idiosyncrasies played into performance practice, now audience needs and ensembles' approaches to more recent trends can dramatically affect the event itself.[8] This brings out concerns of blasphemy and aligns closely with complaints regarding the loss of sacredness in a ritual that continues to be the pillar of gnawa identity, even when that ritual is no longer likely to be the main mode of engagement with the gnawa community or its music.

The advances—a loaded term in itself—made by gnawa music within the larger Moroccan music scene have brought opportunities and opportunism to the community. As described earlier in this chapter, monetizing skills or inviting "outsiders" into ritual are not practices specific to the postindependence period, yet they have certainly accelerated with national tours, major music festivals, national and global media circulations, and international recording sessions. Through this opening and audience expansion, a purposeful vocation can turn into a viable professional occupation. This shift could be blasphemous in itself. Yet when the successes of this adjustment bleed into the sacred event to render spiritual content differently, even stronger reactions follow. This, of course, all assumes that there is a capital A authenticity to be had—that there is something that can be transgressed.

I argue, following Appadurai, that this contemporary situation is an example of "enculturation in a period of rapid culture change" (1996, 43). The target is constantly changing as the object of study—in this case, the gnawa ritual—shifts, as does the perspective of community members or the researchers watching it. Ideas and ideologies of the sacred, not to mention heritage and piety, expand and contract over time. This is compounded by the fact that the audience itself is and has been in a state of dramatic flux. This growing fame and recognition shows a mechanism by which audiences expand, and when they do, they do not only include like-minded listeners. In a way, the successes of musicians like Yassine as described in the previous chapter prove the point. They are able to find work, though it is a struggle. This means that there are clients who are not as concerned about a "lineage of authenticity" or are at least willing to deemphasize their need for experience when faced with economic struggles. A cheap ritual can still "count." As long as it does not fail.

An audience that is unconcerned with, or is less concerned with, authoritative strands of authenticity can be similarly unconventional regarding the music and musical experience it demands of its performers. Therefore, an examination of the sonic elements of history and contemporary social life illuminates an overlap between the sacred and the secular realms in Morocco. The constant fluidity between these two alleged poles permeated my entire research experience, and it was only when I abandoned attempts to delineate "sacred" or "secular" performative styles or contexts that I could begin to approach the complexity of what listeners were experiencing when they heard this music.

Appadurai describes globalized culture as fractal (1996, 46). This growing network of an audience is exactly that, splitting along unexpected lines. Mass media allows for "a wider set of possible lives" than ever before (53), and the popularization of gnawa music, as well as the extreme diversification of its audiences, has certainly expanded the net of possible rituals to accompany those lives. He argues that culture is not a collection of habits, a substance, but is a "dimension of phenomena . . . that attends to situated and embodied difference" (13). While many argue for a substance of gnawa authenticity—a thing that is authentic—I prefer to highlight these fractures, the measures of difference that come into discourse through arguments over appropriateness and authenticity. As a marker, musical activity serves both performer and listener. Taste generates love and disgust, going so far as to identify the spiritually acceptable and the blasphemous within a tradition that is itself considered demonic to many in Morocco. The role of mass media and musical output, therefore, adheres this population together either as antagonists to more conservative renderings of Islam or as notable examples of diversity or Moroccan identity. Simultaneously, however, media and music produce fissures within the community itself.

In the case of *marsawiyya* style—described in detail in the following chapters— we see ritual aesthetics that have been and continue to be influenced by outside sources. This influence is manifest through audience and client demands and is therefore heavily affected by economic and professional concerns. Furthermore, the aesthetic changes are not simply affecting the ritual's musical content, they are subtly altering the ways in which musicians and clients understand the spirits invoked through the healing ceremony itself. With a slow removal of history from popular understandings of these figures' biographies, those who maintain their knowledge of the revered men and women and can outline specifics from the local Islamic past are in a position to stake a firm claim of tgnawit based on their Muslim piety. Similarly, those who emphasize a control over dangerous and mysterious iterations of these same spirits demonstrate a powerful closeness to the "blackness" of their African heritage. Finally, those who achieve success through the spectacle and virtuosity—be it through a command of the spirits, their musicianship as demonstrated through the higher and faster marsawiyya style, or both—stake their own share of tgnawit, one reinforced democratically, in a sense, by their large audiences.

Notes

1. The Interzone period in Tangier's history from 1923 to 1956 refers to a time when the city was controlled by a treaty of foreign governments. This was also a time when American and European writers and artists lived in the region, including Paul Bowles and William Burroughs.

2. The performance described was broadcast on the Maghrabia television station. Many versions have been published on YouTube and elsewhere, though the highest-quality video and audio recording at the time of this writing can be found at https://youtu.be /LyCL3IFLgDU.

3. The 'ud is a plucked stringed instrument most commonly associated with Morocco's classical Andalusian tradition and eastern (Egyptian, Syrian) musical genres. It has six courses of doubled strings, though the lowest is often a single string.

4. *Sama'* is a genre of sung religious poetry. It sits firmly within Sufi practice, though debates circle the use of musical instruments and percussion.

5. Mulay Ismail Salsouli composed poems infused with technology, such as "Khsam l-portable," framed as a debate between a cell phone and a landline, a back and forth full of humor (see Magidow 2013, 123–24). This example was provided to me on more than one occasion by singers demonstrating their genre's contemporary viability.

6. A number of similar performances from satellite broadcasts appear on YouTube: one example is https://youtu.be/n8y3ojsBcJ8. In the opening, the emcee announces the poem, which begins at 16:25, as being in a "gnawa rhythm" (iqa' gnawiyya).

7. This event occurred at the Fez Festival of World Sacred Music's Boujloud stage, which features music aimed at local audiences. The paid events tend toward international artists and attract the crowds of European and American tourists as well as wealthy Moroccans.

8. Perhaps not surprisingly, these concerns impact vocations far beyond music and ritual. A recent article by Orit Ouaknine-Yekutieli (2015) poses similar questions about the artisan craft industry of Fez.

6 Light Rhythms and Heavy Spirits

February 2, 2013

TODAY STARTED WITH *my first shower in what felt like ages. It took some time to find some soap, but it was certainly worth the trouble. I had arrived in Sidi Ali with the hope of finding Bin Salem, an older gnawa ritual leader from Meknes who supposedly taught everyone "of a certain age" throughout the northern part of the country. Last night I realized that I already knew him: we had met in Sidi Ali two years ago when ʿAbd al-Rzaq had invited me for my first visit to the mountainous pilgrimage site. He was sweet, funny, and approachable then. I remember him joking about his lack of teeth after I had offered him some peanuts. I walked down the streets that ʿAbd al-Rzaq had pointed out to me the evening before, asking for some help finding the two mʿallemin. Of course, people from Sidi Ali who choose not to leave town and rent out their apartments during the pilgrimage week see ritual musicians everywhere. It is nearly impossible to pinpoint a specific one. After a while, I gave up the search. Or, rather, I took my quest to the nearest café. Who knows, perhaps I would find him there.*

While in the small town's main square—a space situated in the shadow of an old stone fortress—I stumbled across ʿAbd al-Rafiʿ, a young man who always seemed to be playing with a different hamadsha *troupe. He invited me to join his makeshift ensemble for a procession from the taxi stands to the tomb of the hamadsha patron saint, Sidi Ali Bin Hamdush. A young* muqaddim, *a hamadsha ritual leader, dressed in red (whom I recognized but did not know) was processing in front of a group of musicians carrying four* guwwal *players (large clay drums held over the shoulder), two more percussionists each carried a* taʿrija *(a small clay drum held in one hand), and four* ghita *players (oboe-like wind instruments that are extremely loud) followed, separating the performers from the mass of people behind them. He also had two younger kids with him in the front who were holding a large green cloth to catch monetary gifts from passersby. Another pair carried two flags. A few performers were huddling and trying to find the person with the best video device to record the descent. (My iPhone won—that is, until it ran out of space.) Putting in the wax earplugs that I bought from the local pharmacy, I felt prepared to do this all day long. We kept stopping and starting, moving slowly from the tents near the pharmacy to the main square, down through the tight market, and to the tomb of Sidi Ali. We constantly paused to bless people who had put money in the blanket, using refrains familiar to those that punctuate gnawa and hamadsha rituals. At* one point the muqaddim looked up and blessed an older woman who was leaning out of her second-floor window. She threw change down to the street below her in gratitude. When everyone stopped moving, the ghita players went into heavily ornamented melodies played over a long drone that showcased both impressive circular breathing techniques and ear-splitting volume. This walk went on for a little more than an hour and a half, until we reached the tomb, which was closed for renovations.

I wandered around after this, renewing my desperate search for Bin Salem. While descending, we had passed M'allem Rida Stitu's gnawa group, from Tangier, whose members wanted me to sit with them, but when I arrived up at the café again, they were gone. Another missed connection. I saw Yassine (introduced in chapter 4) and Said (Rida Stitu's brother) during the short walk, who told me that they had a house "down at the bottom." While I was bothering people on the road, asking if they'd seen a gnawa group (of course they had) or knew where this house was, a woman gave me a round of bread. It was blessed from the baraka of the week's events at Sidi Ali. A familiar feeling of reverence came to me, as it usually does during the rituals themselves, while I ate this gift. I eventually found some members of Stitu's group and Yassine's friends at different tables of the same café (far from "the bottom"). Needing a rest, I joined them for yet another coffee. Or maybe it was a mint tea.

I went with Stitu's group back to the main square, where the members began to perform parts of the 'ada, the outdoor entrance portion of the gnawa ritual, after lots of picture taking, of course. There were a handful of gifts: what I assume to have been family members were carrying covered woven baskets, the kind used to roll bread dough, from the main square to Lalla Aisha's cavern. The descent crossed the path of the one I had taken earlier, steering toward the supposed she-demon and away from Sidi Ali's tomb. We moved more quickly and without as much starting or stopping as we wound through the tight sheep stalls that line the muddy roads to the cave. At the bottom of the hill, the people who were carrying the baskets of gifts for Aisha continued through a series of gates and past a sign requesting that no one take pictures. The group members chatted, turned, and returned to where they had begun, ready to start again when another family needed their services.

By now it was well after dark, and I continued to look for Bin Salem, hiking back up toward the houses at the top of the hill. On the way, I saw 'Abd al-Rafi' again, who wanted to play pool; wanted to bring me to 'Abd al-Latif, a hamadsha performer to whom I still owed a visit; and just seemed to need a reason to meander through the streets. The pool hall was packed, so we continued on to the house where 'Abd al-Latif was performing in a hamadsha 'ashiyya. The group had just finished, but I said hello and enjoyed some short conversation with the members. After helping them carry buckets of olives downstairs, I continued my search for Bin Salem and 'Abd al-Rzaq.

After passing a few more houses, I saw a flash of 'Abd al-Rzaq's ever-present scarf disappearing into a doorway. I asked (and thoroughly confused) a young girl who was out front, and she let me go in. (I assume that there are not many Arabic-speaking white people asking about gnawa musicians' scarves in Sidi Ali.) I entered to find Bin Salem and 'Abd al-Rzaq sitting outside a small room where Hamid, 'Abd al-Rzaq's brother, was playing the final songs of a ritual. He was working through the women's portion before ending with Aisha. I talked to the two m'allemin, joking and laughing. Bin Salem, I learned, grew up with 'Abd al-Latif Makhzumi, whom I met in Marrakech. They look like, but are not, brothers. He traveled the country when he was twenty or so for a decade or two before settling down. He now lives in Casablanca and is proud of the fact that he does not own a cell phone (which drove me crazy when I tried and failed to find him in Casablanca later). He broke five of them and that was enough to convince him that these newfangled gadgets just weren't worth the trouble.

We went back to the house that they were renting and sat for a while. It was much larger than the tight room where Hamid's event had concluded a few minutes earlier. I loved Bin Salem's energy, his happy demeanor. He laughed easily and often, showing his toothless gums as he slapped his knee, joking with everyone sitting around him. He left an impression on me two years ago, and I was glad to see him again. At the end of the long day, however, I learned that he was not "that" Bin Salem. My search continues. . . .

Entertaining Listeners

While in Fez, I was struck by the fluidity of experience described by listeners, whether audience members or ritual participants. Some would fall into a trance while standing in the main square of the Essaouira Festival of World Music, listening to gnawa music, requiring their friends to suddenly embody the traditional roles of nontrancing listeners at healing ceremonies: holding the now-possessed bodies up and keeping them safe by making space in the tight crowds. Conversely, in ritual many listeners danced and laughed, making obvious their enjoyment and love of the music and ignoring the trancing bodies in front of them.[1] The healing event was fun. Every listener and performer engages this individual improvisation to some degree, eliding fun into a weighty ceremony. It provides an important counterweight to suppositions of clear sacred and secular potentialities within performance (either musical or otherwise). When individuals discipline their own bodies (Kapchan 2009), educate themselves (Hirschkind 2006), or publicly enact their ideals and attitudes (Mahmood 2005), binaries such as sacred and secular fail to represent the wealth and diversity of actualized experiences present in concerts or rituals. Just as ideals about piety and appropriate behavior inform the identity of certain fundamentalist movements within

Islam (Bayat 2007), individual tastes and perspectives allow for vast creative expressions of what Islam is and should be.

As musicians in Morocco conflate popular and sacred sounds, ritual becomes a malleable part of the Moroccan popular culture industries. Audience desires (healing, catharsis, fun, and so on) and performers' goals (maintaining traditions, appeasing spirits, and making money, for example) illuminate the fluid boundaries of Morocco's diverse music scenes. In this chapter, I show how ritual musicians borrow aesthetic elements of popular music and the spirits of other brotherhoods to negotiate the desires of their listening and trancing audiences against the aesthetic requirements of possessing spirits. I demonstrate ways in which gnawa musicians blend the boundaries between ritual and entertainment by adeptly integrating music and spiritual content from a wide variety of sources into their performances. These innovations are often done at the behest of audiences, leading to a quickening pace of change within these scenes that is dependent on dominant popular tastes. The line between ritual and entertainment is not firm; it is fused within the experiences of listeners, the goals of performers, and a changing understanding of the possessing spirits.

As in Jonathan Shannon's descriptions of musicians who "improvise modernity" (2006, see chap. 5), these individuals navigate their way through performances, constantly working to determine the needs and wants of their listeners. They recognize the importance of the international distribution of material and ideas while providing a nuanced understanding of local decisions. The rise of festival settings for musics, including that of the gnawa, highlights the global pressures on local artists. This is especially apparent when dealing with the economic potentialities of tourism markets (Baldassarre 2003; Schaefer 2009). The results of these combined pressures in staged performance are well documented for the gnawa (Sum 2011, for example). Gnawa ritual leaders compete for clients either by accommodating the requests of their ritual audiences—borrowing from the popular music aesthetics of the previous chapter—or refusing to manipulate their sound and therefore reifying their claims to authenticity.[2] This becomes especially important when those listeners are possessing spirits required for the successful outcome of a ritual.

These gnawa musicians strive to accommodate an increasingly globalized audience of local Moroccans. They encounter tastes influenced by globalized musics, including American pop stars' and electronic dance trends. Some go out of their way to directly engage foreign audiences in festivals, on international tours, or through recording, but most deal more explicitly with the young and old of their own neighborhoods or regions. They focus on their clients and the friends and families present in ritual. Shannon's improvisation—like Goodman's (2005) understanding of Kabyle cultural politics and Silverman's (2012) approach to Romani pragmatism—examines how musicians and other actors reorient their artistic products for new audiences. Studies like these interrogate musical experiments that are simultaneously oriented toward local and international audiences, policy makers, nation builders, and others. Not always transparent, however, is how the ritual content has shifted in response to these pressures.

The music of the ritual is often described as something unchanging, a symbol of past communal experience.[3] I argue that the musical aesthetic is a malleable reflection of these changing influences and an audible signal that performers not only consider novel audiences (like uninitiated foreigners) but also adapt their ritual performance practice to better address more pervasive trends in their local clients' tastes. In the sections that follow, I outline three changes that illuminate the influence of new audience tastes. *Marsawiyya* style brings ritual practice closer to the pop music loved by so many audience members. The *flali* rhythm's appearance in the gnawa repertoire shows the further adaptation of dance rhythms. The incorporation of Lalla Aisha from the hamadsha brotherhood demonstrates a willingness to cross lines between brotherhoods to appease audiences. These innovations are reflected in performances at a pilgrimage to Sidi Ali, the setting for an equally poignant example of popular musicians adapting musical and spiritual content from the gnawa ritual for their own concert audience. The winding processions and close proximity of brotherhoods and musical ritual practices that wove through that day-long search for Bin Salem provide a fertile ground for audiences and musicians to innovate—or even demand—these shifts in sacred performance practices. As this chapter concludes, the tight spaces and permeable boundaries of Sidi Ali's noise can even reflect back into ostensibly secular musical sounds, blending ritual and entertainment in surprising ways.

The public space of popular music is an arena for these varieties of personal Islamic practice. Gnawa music, like other ritual sounds in Morocco, exists as popular music, bought and sold as MP3s and CDs.[4] Straight ritual recordings appear alongside studio adaptations by artists like Hamid al-Qasri. Fusion projects abound where rappers make use of samples or bring ritual leaders into the studio. Non-gnawa artists work with or borrow melodies and instruments from gnawa musicians to color their own sound, and therefore expand their own audiences by incorporating the unmistakable timbre. Although gnawa musicians saw drastic changes in how their music circulated through the popular music industry thanks to artists from Nass al-Ghiwane to recent gnawa reggae performers, audiences took note and began requesting similar cross-pollination within ritual. Musicians honored their requests for songs and styles borrowed from popular music or other unrelated brotherhoods.[5] Listeners who are invited to the ceremony by clients and their families (or who simply wander in when they hear the sound from the streets) view the performance as a sort of entertainment. This confluence of entertainment and healing ritual drastically influences the pressures faced by musicians. They must now cater to two different, yet overlapping, listening audiences. Those who are especially adept at navigating these pressures gain prestige from their ability to connect with ritual participants in both entertaining and healing modalities. It is a new type of virtuosity—measured in fame, popularity, and skill in negotiating audience expectations throughout this new milieu—that animates the construction of a simultaneous concert and ritual space. For those present, the ceremony becomes an arena for the individual expression of diverse modes of listening that highlight competing, even conflicting, ideals.

Ritual musicians innovatively respond to their demanding audiences by drawing from popular music and other non-gnawa sources, even going so far as to borrow spirits when necessary. This type of audience engagement is not exclusive to the gnawa, as we see a hamadsha leader excitedly participating within a gnawa ritual and popular musicians incorporating possession into their own concerts, nor is it likely to be as novel as these historical descriptions imply.

The Marsawiyya Sound, Demonstrated

Marsawiyya is a gnawa style and repertoire originating around Casablanca, in the Marsa region of the country. Long recognized as a center for *'aita*, a type of regional popular music, the region became synonymous with upbeat dance songs. As the recording industry expanded from a localized to a national phenomenon, 'aita's violin melodies and complex percussion rhythms spread across the country (see chap. 5; Callen 2006). Marsawiyya is conceived as a new gnawa performance practice, different from largely unknown earlier practices. There are several common characteristics used to define marsawiyya in relation to the older practices: (1) faster tempi, (2) the higher vocal and instrumental tessitura, (3) the increased use of instrumental accompaniment patterns independent from the vocal line, and (4) its changes to the songs that make up the repertoire. M'allem 'Abd al-Wahid Bradi Stitu from northern Morocco, one of the primary teachers of Hamid al-Qasri of Rabat—the gnawa musician famous for his studio recordings, concerts, and televised performances mentioned earlier—claims to have brought the marsawiyya sound to his part of the country. Stitu, who now lives in Brussels, avoided discussing his role when I met him in Meknes. Instead of answering me directly, he had me speak with the many group members, family, and friends who joined him for his visit. They all sang his praises, stating that he did, in fact, bring marsawiyya across the northern part of the country, but they avoided giving me specifics. He became more animated as he described his work with Qasri's early career, pointing out his own influence in Qasri's fame. Most descriptions of this history that I learned through interviews supported this claim, locating the rise of marsawiyya in the 1950s or 1960s, just after Morocco's independence.

Without exception, every member of the gnawa communities of Fez, Meknes, Marrakech, Rabat, Casablanca, and Essaouira whom I spoke with regarded marsawiyya practice to be musically different from what came before it. It is a style conceptualized as vastly removed from an undefined older set of performance practices squarely because of its newness. The specific details of how the change took place in Fez and Meknes were recounted to me in different versions according to each speaker's ritual, musical, and historical knowledge, but the overarching story remained consistent and likely has parallels across the country. A m'allem known by the honorific title Ba Blan moved to Fez from the south, where gnawa music and ritual have historical roots from major slave trade centers of the past.[6] He brought the older style of ritual performance practice to Fez (now called both *fassiyya* and *sudaniyya*) two generations ago, yet it was the marsawiyya sound that became influential with his apprentices and others of the next generation. During my research between 2007 and 2013, three m'allemin remained who had memory of this shifting time period. M'allem Aziz wuld Ba Blan of the Mulay 'Abd Allah quarter, Ba Blan's grandson, continues to be the most conservative and does not claim to know marsawiyya. He is the only m'allem in Fez of his generation (roughly fifty to seventy years old) who has not changed his playing style and the only one who turned down requests to play popular borrowed songs in rituals I witnessed. According to 'Abd al-Rzaq, M'allem Muhammad Bujma, who lived in Oued Zghun near the Tijaniyya *zawiya* in the *medina*, played the older style "until times changed" and enough clients desired marsawiyya style that he switched his playing to accommodate them. Bujma passed away during Ramadan in 2012. The third, M'allem Hamid of the Fez Jdid quarter (not 'Abd al-Rzaq's brother), is now the most well-known elder m'allem in Fez. He, like Bujma, learned marsawiyya performance practice after originally learning the older styles. Others who currently live in Fez, aside from some *drari* who perform exclusively with M'allem Aziz, learn only marsawiyya because of its dominant popularity. As the client population requesting the older style shrinks, "specialist" groups like those of M'allem Aziz or M'allem Hamid are sufficient to satisfy the market.

After roughly two years spent in Fez working with M'allem Aziz and M'allem 'Abd al-Rzaq, a lifelong apprentice of Bujma, I finally made the acquaintance of Hamid in Fez Jdid. Fifty-four years old when we met in late 2011, Hamid is one of the more active ritual leaders and performers from the city in the national circuit. He regularly appears across the country in festivals, and he has seen his pupils gain commercial success nationally as well as internationally. A dark-skinned, quiet man with a relaxed and patient demeanor, Hamid is an example of a m'allem who laughs easily yet demands complete respect for his work and his tradition's music. M'allem Hamid performs almost exclusively in marsawiyya, but the fact that he learned enough fassiyya from M'allem Aziz to negotiate a ceremony lends weight to his reputation, placing him within Ba Blan's musical lineage. In one conversation described below, Hamid did something that few others were able to do for me: he performed short segments of one piece of the ritual in different styles to show the musical differences between them. His demonstration highlights his perception of marsawiyya performance practice as a dramatic shift from that which came before.

As with many similar conversations, we fell into the topic of fassiyya style by way of a tirade against changes in the ritual tradition. Hamid, like so many older m'allemin, lamented a diminishing quality of the ritual ceremony. It is rarely the musical content's shift per se that captures the frustration of elder leaders. Rather, it is the shortening of the ritual that gets cited for upsetting the traditional balance of the ceremony (see also Hell 2002, 351). The balance of seven distinct groups of seven spirits "opening the door" followed by seven female spirits "shutting the door" used to take two to seven days. Hamid's description, that the two-day musical event was a part of a weeklong wider ceremony, identified two long ritual evenings lasting from sunset until 5:00 a.m. The other five days of the week were spent procuring and ritually sacrificing animals, cleaning, celebrating, and decorating the body with henna, and, interestingly, they included musical performances of other ritual traditions ('*issawa, jallaliyyat, 'arabiyyat,* or others). This fassiyya ritual, therefore, consisted of far more than just gnawa music. Instead, the music was part of a much larger ceremonial complex, one that, according to Hamid and so many others, eclipsed the single afternoon or evening event that characterizes contemporary marsawiyya events. (Other elders described seven-day events composed exclusively of gnawa music. There was likely a variety of options for clients hiring musicians at that time, as there is now.)

Marsawiyya events, in turn, are shorter and most frequently consist of a repetition of only the most well-known segments of each spirit group's repertoire. These last from the late evening (10:00 p.m. is a common start time) to early morning (sunrise brings the final segment of female spirits in the region around Fez and Meknes). Often, they are compressed even further, adapted from a *lila* to an 'ashiyya that extends only into the middle of the night (see chap. 2). Elders decry the relative void of necessary ritual knowledge, contrasting their own awareness and memorization of a deep repertoire of songs—enough to fill many nights of music—with the shallow memories of the stereotypical younger artist who can play only two or three songs for each spirit. It is in discussing the impoverishment of the repertoire that conversations move from ritual to music. Because marsawiyya artists know fewer songs, they concentrate on learning those that are popular. "They live in capitalism [*maliyya*]," Hamid opines. Abdelhafid Chlyeh cites Abdelatif, a m'allem from Marrakech, who similarly decries young performers who "ignore our true traditions and consider this craft [*métier*] uniquely as business [*un fond de commerce*]" (1998, 67).

This orientation led to musical changes, the popular aesthetic that animates much of marsawiyya style includes a high vocal tessitura, for example. The ideal m'allem of fassiyya style possessed a low, booming vocal quality. The ideal marsawiyya sound, influenced by popular artists like Hamid al-Qasri, more closely approximated the high nasal sound of Casablanca's 'aita or reciters of the Qur'an. Hamid described other aesthetic shifts as he began to tune a *hajhuj* chosen from the many decorated instruments that sat in the corner of his dark first-floor room in Fez Jdid. Importantly, the higher-pitched vocal sound required a higher pitched hajhuj. The instrument, as described by Hamid, is pulled tightly for marsawiyya performance, creating a sound that he labeled *nhasiyya*, "metallic" or "brassy." Others described the high tuning as "choked," accompanying the description with hands wrapped around their necks. When he prepared his instrument for the short fassiyya demonstration, Hamid placed the strings roughly a minor third below a typical marsawiyya tuning. Paired with Hamid's low voice, this change lent a rough growl to the ends of phrases that descend to the lower range of the instrument, a sound far removed from that of the more ubiquitous higher-pitched marsawiyya.

Hamid played a short introduction. He was singing the fassiyya version of "Ghumami," one of a handful of songs named for that spirit, which typically appears alongside the repertoire for Sidi Mimun. This group, making use of black fabrics and *jawi kuhl*, or black incense, appears second in the ritual as performed in Fez, just after the white descendants of the Prophet. The contour of this melody opened with an ornamented and syncopated octave descent (see example 6.1a). His example shows a melodic motion downward, accentuating the bottom half of the scale. This is a notable feature, as fassiyya performance practice is often described as "lower" in pitch or "heavier" than the more recognized marsawiyya. Similarly, the hajhuj accompaniment drops to the lower octave with an abrupt C–D–C that pulls the listener's attention downward (see example 6.1b).

Hamid then performed "Ghumami" in marsawiyya style. He, once again, played a short introduction before exposing the melody, the segment that would accompany the drari as they sing the chorus. This hajhuj line (example 6.2) was distinct from that of the fassiyya version. It is slightly more agile: syncopations lightened Hamid's right-hand strokes throughout the passage. It opened with a D to F figuration that rose up to a high C, whereas the corresponding segment of the fassiyya version rocked between G and D, rising to an A before falling back down. The fassiyya version reinforces lower pitches while the marsawiyya utilizes a contour and playing style that carries a "lighter" sound, traversing the entire range of the instrument. The surprising part is that the "heaviness" or "lightness" does not appear to be born exclusively from pitch selection: contour and timbre ground or lift the music throughout each example. This melodic agility came through even though Hamid had not bothered to tighten his instrument back up to the nhasiyya range before demonstrating marsawiyya.

These musical changes—the adaptation of 'aita's lightness and agility—led to a rise in virtuosity. Performers like Fez's M'allem 'Abd al-Rzaq could gain respect as skilled instrumentalists, adept at using a high-energy playing style to invoke

Example 6.1. Excerpt from M'allem Hamid's example of "Ghumami" in a fassiyya style.

Example 6.2. Excerpt from M'allem Hamid's example of "Ghumami" in marsawiyya style.

and invite spirits within ritual. Others like Hamid al-Qasri would enhance the clarity of their instrumental sound by switching from intestine to nylon strings and recording pristine virtuosic versions of the most famous gnawa repertoire in studios and on stages, leading to new models of success.

Dancing Spirits and Clients

While some songs within the closing segments of the ritual, dedicated to female spirits like Lalla Rqiyya, Lalla Mira, and others, have melodic structures that follow standard gnawa musical characteristics, most marsawiyya performers adapt the flali dance rhythm to further separate this repertoire from that of the rest of the ritual. Lalla Malika's songs and story gives insight into why her music carries a close relationship to popular dance styles. The history I recount here was given to me by 'Abd al-Rahim Amrani, the previously introduced hamadsha leader who takes great measures to expand his own audiences, as described below. All versions of Malika's history agreed that she was either wealthy or royalty and that she loved to dress in chic clothing with expensive jewelry and dance, but 'Abd al-Rahim's telling is unique in that it offers more details and localizes her history to the city of Fez.

> Lalla Malika was from an Algerian Jewish family. She lived here in Fez, in the *mellah* [Jewish quarter] Back in that time, there was no *ville nouvelle* [French new city], just the *medina*, which was occupied by Muslims, and Fez Jdid, which included the mellah. Drinking and smoking *kif* was forbidden in the old city, so those Muslims who wanted to do such things went to the mellah. Lalla Malika loved to dance and drink, as did her family. But there was an older Muslim man from the family of Bin Kiran who loved her. He was wealthy and showered her with gifts. She didn't want to give up her freedom, but a friend came and told her that she should stop drinking and dancing and marry this man. She lived for one or two months without her former freedoms as his wife until she started to truly miss her past activities, so she decided to try something, a trick. She pretended that she had fallen ill and would not eat or drink anything. After a month, her husband brought a Jewish doctor [*fqih*] to the house. [7] She explained to him that she was not sick, but was only trying to find a way to win back her freedom. The doctor told the husband that she requires an hour each week to sing, dance, and drink in a beautiful space, to have a party, and she will be well. The husband relented and allowed it. Malika went down to the garden and laid out carpets, arranged flowers, and invited artists. She brought her family and that of her husband, and this weekly party became a tradition. This is why people now say that they need a "Malika's hour" [*sa'at malika*] to relieve their sicknesses. (Amrani, personal communication, 2013)

While I had never heard of the concept of a "Malika's hour," the story has a familiarity to it. It follows a trajectory similar to other Moroccan storytelling ideals, especially in regard to the woman-as-trickster. When I retold this story to gnawa m'allemin in Fez, asking them about their thoughts, they found it interesting and did not contest the details. Malika's invitation of artists, laying out of carpets, and arranging of flowers in the garden for a party is notable and influences the sound of the music that animates her section of the ritual. Much of her music uses an adaptation of a popular rhythm for the hajhuj, highlighting her desire to dance. Furthermore, upon reaching her songs during the ritual, near the end of the evening and often after sunrise, all the women present get up and dance with Lalla Malika. This is the only point of the ritual where nontrancing members of the audience participate so directly, and the room shifts abruptly from that of a sanctified space to a postwedding celebration's dance floor.

During this segment, the *qaraqib* maintains a triplet rhythm while the hajhuj adapts the flali rhythm heard in much popular music, especially at weddings. The rhythm allegedly comes from the Tafilalt region of the country, in the southeast near the desert cities of Errachidia and Rissani. It is a rolling 6/8 that shifts between a duple- and triple-meter feel based on a pattern of accent placements. The hajhuj mimics this feel of the *bendir* (a large-frame drum with a snare) or *riqq* (a smaller-frame drum with tambourine-like jingles that appears in much Middle Eastern music), instruments that are commonly used to play this rhythm in other dance genres (example 6.3). Melodically, "Lalla Malika" emphasizes this constant hemiola and the audience invariably responds by singing along (example 6.4). This flali hajhuj line continues through many of the songs in the women's segment and also appears at rare points of other ritual segments. "Ulad Lalla Fatima," for example, closes the *shurfa'* segment of white-clothed spirits with noble links to the Prophet Muhammad using this rhythm. It does not appear in the fassiyya form except when requested by the audience, making this adaptation a reminder of the difference between marsawiyya form and those other styles that preceded it.

New rhythms and faster tempi, according to those who played gnawa music before the onset of *marsawi*[8] dominance, drastically changed the ritual. Instruments are now tuned tighter, vocals are higher in pitch range, and rhythms are increasingly focused on getting people (and spirits) to move in ways more appropriate for the wedding than the lila ceremony. Interestingly, some elders note a metaphorical link between the lila ceremony and a wedding, begging the question of whether these changes represent the contemporary life of foundational elements of the tradition.[9] Audiences celebrate and reward innovation and virtuosity through larger monetary gifts in ritual, concert attendance, or the purchase of MP3 and CD recordings. Those who disapproved of these shifts increasingly claimed that ritual leaders were becoming performers in a spectacle. Such musical changes demonstrate that musicians were beginning to view listeners more broadly, looking beyond ritual participants and searching for new audiences and new economies of sacred music. On a smaller scale, they became more willing to establish themselves as entertainers for those present in ritual who were not trancing, not possessed, and not in need of healing. The integration of the song

Example 6.3. The flali rhythm and variation characteristic to 'aita music as demonstrated to me on the riqq by 'Abd al-Latif, a professional percussionist active across a number of genres. "Dum" is a right-hand open stroke on the middle of the drum head, "tek" is a right-hand stroke on the edge of the drum head, and the "zilj" is a stroke using either index finger in the *zilj*, the metal jingles attached to the rim of the instrument.

Example 6.4. Excerpt from M'allem Aziz's performance of "Lalla Malika" featuring the hajhuj's rhythmic adaptation of the flali pattern.

"Aisha Hamdushiyya" during an annual pilgrimage forty years ago, and its subsequent rise to become arguably the most potent segment of the gnawa ritual, clearly demonstrates the willingness of musicians to go beyond simply adapting musical styles to appease their audiences: they would welcome new, and powerful, spirits.

Borrowing Songs and Spirits in Sidi Ali

Sidi Ali, a small Moroccan mountain town north of Meknes, hosts an annual pilgrimage attracting ritual performers and popular musicians. Setting up makeshift venues in tents, rented apartments, and half-finished basements, adepts from a variety of semi-marginalized traditions participate in ritual healing. Various types of music and dance animate the events, which are usually open for anyone interested in watching. Interspersed between the makeshift rituals are equally temporary nonritual popular music venues. An unfinished second floor between two taller buildings stands in as a nightclub with a large tarp strewn across the gap, long and tangled extension cords suspended in midair. When I witnessed these pop-up nightclubs in 2013, they seemed almost as pervasive as the sacred activities that they overpowered with their speakers.

The pilgrimage is oriented around a pair of holy sites that are linked to the history of the hamadsha Sufi brotherhood's founder. 'Abd al-Rahim Amrani described Sidi Ali Bin Hamdush, his brotherhood's patron saint, as a student in Fez during the seventeenth century who fell into an ecstatic trance and became Sufi. Hamdush left Fez and walked to the site of the current town where he settled near a spring and began to incessantly recite prayers, tying his hair to a tree so he could not fall asleep. Sidi Ahmed Dghughi, a professed thief, came to him and entered Sufi life. Eventually, the master sent Dghughi to West Africa to see a king, who presented the traveler with a young woman named Aisha as a gift for Sidi Ali. Upon his return, Dghughi found that Ali had died. Aisha began to work miracles, becoming famous until she suddenly disappeared. Her cavern, just downhill from Sidi Ali's tomb and shrine, became a place where one could bring a sacrifice, light candles, and be healed. These two points constitute the main pilgrimages to Sidi Ali during the festival, which follows the celebration of the Prophet Muhammad's birthday each year.

The loudest ritual events during the festival time are descents to Sidi Ali's tomb by troupes of hamadsha musicians. These troupes play music from the climax of their ritual as they process for up to an hour and a half through town, like the one that opened this chapter. The start-and-stop walk winding through the markets gives leaders an opportunity to chant blessings in exchange for small change. The gnawa, whose music and ritual work differs greatly from the hamadsha, orient their shorter descents toward Aisha's cavern. Individual families or small groups hire gnawa musicians to bring gifts of food, milk, meat, and candles to the spirit. These two, along with other traditions' representatives, get twisted up, crossing paths in the main square or in the small dirt paths between the sites or when squeezing through the tight market areas that line the two routes. The evenings feature rituals of varying length, depending on the hosts' ability to pay for musicians, paraphernalia, and sacrificial animals. Each tradition follows its own practices, but in all cases, the events occur in spaces that fail to "hold in" the sound. Walking past these tents, dirt patches, unfinished concrete buildings, or rented-out apartments, therefore, allows a nonparticipatory listener into these sacred sounds as they dovetail one another, prefiguring musical interactions that I describe in the following pages. In many, but not all, cases a casual uninvited listener can spectate, or if possessed by a spirit, he or she may fall into trance. This confluence of spiritual power and flowing music was germane to the genre's transformation out of marginality.

The pilgrimage to Sidi Ali is historically a hamadsha event, with the gnawa beginning to attend in the mid-1970s.[10] In these close quarters, audiences mingle,

Example 6.5. A) Common pitch collections in gnawa repertoire. B) Pitch content of "Aisha Hamdushiyya" borrowed from the hamadsha. C) An excerpt from the hajhuj melody of "Aisha Hamdushiyya" as played by M'allem 'Abd in Sidi Ali in February 2011. Note the 6/4 measure, implicating an additive conception of the meter when the song is adapted by the gnawa: "playing in one."

leading to songs and spirits filtering between ritual practices. According to a number of sources, "Aisha Hamdushiyya," a powerful song that ends ceremonies, entered the repertoire when an audience member requested that a gnawa ritual leader from nearby Meknes named Sidi Omar perform a hamadsha poem during a ritual. He did not know all the text and only recited one stanza of "Dman al-Blad," which quickly became the famous gnawa version of the song. Distinctly non-gnawa musical elements were introduced through this piece. First, it is in a loose five-beat meter, not the standard duple. Hamadsha performers tell me that the gnawa could not play the difficult rhythms and therefore "played it in one." Second, the melodic content is based firmly within a typical hamadsha scalar pattern, unlike the pentatonic melodies of the gnawa. "Aisha Hamdushiyya" uses a modality related to *hijaz* (called *hijaz al-kabir* in Morocco) and centers on half steps and augmented seconds for color and structural movement (example 6.5).

In this song, the shared history between Aisha and Sidi Ali bin Hamdush of the hamadsha brotherhood plays out musically. The majority of the gnawa repertoire shares a set of musical elements, including consistent rhythmic and scalar patterns. The open pentatonic sound, a tonality that often avoids the third scale degree and therefore is neither distinctly major nor minor, flows over a limited set of accompaniment patterns performed on the hajhuj. This aural consistency gives space for creativity and interpretation. "Aisha Hamdushiyya," however, is heavy (*tqil*), gripping listeners and bringing many of them into simultaneous, yet individual, trances. Whereas the rest of the evening sees a small handful of trancing bodies for each spirit, this song often entangles half of the room in violent, loud trances. This weight comes, in part, from the spiritual power of Aisha herself. She exists throughout Moroccan folk beliefs but is primarily associated with the hamadsha and remains popular among the poor. In the gnawa ritual context, this experienced "heaviness" also derives from abrupt musical changes. "Aisha Hamdushiyya" introduces a new scale and meter after a long evening of sounds that had, up to that point, felt familiar. The performers put down loud qaraqib and clap while the hajhuj settles into the five-beat pattern, emphasizing a longer melodic phrase in a scale that oscillates between a natural minor (on D) and major (on F), featuring dissonant half steps (example 6.5b and c). Aisha's presence in the gnawa ritual invites new aesthetic and spiritual ideas.

The hamadsha, a group experiencing few of the commercial opportunities seen by the gnawa in recent decades, reacts in turn as ritual leaders from that tradition, most notably Fez's 'Abd al-Rahim Amrani, perform the hamadsha tune alongside famous gnawa artists. He uses every performance, even those in ritual settings, as a circumstance in which he can follow the model of making the sacred entertaining, performing the aesthetic pleasure of his audience. In early 2013, he hosted a gnawa ritual in Meknes and hired Rida Stitu's ensemble to perform. During this event, Stitu invited Amrani to sing with the gnawa troupe during "Aisha Hamdushiyya," asking him to expand the text and complete the poem. Although these types of invitations were common for him on stages (he had just sung with Hamid al-Qasri in Casablanca a few months previous and worked with Paco of Nass al-Ghiwane earlier in his career), the fact that this was during a gnawa ritual gave him tremendous pride; it was something he had never done before.

The attempt to appease an audience member's request of a song from a different tradition turned into an integral part of ritual because audiences found it powerful and compelling. Its incorporation led to a novel climactic ending of the event, during which the lights are put out and most women in the room enter into noisy, simultaneous trances. Not only did the gnawa borrow the sound of the hamadsha; they borrowed the spirit of Aisha. In turn, a hamadsha leader adapted to align with public taste and forward his career. Furthermore, this is not the only example of borrowing songs from other traditions. Many m'allemin identified other pieces from the gnawa repertoire that are from the jallaliyyat, hamadsha, and popular music. While some performers resist the most extreme changes in ritual practice—using amplification, shortening rituals, adding repertoire, or expanding the ensemble's size, for example—most make the shift. Fewer and fewer clients remain who demand the older style, resulting in fewer m'allemin who specialize in its performance. Furthermore, these integrative strategies are not exclusive to the gnawa. Popular musicians have been following the lead set by Nass al-Ghiwane and incorporating gnawa performers, rhythms, melodies, and texts into virtually every major genre of Moroccan music. Yet one evening's concert in Sidi Ali shows the extent to which popular musicians reciprocate the borrowing, again in order to appease both audiences and the spirits residing in the small town, including Lalla Aisha.

Audiences, Listeners, and Believers

The gnawa ritual is largely an urban phenomenon. While many small towns have communities, the most recognized centers for these activities include major cities like Marrakech and Rabat. Essaouira's history rose and fell along with the city's port during the precolonial and colonial periods, but it is currently resurgent thanks in no small part to the gnawa community. It now hosts the Essaouira Festival of World Music, which features regional artists performing alongside international stars as described earlier. Other cities like Fez, Meknes, and Tangier in the north, or Merzouga and those of the Tafilalt region, have their own communities of gnawa practitioners and participants. Each has its own local ritual dynamics and history. They largely share the overall trajectory of the ceremony, but each region has its own subtle differences. The order of the segments may change as you move around the country, or some spirits may be included or omitted because of local connections or a nearby shrine.

Networks of musicians are not limited to neighborhoods or city limits, however. Pilgrimage sites like Sidi Ali, near Meknes, bring performers and potential clients from across the region. Old friends sit at cafés and reminisce about their years of traveling together decades ago. Others come to make new friends or, in the case of younger performers, reconnect with those in their virtual (Facebook or Twitter) networks. I met a young man from Agadir in Sidi Ali in 2013 who had come from nearly five hundred miles away to rent a small space. He converted it into a ritual venue that combined with a dance hall and performed constantly using a large PA system and speakers set up in the corner. It served as a hub for those who loved to listen and dance, perhaps occasionally falling into trances. I sat in the corner of the room talking to some of his friends from all over the country. They, like the older men and women flooding the coffee shops and turning this sleepy town into a standing-room-only venue, were meeting new people, retelling old stories, and hashing out worn debates while reveling in their shared tastes and using cell phones to add each other to their social networks. They talked shop and made tentative plans to visit one another's hometowns, hopeful stints of couch surfing that could facilitate meeting more fellow young gnawa musicians and fans.

One Sunday evening during the pilgrimage, I ran into Yassine, the young performer introduced in chapter 4. After walking past hamadsha performances and the beginnings of overnight gnawa rituals, I heard Amazight music, popular in the interior region of Morocco, coming from under a large tarp hung over an open space on a street corner. I pulled Yassine back and paid the 20 dirham (roughly $2.50) for us to enter. The group consisted of three percussionists beating out variations on the flali rhythm described before, two interchanging violinists, and the *lotar* musician whose playing had caught my attention. The bulk of the performance featured the singer interjecting between pop songs improvised comments about men in the audience. She followed the chants by climbing through the growing crowd, standing in front of a man, dancing with her belly in his face for a few moments, collecting her small tip, and moving on to someone else. Other women would get up and dance with her, and she wowed the audience with an occasional somersault, her long dark hair flying through the air.

Then the lights and amplifiers went out. A complex web of extension cords was interrupted by a short in a bulb, creating a puzzle akin to finding the dead light on a Christmas tree. During the half hour that it took to find and replace the bulb, the performance took a surprising acoustic turn. In the darkness of the tent, lit only by the flame of a propane tank heating Nescafé, the music gave way to a playful mimicry of the concluding segments of the gnawa ceremony. The crowd whispered, some jokingly, others fearfully, of Aisha. The violinist, Tariq Wuld Gazar of Casablanca, took the opportunity and yelled, "Give me Qasri!" referring to the heavily recorded gnawa m'allem. He then began to play a song about Aisha by popular artist Said Senhaji. "Mulat al-lila," a phrase borrowed from the ritual that opens the song, firmly connected his pop group's performance with a ritual climax. The women, especially the lead singer, laughed and joked throughout. They mimed the trance, undoing their hair and swinging it up and down.

Men and women mocking the ways in which women trance in ritual punctuated my recordings of the energetic close to the acoustic short set. Yet other women entered into trances during these pop covers in the dark, requiring the care of the audience's front row as they fell to the ground. Like the interactions between gnawa and non-gnawa elements that came together in "Aisha Hamdushiyya," this moment illuminates the constant flow of musical and ritual ideas between popular genres and ceremony. Marsawiyya-style performers used dance music ideas in ritual settings, and now those popular music artists were borrowing back some of those very same influences.

Deborah Kapchan describes experiencing *nashat*, energetic pop dance and music, as "intoxication," not one resulting from alcohol, but from "a moment when ecstasy circulates among members of a group" (2003, 264). She tellingly uses the same metaphor of intoxication to describe gnawa ritual experience in her later book on the subject (2007). This shared terminology speaks to not just the similarities but also to the overlaps between performing to entertain a crowd and to appease a spirit. The darkened room in Sidi Ali hosted a popular music group incorporating content from gnawa ritual, opening a space for listeners that was simultaneously fun and therapeutic. A woman fell to the ground possessed while others danced, laughing. I felt the air as alternately heavy with sacred weight and light with dance and humor. The actions of listeners defined the music and context as either a ritual or a concert, individually. Or, better put, they allowed it to be both, to be open and unbounded, pitching their own defense against rigidity in religious practice.

Authenticity in performance practice is not something created only for and by international circuits, the labels, and centers of distribution for the "world music" scene. Although elements of authenticity are important for the sales of music like that which comes from the gnawa ritual abroad, the maintenance of an authentic authority over the therapies of the ceremony are important for performers looking for local opportunities. The appropriateness of certain performative turns, like the adoption of marsawiyya style or the inclusion of Aisha's music, is constantly debated locally by performers, clients, and many others within and outside the gnawa community. Importantly, these local debates are not easily settled, as measures of authenticity are different for individual listeners. "Intoxication" belies a variety of aesthetic practices for a wide range of potential audiences, whether human or spiritual. Lalla Malika and many of those listening to her music want to get up and dance. Some clients want spectacles to prove authenticity. They want to see trancing bodies during a ritual dripping hot wax down their backs or eating raw meat; they want the types of demonstrations of possession that some troupes' drari emphasize. Other listeners, like those who hire M'allem Aziz of Fez, decry the rampant disrespect that these types of practices imply and focus on what they see as a performance practice steeped in a tradition, a trance-based practice more akin to intellectual Sufism with authenticity derived from piety and demonstrated by the fact that the performer recently returned from a pilgrimage to Mecca. Increasingly, it is the ability of a performer to fully engage those present, whether client, listener, or spirit, that earns him authenticity and future work. In this climate, it follows that the strategies outlined previously have been influential throughout the country, beyond individual neighborhoods.

The utility of authenticity as an analytical term is processual. It is more interesting to see how it is conferred and how it shows the values of different marketplaces. The "sympathetic mediation" (Erlmann 1996) of local and global—not to mention ritual and entertainment—appears throughout these pragmatic moves made by gnawa practitioners as they attempt to identify and play to the values of their audiences. The lila ritual and Sidi Ali's pilgrimage serve as focal points for the playful interactions that permeate Morocco's music scenes. The innovations described in this chapter illuminate how audiences compel artists to borrow and toy with diverse musics in novel settings. In semi-open concerts and rituals, participants negotiate the ethics, efficacy, and value of these traditions as both powerful transformative experiences and entertainment. Furthermore, the very public nature of being in these settings makes them an effective marker of how each listener individually navigates his or her own way through the relationship between the everyday and sacred spheres of life. Yet many of the distinctions between styles of gnawa performance reside as much within discourse as they do within practice. I now turn to a closer look at what different performers and audiences listen—and respond—to when hearing fassiyya and marsawiyya rituals. The narrative of gnawa history in Fez tells a story of departure as the most widely respected musicians turn toward the needs and wants of their local communities, leaving a ritual that is fraught with questions of authenticity and heritage.

Notes

1. There is a portion of the ritual, described in the following pages, in which listeners (especially women) are expected to get up and dance whether possessed or not. This segment, which coincides with the music for Lalla Malika and Lalla Mira, appeases the possessing spirits who, themselves, loved to dance while alive.

2. Tamara Turner, in her 2012 thesis, points toward one specific ritual leader's ethical directives as he defines his authenticity through music and timbre, countering the changes he sees in other (often younger) performers. When I spoke with this m'allem, 'Abd al-Latif of Marrakech, he would often embark on passionate declamations about how new musical aesthetics betrayed inappropriate priorities in younger artists more interested in fame than faith (see chap. 8 of this volume).

3. Most young gnawa artists describe their music thus, especially those who have not spent considerable time researching the music's various regional differences. Some respected elders, such as 'Abd al-Kabir Marshan of Marrakech, similarly describe the ritual as unchanged (personal communication, 2011).

4. Shops that sell gnawa recordings in Fez often include a far greater selection of 'issawa and hamadsha recordings. They also feature a wide variety of musical practices more directly linked to elite forms of Sufism or mainstream Islam: *sama'* in its standard (unaccompanied) form, with instrumental backing, and in a "modern" (*'asri*) variety that is highly produced using electronic instrumental sounds and beats.

5. The gnawa have a history of influence with other Sufi brotherhoods in Morocco, especially those that deal extensively with trance-based healing. See el Hamel (2013, 282) for a discussion of these influences in relation to the gnawa's status in Morocco. See Crapanzano (1981) and Nabti (2007) for details on how the hamadsha and 'issawa have each brought elements of the gnawa ceremony and spirit pantheon into their own ritual practices.

6. The meaning of Ba Blan's title is the subject of intriguing possibility in itself. While I have not been able to confirm it widely, some have told me that the term *blan* is an adaptation of Bilal, the name of the adopted saint of the gnawa, Sidi Bilal. Sidi Bilal was an Ethiopian slave or servant freed by the Prophet Muhammad who was renowned for his beautiful voice. Upon the reconquest of Mecca, he was the first to give the *adhan*, the call to prayer, gathering believers for worship. His African heritage and the significance of his voice has made him an important symbol for Afro-Muslim groups across the continent (see Jankowsky 2010). The "Ba" in his name is a common term used for a father or grandfather. This respectful prefix appears with all of the m'allemin of his generation. Further, the "wuld" in M'allem Aziz's name means "son of." Here, it refers to the fact that he is the descendant of Ba Blan, but elsewhere it can locate a m'allem: 'Abd al-Latif wuld Sidi 'Umara (better known as 'Abd al-Latif Makhzumi) is from the Sidi 'Umara neighborhood of Marrakech.

7. The term *fqih* is usually reserved for a Muslim religious scholar, some of whom do healing work using the power derived from their faith and knowledge (see Spadola 2014). Here Amrani uses the same term to describe a Jewish scholar/doctor.

8. Marsawi is the adjective form of marsawiyya and describes musical content that makes use of marsawiyya style or those performers who perform in that style. It more literally describes people from the Marsa region of Morocco, the origin of marsawiyya performance practice as described here.

9. See, for example, Al Ayachi's discussion during an interview with Viviana Paques (Willemont 2011).

10. According to 'Abd al-Rahim Amrani, the hamadsha leader, and Lalla Fatima, the daughter of a prominent gnawa muqaddima in Fez, the gnawa first came to Sidi Ali during the pilgrimage in 1974, when Sidi Omar brought his troupe from Meknes, described later in this chapter.

7 Fighting New Demands

As I sat with Fatima, a muqaddima whose mother served in the same role, she compared the ritual music of today with what she remembered from her mother's ceremonies:

> There is one tgnawit across all of Morocco. There are just people who add to it, like Sidi Omar who added hamadsha or those who added "Mulay Hamid" at the people's request. The people do not know [matalib al-nas]. This is why the gnawa change [tighiru], but there is only one path [tariqa wahida]. The path has other routes like shamaliyya or that which appears in Rabat and Casablanca [marsawiyya], but there is only one set of mluk. . . . The clients do not know. Now why do people add "Mulay Hamid"? Because people ask for it. . . . and the people are not holy in faith [masalih]. . . . There were those who would ask for things [make song requests] and then they [the m'allemin] would play them.

The muqaddima here does not blame audiences or opportunistic performers for the drift toward a more commercially inclined ritual practice. Instead she identifies the interactions between them as the cause. The audience (jamhur) is faulted for not knowing or not understanding what M'allem 'Abd al-Rzaq called "the gnawa sciences" ('ulum al-gnawiyya). The m'allemin did not take on important roles of leadership in maintaining the purity of the musical practices. Everyone failed, according to Fatima, in keeping faith central to the ceremony. Now we have added repertoire and new styles of playing that are based solely on the whims of the unknowing audience.

Sidi Omar, whom she mentions, was the m'allem in Meknes who appended "Aisha Hamdushiyya" to the ritual. According to Fatima, when he was originally asked to do this, he declined, noting that he was not hamdushi, but gnawi and as such, he did not play hamadsha songs. Yet he relented during an event hosted by her mother, Aisha bin 'Abd al-Rahim Flali Hakim. Once he added the hamadsha song into his repertoire, it stuck; it took off in popularity and gained prominence across the entire community. Something similar happened with another song, "Mulay Hamid." Unlike the repertoire that surrounds these new additions, according to Fatima, "there is no tgnawit in these." The people of Fez were addicted (mbli) to the hamadsha, bringing that tradition's sounds with them into the region's gnawa ritual.

As 'Abd al-Rahim Amrani explained, these types of innovations are responses to monetary opportunities within ritual. "[Alongside 'Aisha Hamdushiyya'], you can even have Aisha TV or Aisha Radio!" He said once, before singing an

impromptu and improvised "Aisha Obama" about the then American president.
The skill sets necessary for garnering tips is now more closely related to those of the
street musician pleasing café patrons, a job held by many—if not most—gnawa
practitioners at some point in their careers. "This is the problem," Amrani declared.
"Money!" Fatima added, "There was a lila *with gnawa and the audience wanted*
"Blonde Aisha (Aisha Zara)."[1] *The import of pleasing audiences rises as gnawa*
m'allem–hood *becomes a full-time occupation.*

The Codification of *Marsawi* Musical Style

In previous chapters I discussed extramusical dimensions of gnawa practice in
order to place the musical and religious content of both ritual and public performance into their dynamic contexts. My argument, that this music has and continues to change in the face of these pressures, is not a new one, but my goal is to add
depth to the work of previous authors by more directly engaging musical content
and discourses about it. Timothy Fuson (2009), for example, notes the interplay
between gnawa music and other Moroccan rhythms, cites additive forms to note
the elasticity by which ritual moves, and locates the crux of his thesis—interaction
between moving bodies and performed music—in close musical and video analysis. Two articles from Maisie Sum use transcribed melodic lines as performed by
different ritual leaders in ritual and on stage to draw connections between setting, audience, spiritual presence, and performance practice (2011, 2013). Other
scholars, including Richard Jankowsky (2010) in his work with a related cultural
practice in Tunisia, have also used close analysis to strengthen observations about
these types of music and ritual.

In this chapter, I historicize the most prominent contemporary version of
gnawa music. While artists sing and play differently—based largely on regional
variations, linguistic differences, individual goals, or aesthetic preferences—the
past three decades have seen a rise in an overwhelmingly consistent approach
to marsawiyya, the style and repertoire of songs that make up most contemporary rituals. This branch of what used to be a full tree of stylistic diversity is now
the norm throughout the country and across most age groups. This chapter concludes by reflecting back on the dichotomy of stylistic performance practices in
Fez and the oppositional relationship between the previously dominant style, *fassiyya*, and marsawiyya. By comparing recent performances of each, my analysis
draws conclusions regarding discourse on the past, a subject that returns in chapter 8. These forms of ritual performance are more similar than descriptions such
as those of M'allem Hamid from the previous chapter, which situate this oppositional relationship between styles in terms of heaviness, imply. To the contrary,
melodic material often differs between them, but in terms of rhythmic motion—
a proxy for heaviness or lightness—they are not far removed from each other.
The focus on rhythmic elements of gnawa performance practice is not meant to

diminish the import of the melodic material. Instead, the analysis points toward the increased importance of things like tessitura, contour, and repertoire choice in creating and maintaining this sense of "heft" and "lightness" in performance.

When I interviewed gnawa practitioners, both young and old, they consistently described changes—like the characteristic rolling *flali* dance rhythm that was adopted by the gnawa in the women's section of the ritual or the high tessitura of the voice that I most often heard cited as a fundamental musical element marking significant transformations within the sound of the ritual—as having happened *shhal hadi* ("Oh, so long ago"). The speakers unvaryingly made a hand gesture, waving backward over their shoulders. It seemed to say, "This is forgotten ancient history!" At this point, I would ask, "How long ago?" After a moment's pause they would reply, "Thirty years?" or "The 1970s?" The dates that I was given were almost always guesses, answers in the form of questions, but they were also consistently placed around the early or mid-1970s. My aim here is not to create a definite timetable of this musical development, but it is worth pointing out that these hazy memories locate a period that neatly aligns with changes in the music industry's notice of gnawa music and its explosion into domestic and international marketplaces.

My many conversations about marsawiyya circled around two major aesthetic shifts across the country. The first, beginning during the end of the colonial period, saw the regional style gain influence nationally while other styles, such as fassiyya (from Fez), *shamaliyya* (from the northern mountains), and *sudaniyya* (from the southern regions), became less often requested by ritual clients. As audiences and those who required healing hired gnawa groups who performed this faster, higher, more exciting marsawiyya style, ritual practitioners adjusted by learning it. Later, in the 1980s or '90s, Hamid al-Qasri began to appear on television. Nationally broadcast shows offered peeks into regional styles, introducing Morocco to its own diversity of traditions. Qasri then went into the recording studio and began producing hi-fidelity cassette tapes of gnawa music. These recordings presented shortened versions of ritual repertoire and did not include as much ambient sound and the recording "noise" present on the few other recordings that existed, becoming popular successes. Qasri's innovative style and clear studio sound in particular spread quickly, heavily influencing a generation of young artists who began learning these songs from the CDs instead of through the apprenticeship system. The change in distribution technology made these two stages of marsawiyya's rise quite different: the first happened mostly in the context of ritual performance and was incremental and slow, while the second phase separated the music from its clandestine past, disassociated it from the ritual atmosphere, and had a more fundamental impact on a younger generation of performers and audiences. Both phases affected major changes in contemporary ritual practice. Without exception, the gnawa m'allemin and *drari* in Fez regard marsawiyya practice to be musically different than what came before it, something newer and distinct from an undefined older set of performance practices. The specific details of this change depended on who was speaking and were influenced by ritual, musical, and historical knowledge, but the overarching story remained consistent. After M'allem Aziz's grandfather Ba Blan brought the older style of gnawa ritual (sudaniyya) to Fez, where it may have changed or was simply renamed fassiyya, his students began to pick up the marsawiyya sound.

My argument here is that marsawiyya is conceived as a new practice, different from a largely unknown earlier practice. Statements abound regarding the higher tuning and faster tempi of marsawiyya when compared to fassiyya, claims that my analysis of contemporary performances dispute. Not surprisingly, as I explore below, the relationships between these two practices are not so clear. In this chapter, I revisit those common characteristics that practitioners and audience members most often use to define marsawiyya in relation to the older practices: (1) its faster tempi, (2) its higher vocal and instrumental tessitura, (3) the increased use of instrumental accompaniment patterns independent from the vocal line, and (4) changes to the songs that make up the repertoire. Note that these claims do not stand on their own as statements about marsawiyya. Instead, they compare it to fassiyya, a style that many of the m'allemin have little or no experience with, yet one that they universally conceptualize as *tqil* (heavy) compared to what exists today. In Fez, while these two styles are defined in opposition to each other, one is omnipresent in ritual and public performance while the other is rare. This relationship informs the analysis that follows. First, I outline the characteristics of marsawiyya that Fez's m'allemin described. I then compare performances of marsawiyya to one in the fassiyya style using the characteristics cited earlier as loose guidelines. In an analysis focused on tempo and accompaniment patterns, I identify consistencies and inconsistencies between discourse about music and the musical performance itself. A close examination of general and specific tendencies within marsawiyya performance draws out larger patterns—be they melodic, rhythmic, textural, or contextual—and lends depth to descriptive comparisons between performers and performative settings. In the following sections, I use a recorded performance to present some of these internal structural patterns.

A Marsawi Performance in Fez

Throughout my time in Morocco, I had frequent opportunities to create recordings of ritual ceremonies, both *'ashiyyat* (evenings) and *lilat* (nights). Always invited by the m'allem, I was afforded the privilege of leaving my portable recorder in front of the performers, leading to eleven complete or nearly complete recordings of different events in Fez, Meknes, and Sidi Ali between 2009 and 2013. This, when added to the wealth of recordings made by gnawa performers themselves that are readily available in markets—usually of a low quality from cell phones or ethnographic recordings made by previous researchers that were given to the performers—and demonstrations occurring during my interviews (like the examples from M'allem Hamid described in chapter 6), provide me with an array of examples from different performers in various settings and from diverse regions. These ritual recordings document events that unfold in relation to ritual needs. Musicians adjust their performances throughout the event based on the present sprits, the tastes of the audiences, and other extramusical concerns that can be as banal as mint tea not being ready for serving or a smoke break. These small adaptations and larger concerns regarding the time required to "work the spirits" account for the extreme flexibility of gnawa formal musical structures. M'allemin repeat segments, return to melodies, skip songs that will not further the ritual's needs, or otherwise change the musical content based on specific practical concerns.

These ritual concerns do not change the fact that there is a core set of marsawiyya songs. With each colored set of spirits, there are certain pieces that remain almost universally present in ritual. Some sets of spirits have a larger number of these songs (like the white *shurfa'* or women's sections) while others only have two or three. These songs, however, constitute a canon of marsawiyya practice, one created in part by the changing learning practices described in chapter 4 and the prevalence of successful commercial artists who repeat a small group of "hits." In an effort to best capture a recording of the most consistently present marsawiyya melodies, I paid M'allem 'Abd al-Rzaq to perform an 'ashiyya split over three days. He brought two of his longest-tenured drari, Muhammad and Rashid, both of whom also perform with M'allem Hamid and M'allem Aziz and were with M'allem Bujma before his recent passing. Because of the small number of expert drari, the recorded sound clearly highlighted the voice and *hajhuj*, and the *qaraqib* rhythms were tighter than they often are in groups of five to seven. There were no possessed adepts who tranced during the events, meaning that the group progressed from one song to the next without the extensions or returns that breathe so much life into ritual performance. The result was much closer to a staged event than a ritual, but one that gave me short examples of the melodic movements through the complete ceremony. The remainder of this chapter is based on my analysis of these distinct songs from the spirit-inducing mluk segments of the ceremony. I am not including the *'ada* (the opening procession) or the *fraja* (the entertainment portion of the event) here.

The music is organized in songs, sets, and sections. Songs in gnawa music are generally equated to spirits: each piece of music within the mluk portion of the ceremony relates to a specific possessing figure, color, scent, and so on. Yet most spirits have a great deal of musical repertoire that can animate their trances. Similarly, some colors are identified with a group of spiritual figures who come and go, both named spirits and unnamed ones. Because of the wealth of musical ideas that can pass freely through a segment of trance, I adopt a smaller analytical unit here. What I call a song may be a long call and response with four or five verses, a bridge, a return to the first melodic idea, and a coda-like tag. It may also be just a thirty-second call and response. I take the defining factor, for my analysis, to be the long vocal pause and instrumental segue, or interlude, that signals one ending and another beginning. This interlude usually features an increase in tempo: the following song is almost always a few metronome clicks faster. I define a set as one or more songs that increase in tempo before a break. The pause allows the group to reset to a slower tempo and begin a new set. It may be a three-second moment where the drari stop, look at each other, and start anew. It may also be a smoke break or a period where a group member rises to recite blessings for those in the room (or for family members who are elsewhere, but "call in" by phoning people who are present). The defining factor is the resetting of the tempo from fast to slow. Sets only increase in tempo, and single songs that move through the full range from slow to fast before a stop—like "Hammadi" in this performance—can constitute their own set.

I call all of the sets that speak to an individual collection of spirits a section. The spirits are organized most obviously according to color. Each collection of spirits under one section is consistent in their color and incense needs, save for a few exceptions that are mostly within the women's section. The sections are typically named for either the color or the primary spirit. The black section is often called Sidi Mimun, though Lalla Mimuna, Ghumami, and others may be the subject of songs performed during that time. There is usually a logic to the combinations: Mulay al-Tahir, for example, described to me that Sidi Mimun, Lalla Mimuna, and Ghumami were siblings who lived in and around the Tamesluht and Marrakech regions. Sidi Musa and the other spirits of the blue section have relationships with water or, in the case of the *samawiyyin*, the sky. The shurfa' wear white and trance to sandalwood brought from Mecca. They are holy: the group's name identifies them as "descendants of the Prophet." Other sections are populated by spirits from the forest (brown), butchers (red), other prophets such as Abraham (Ibrahim, green, the color of Islam), and so forth.

Songs, sets, and sections are not consistent; they can differ by region, by performer, or by context.[2] The songs and spirits within each section are stable, however, with one exception that I found: "S'adi bil-Wali Jani" appears in the shurfa' section of performances in Fez (both marsawiyya and fassiyya), though the song appears in the Buhali (multicolored) section of performances elsewhere, most notably in the popular Rabat-based performances of M'allem Hamid al-Qasri. The sections themselves appear in various sequences throughout the country. There are specific songs that define the section and therefore appear in performances by different m'allemin in different settings, constituting a sort of "greatest hits." The majority, however, are fluidly included or omitted depending on time requirements, the audience's response, ritual needs, or the m'allem's preferences. With or without all songs, though, sets generally progress in the same order. The slowest songs move to the same middle-tempo songs and on to the fastest closers, with lesser-known intermediaries added or dropped as needed. Therefore, in a shortened performance, like an 'ashiyya, a set in the shurfa' section may be four songs long or, in a longer event, it could be extended to seven or eight. Those same four songs would arrive in the same order, but with the others inserted between them. A set from one segment will never enter another segment unless there is an extreme ritual need, such as a spirit from the previous segment that remains unsatisfied and continues to control a trancing body. In this case, the group may return to the previous segment to play another set before moving back to the normal progression.

When speaking with gnawa musicians, I find that there are few clear terms used to describe rhythm and tempo. Perhaps because the qaraqib rhythms are the first things that a new musician learns when entering the gnawa tradition, they are internalized through listening and repetition, not verbose didactic teaching. The fluidity between the distinct patterns that I identify here implies an understanding of and ability to perform the innumerable micro-temporal variations that result as one rhythm slowly shifts into another over a period of minutes. Richard Jankowsky's graphic depiction of Tunisian *stambeli* rhythmic shifts appeared in print as I was grappling with similar temporal movement in Morocco, and he aptly identifies the close link between the traditions (2010; see also 2013). His description of attacks getting closer together as tempi increase, moving from what I deem an eighth note followed by two sixteenth notes to an eighth-note triplet is roughly equivalent to one specific type of movement that I describe below. It is worth noting that my use of Western classical terminology hardly implies a clear perception. Within Western classical music itself, it can be impossible to determine the difference between a duple or quadruple meter, and the same is true here. These terms stand in as less-than-ideal representations.

'Abd al-Rzaq's performance comprises five distinct qaraqib rhythms and a handclap. These fell into three clear categories: three-stroke qaraqib rhythms, four-stroke qaraqib rhythms, and the hand clap, which articulates a quarter-note pulse. By three- and four-stroke, I refer to the number of qaraqib articulations within each cycle, what I hear as each beat. As described below, there are duple and triple three-stroke patterns, just as there are duple and compound four-stroke ones. The metric feel of this music changes as the songs in a set progress. Aside from rare moments when the m'allem tells his drari to put down the qaraqib and begin clapping, there is never a switch between types mid-song. Furthermore, there are only two instances of a single song in a three- or four-stroke rhythm framed by songs that feature the other type within the same set. Both instances involve one of the longer songs in the repertoire—which helps them stand on their own—and both are bounded by pauses in the playing before and after, easing the transition and keeping the drari from having to change types on the fly. Within both three- and four-stroke patterns, however, there are multiple rhythms that do shift fluidly mid-song or mid-set. Three-stroke patterns are not always in triple (3/4 or 3/8) or compound (6/8 or 12/8) meters, and they often elide a duple feel and a triple feel within an individual set. The four-stroke patterns always subdivide evenly, with the first and third strokes creating a regular eighth-note feel, but the placement of the second and fourth strokes can dramatically affect the feel of the groove. These patterns are often called *iqa'*.[3] While it is possible for a single member of the group to improvise above other performers' iterations of one of these patterns, the improvisation always accentuates extant features of the iqa'. This becomes an improvisation by omission, where notes are accented because others are left out. Such improvisations do not overtake or alter the underlying groove.

Figure 7.1 shows rough approximations of the common rhythmic patterns that I describe below. Thirty-five percent of the songs played during the mluk segment of 'Abd al-Rzaq's performance were in three-stroke patterns. I discerned between the two easily notated rhythms based on the feel of the meter: the eighth-note pattern with two sixteenths had a distinct duple feel—and from this point forward I will refer to it as the "duple" three-stroke pattern—while the triplet did not. The triplet was not always even, however. The triplet pattern generally appeared in the faster songs, as it had an average tempo of 144 beats per minute (BPM) compared to the duple pattern's average tempo of 107 (see fig. 7.2).

The four-stroke patterns account for fifty-eight percent of the songs in 'Abd al-Rzaq's performance. There are three main patterns. The first two are palindromic, with a long-short followed by a short-long. The metric feel marks the difference between them. The first, which I call the "march," has a strict duple feel, with tight thirty-second notes in the middle of the pattern. This has the aural effect of a cluster of activity surrounding the middle of the beat, the "and." It is march-like in its precision and occurs in sixteen percent of the songs. The second forms a hemiola, a superimposition of duple and triple metric figures. An eighth note–sixteenth note figure is mirrored back in the second half of the figure. The two halves of the beat maintain a duple feel, yet the eighth/two sixteenths/eighth grouping layers a triplet feel above it. When listening, I distinguished between these two based on the presence or absence of the triple feel of the hemiola. When it was absent, but the second half of the cycle was not even sixteenth notes, I categorized it as a march pattern.

The third four-stroke pattern came at slightly a higher average tempo. As the pace quickened, the second half of the patterns evened out, eliminating the mirror-image character of the march and hemiola rhythms. The first half remained fluid, however, and while I approximate it as an eighth-sixteenth triplet figure followed by two sixteenths, the identifying characteristic of this pattern was the distinct evenness of the second half. When it unfolds underneath hajhuj and vocal melodies, the heavy first stroke clearly articulates the beat. Whether or not there is an actual increase in volume, the players "lean" on that first stroke in a way that

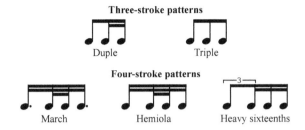

Figure 7.1. Common qaraqib rhythms.

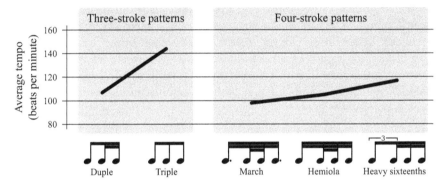

Figure 7.2. The rising average tempo of successive qaraqib patterns.

makes its duration audibly longer than the second stroke, which is slightly delayed as if it were a pickup to the second half of the pattern.

This performance and my observations from others suggest a close link between rhythmic pattern and tempo, likely due in part to the physical limitations of the qaraqib at high speeds. A prominent feature of gnawa music—and of many other types of music in Morocco—is an acceleration extending throughout songs or sets of songs that increases in intensity toward their conclusions. As a set progresses, both in three-stroke and four-stroke rhythms, the tempo rises until it reaches a point at which the rhythm becomes physically unsustainable. The rhythm then morphs into one with more evenly spaced beats: an eighth note followed by two sixteenth-notes becomes an eighth note triplet, for example. I recorded the tempo at the beginning and end of each of the distinct songs played by ʿAbd al-Rzaq. A gradual increase in tempo makes these numbers approximate, as I notated moments where the group was rhythmically tight, generally occurring just after the hajhuj introduced the melodic material that composed the next song, before the voices entered. Some sets conclude frantically, and I attempted to get a tempo as late as possible before the performers stopped or moved on to the slow first song of the following set.[4] The sung portions of songs generally have stable tempi, and it is in those closing instrumental segments that the groups accelerate, reaching toward the one that follows. The relationships between slow and fast and the invocation of different patterns at various points of the ritual illuminate the relationship between old and new styles. As the analyses that follow demonstrate, these rhythmic transitions speak to musical change in a number of ways: not only do they point toward the incorporation of outside influences within the newer marsawiyya style, but they also highlight a disconnect between common understandings of the older fassiyya practice and how it appears in performance, at least today.

This is the core of gnawa rhythm's complexity. Three-stroke sets open with a duple rhythmic feel, a groove mirrored in the hajhuj and vocal melodies. As they accelerate, they shift toward a triplet pattern. Conversely, four-stroke patterns elide into more even figures (like the "heavy sixteenth" pattern) where the first half of each group of strokes struggles to maintain what came before despite the level of difficulty in articulating identifiable rhythms on the qaraqib at high speeds. There is an infinite range of metric variation that passes by while these transitions happen. Because it is a three-stroke rhythm here, the accent changes hands each cycle (RLR | LRL). Four-stroke rhythms, which always see the accent on the same hand (RLRL | RLRL), are moderately easier to play. They tend not to accelerate toward the same speeds heard with the triplet pattern due to the upper limits of ensemble members' dexterity. It is therefore easiest to see the compression that links these different rhythmic patterns in the three-stroke progression. Figure 7.3 graphically represents the duple and triple patterns at their average tempo from this performance (107 BPM and 144 BPM, respectively). The duple pattern's sixteenth notes (the second and third of each set of three) are roughly the same distance apart as the individual articulations of the triplet pattern. There is an upper limit beyond these average tempi, but as speeds increase, it is largely the first of the three strokes that "gives."

Musicians also occasionally clap. There are two main types of clapping that happen throughout a ceremony. Both are participatory as the group invokes members of the audience to actively and creatively contribute. The first is a steady clap, an articulation of the song's pulse. This happens during "heavier" moments of the marsawiyya ceremony, most notably during the performance of "Aisha Hamdushiyya" in the dark near the end. It also appears during borrowed songs where the qaraqib rhythms described above do not fit particularly well. The m'allem can also take advantage of the aural heft that comes when the drari put down the qaraqib if he feels that the spirit or audience may respond well to the change. A drari occasionally uses the qaraqib—beating out the pulse—to engage the audience or spirit while the group is clapping, adding a touch of showmanship. The songs that featured clapping regularly signaled musical change. Songs with clapping appeared right before a stoppage or as a bridge between the conclusion of a set of three-stroke and four-stroke songs. As such, the tempo of

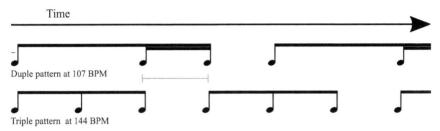

Figure 7.3. Spacing between strokes in the duple and triplet rhythms at the average tempo of each. The gray line shows the similar distance between close articulations. Note that this is an abstraction; actual distances between strokes are rarely mathematically even.

moments of clapping were consistently very fast. Average starting and ending tempi for these songs were 138 BPM and 157 BPM, respectively, much faster than that of any other patterns aside from the triplet figure. At these speeds, physical limitations would obscure the clarity of four-stroke patterns. The textural intensity lasts for one song before the musicians pause and restart slowly for the beginning of a new set.

This accompaniment clapping is rare, appearing in only six percent of Rzaq's marsawiyya performance. In the fassiyya performance that I address later on, the clap only appeared in one of thirty-eight distinct songs. This particular song was after a conclusion of a section, when the trancer asked that the group return to the song so that he could continue. He was in the midst of a possession that required him to burn two handfuls of large candles and drip the wax along his arms and down his back. When the group ended early, he encouraged the m'allem to begin again and paced the room asking for donations in exchange for *baraka*. It is possible that the group did not pick the qaraqib back up for nonmusical reasons: they had just concluded a long segment of the ritual and were nearing the end, ready for a break. Because of the relative rarity of this type of clapping in fassiyya performance, it is most likely an innovation used in marsawiyya performance practice, one of the many markers that distinguishes marsawiyya attention to dynamic musical texture from the previous tradition's musical and ritual consistency.

The second type of clapping is identical to a form of audience participation that extends throughout Moroccan popular music. Listeners occasionally begin to clap on the beat, along with the music, and then improvise to fill the rhythmic gaps. This leads to a groove of interlocking syncopated claps. The thick texture builds a strong sense of the connection between audience members within the room. This clapping can be spontaneous—quickly spreading after one audience member begins—or a member of the group can request it through hand and head gestures. At some times, the ensemble and the audience will intensify a choral passage using these syncopated and improvised patterns while pulling back to more regular patterns for verses. This is a musical innovation seen in marsawiyya performance that was uncommon, if not absent, to fassiyya and other older practices. The same clapping patterns animate *sh'abi* music, wedding songs, and other ritual traditions' musics, leading me to believe that this type of clapping is not germane to gnawa music. It instead signifies a dramatic (and fun) importation of aesthetics from elsewhere. It is also the type of detail that is hazy in memories from childhood, making the likelihood of its innovativeness difficult to confirm in interviews.

In most songs, before the singer or singers enter, the hajhuj outlines the melody. Despite the differences between this introductory passage and the actual sung melody, m'allemin consistently conceptualized the introduction as related to the vocals that follow. Sometimes this melody is identical to the accompaniment played under choral responses; other times it closely prefigures the m'allem's own vocal entrance. Occasionally it is related to the closing patterns of the song form, not unlike the last four measures of a piano part used to identify the key, rhythm, and starting pitches for a church choir. In all these cases, however, interviewees regarded the hajhuj line as central, germane to the identity of the song. When I pulled out my hajhuj and played songs without their introductions, listeners— both adepts and noninitiated alike—stopped me to point out that I had neglected this important part of the performance.

The hajhuj fluidly switches between two main roles after songs begin: for some of the song, it doubles the voice's melodic contour, and at others, it maintains repetitive figures that accompany vocal segments. The latter role occurs when the hajhuj falls into a pattern that underlies a vocal melody. These patterns range from one to four beats but can also borrow elements from the introduction's melody or standard cadential patterns in highlighting major musical events. Each of these patterns is called a *mwima*, literally a "little mother." Mwima figurations develop slowly, creating a consistency between songs that directly relate different grooves and textures within performance. Patterns like the one heard under "S'adi bil-Wali Jani" roll forward thanks to the even eighth-note pickup (see example 7.1e). Similar rhythmic figurations underscore other ritual traditions, popular musics, and sung poetry like *malhun*, making these gnawa grooves all the more familiar to uninitiated audiences.

These figures recombine motives as songs pass, providing aural coherency to the ritual. The opening mwima of this performance, "Rubbi Mulana" (example 7.1a) from the shurfa' segment, augments to form the second one, that of "'Abd al-Nabi" (example 7.1b). The second beat of the "'Abd al-Nabi" mwima includes an extension of the opening phrase from the song before, and the third beat incorporates an idiomatic rocking motion that appears throughout the repertoire. Likewise, the mwima appearing later under "Jilala Bu 'Alam" (example 7.1c) contains the same rocking motion, but without the opening ascent, bringing it closer to other patterns heard throughout this segment. The second half of "Allah ya Rasul Allah Sidi" (example 7.1d), "S'adi bil-Wali Jani" (example 7.1e),

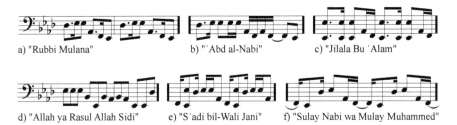

a) "Rubbi Mulana"   b) "'Abd al-Nabi"   c) "Jilala Bu 'Alam"

d) "Allah ya Rasul Allah Sidi"   e) "S'adi bil-Wali Jani"   f) "Sulay Nabi wa Mulay Muhammed"

Example 7.1. Approximate transcriptions of the first accompaniment patterns (mwima) in Abd al-Rzaq's marsawiyya performance.

and "Sulay Nabi wa Mulay Muhammad" (example 7.1f) share these traits and exemplify the close relationships between these motivic structures. This constant return to ideas heard previously facilitates hearing the segment's songs as part of a cohesive whole. It also relates to the common discourse of change, showing flexibility and structural consistency within the repertoire. Similar relationships exist elsewhere, but not everywhere, throughout the ritual.

The stout reactions from musicians like 'Abd al-Latif Makhzumi and Aziz wuld Ba Blan reflect on musical and contextual differences between the ritual of their memories and what they see going on around them in Morocco now. They charge their performances with a political—or at least an activist—cultural heritage by pressing back against practices that feel inappropriate, opportunistic, or otherwise objectionable. While histories, both oral and written, remember days of events leading up to ceremonies that extended through multiple nights, the settings of rituals undertaken by Aziz and others like him now share much in common with those animated by the marsawiyya musical style. Clients of today, even those who clamor for an older musical practice, only require a single evening of ritual activity to satisfy their possessing spirits and their neighborhood's expectations for the event. Because marsawiyya practice allows for flexibility in moving through the spirits, the way it plays out in Fez mirrors the progression of the fassiyya event. So, with no real difference in the length or order, and similar sacrificial activities preceding the evening's festivities, the main point of differentiation between the two performance practices is musical. The distinction between what the musicians play to invite spirits serves an important role, not just for elders or traditionalists, but also as an accepted norm from which innovation can depart. Yet very few performers and almost no listeners outside of small circles know or can recognize fassiyya. The dominance of the new has not only marginalized the old; it has turned the old into something new in its own right. Traditionalists battling against extinction rely on the tools of cultural heritage for both preservation and innovation.

Because the fassiyya is rarely performed today, it is difficult to gauge the continuity between what was and what now exists. Due to the lack of recordings of past fassiyya performances, I am dependent on contemporary performances by the few remaining m'allemin who continue to play this style. Despite efforts toward preservationism, they are subtly influenced by the same pressures that gave rise to marsawiyya. The aesthetic ideals that shifted the gnawa sound and ritual content toward audience engagement impact performances by artists who feature the older practice. A closer look at the music of M'allem Aziz wuld Ba Blan of Fez, the most revered gnawa musician in the city, speaks to the conflicted relationship between descriptions of fassiyya and its sound in contemporary practice. It is far closer to marsawiyya than is generally assumed.

Gnawa History in Fez

Gnawa history in Morocco is complex and contested. The current moment supplies additional challenges thanks to efforts of heritage production across the country and the pressures of the international world music scene. Early on during my research, I learned of the difficulties of doing research on the gnawa in places central to gnawa history. The large number of interested musicians and researchers, not to mention tourists and cultural brokers, make it difficult to discern lineages and influence. Further, the wealth of diverse approaches, family histories, and personalities caused me to appreciate the openness and practicality of the gnawa that I knew in Fez from my previous work. While Fez remains outside of most attention given to major gnawa centers, its gnawa community is not atypical. Where a major influx of sub-Saharan Africans changed the demographics of the slave trade centers of the past, other cities have simpler histories of gnawa influence. The communities grew from individuals and small groups. Gnawa music and ritual took hold and continued to operate across the country in ways that differ greatly from Marrakech, Essaouira, and other major centers. In these cities, international and domestic producers, restaurant owners, and researchers are influential collaborators. Such figures change the tenor of the scene in ways that are distinct to these spaces, not least by giving performers new aims and opportunities for their professional careers. The significant intermediaries facilitate the attitudes lamented by 'Abd al-Latif when he describes young performers as only wanting to go to Casablanca to record, make money, drink— to enjoy the trappings of fame (see chap. 8). This is not to say that similar influences and opportunities do not exist in cities like Fez or smaller towns outside the orbit of Marrakech and Essaouira. I remember running into M'allem 'Abd al-Rzaq in Jnan Sbil, gardens situated near the Royal Palace in Fez Jdid. He and two drari were dressed up in their most ornate costumes, outfits that I had never seen them wear in rituals, posing for photos and supplying short bits of singing accompanied by qaraqib between staged musical performances. He, like most other m'allemin I knew in the city, supplements his income by playing in tourist-oriented restaurants, many of which are tucked away behind tiny doors, only accessible to large, organized bus tours. But the city's musical claims centered on Sufi music, Andalusian music, and other genres largely unrelated to the gnawa. M'allemin in Fez have to find ritual work to earn a living, often in conjunction with something more mundane.

The community is relatively small but growing, and demand is sufficient for a variety of performers to service its needs. Over the last few generations, Fez's gnawa community has changed significantly. In the early and middle parts of the previous century, there were two major gnawa figures. These two main lineages quickly multiplied in more recent decades. While interviews describe a neat and organized system of apprenticeship, it is not immediately clear whether these are nostalgic histories reacting against the complexity of the present. The community was certainly smaller then than it is now, as this was before television, international successes, and the advent of festivals in Marrakech and elsewhere after independence brought exposure to the gnawa.

As described in chapter 3, M'allem Aziz wuld Ba Blan is the grandson of the gnawi who was commonly cited to have brought gnawa music to Fez. Aziz's grandfather, known as Ba Blan, worked for the palace and lived in the nearby Mulay 'Abd Allah neighborhood. According to M'allem Aziz and others, Ba Blan was singly responsible for bringing the ritual to Fez. Coming from the south, he continued to perform in the *sudani* style of the Marrakech region. Because of this clear lineage, fassiyya style is often described as identical to what was going on in the south at the time, but I could find no early recorded examples of either performance practice existed to confirm these statements. Interestingly, one notable difference between fassiyya and contemporary practice in Marrakech is the order of the ritual. Marsawiyya as it exists in Fez and fassiyya share a path through the order of segments that is different from that which is common elsewhere, though the actual songs performed within this larger organization differ.[5]

In describing his own knowledge of the history, M'allem 'Abd al-Rzaq categorized two groups. Ba Blan and those of Fes Jdid who learned from him—including his grandson Aziz—were the *hawsiyyin*, those from the south. This term refers to the Hausa, a West African ethnic group that is also recognized as contributing a segment of the gnawa spirits called the *hawsawiyyin*. These sprits are described as being directly from Africa and having come to Morocco with the slave trade, with the practitioners themselves. Ba Blan's black skin contributed to the respect given to his group. A friend and shop owner remembered seeing the ensemble walk through the streets and recounted to me how Ba Blan's drari were dark, large men who frightened him as a child. They were serious men, obviously not from the *medina*. This ethnic "othering" of gnawa practitioners began early and has continued despite the fact that few contemporary gnawa m'allemin in the city are from the south, let alone descendants of families who lived through the trans-Saharan slave trade.

'Abd al-Rzaq's second category was the *matiyyin*, who were based in the medina. This group's patriarch was Ba Bujma, who lived in the Oued Zghun region of the city, near the *zawiya* for Sidi Ahmad Tijaniyya and not far from the mosque, library, and school of Qarawiyyin. The zawiya serves as a pilgrimage site for those who follow Sidi Ahmed Tijani, a saint who visited Fez during the middle of the eighteenth century. He remains an important figure for West African Muslims, many of whom make the pilgrimage to the nearby site. The neighborhood surrounding the zawiya has been described to me as a place "where all the Senegalese live": dress, food, and names of restaurants all take on a more West African flavor as that community becomes more visible (see Berriane 2015). None made any explicit connections between Ba Bujma and this minority community, nor has anyone connected the gnawa to this specific West African influx. I have heard references to potential connections, however, uttered during wandering conversations. In Sidi Bujida, another neighborhood of the old city, there is a "Dar Senegal," a Senegalese house that appears to be cheap lodging for poor or traveling West Africans, many of whom are single women with children. This space occasionally serves as a venue for gnawa activities, though I have never been able to confirm what, exactly, the rare gnawa musician does there. Oblique answers to direct questions emphasize the lack of a distinct link between Fez's West African population and the gnawa, who identify as Moroccan.

Ba Bujma, who died in the late 1990s, was the grandfather of Si Muhammad bin Bujma al-Flali, known simply as Bujma. The younger Bujma, who passed away during Ramadan of 2012, was ʿAbd al-Rzaq's mʿallem and easily the most respected gnawa of the medina during my past visits. He was a quiet man who ran a musical instrument shop that sold cheap decorative drums and string instruments alongside some of the finer gnawa instruments to be found in the city. Widely known for his authoritative position within the gnawa community, he used his space as an office, giving potential clients an easy way to find him. This is despite the fact that much of his shop's business was with tourists. Members of his group would often sit, smoke, and drink tea to pass the afternoons and evenings hidden behind a curtain on the side of the small room. Bujma learned fassiyya from his grandfather and continued to play it exclusively until the "tastes of the people changed" (*dawq al-nas tawwar*). ʿAbd al-Rzaq went on to tell me that his mʿallem learned marsawiyya in response to the desires of the audience, becoming the premier artist in that style. At this point, fassiyya style, now practiced primarily in Mʿallem Aziz's Fes Jdid, became known as cold (*barid*) in opposition to the changing medina style, which was hot (*skhun*). The development of marsawiyya took hold and now the younger performers from across the city, even those in Fes Jdid, perform Bujma's "medina" style, aligning themselves with the rest of the country.

A story about a lesser-cited third figure from Fez's gnawa history identifies some interesting trends in fassiyya performance practice. Fatima, the daughter of a muqaddima named Aisha bin ʿAbd al-Rahim Flali Hakim who opened this chapter, described her memories of Ba Rami. He lived in Fes Jdid, but on the opposite side, closer to the Jewish quarter than Ba Blan's Mulay 'Abd Allah neighborhood. Fatima remembers Ba Rami as an older man who played hajhuj with just one hand. He would strike the strings with his right hand but would not close his left to melodically change pitches (*makishadsh*). He would hit the leather percussively on down strokes (*tatfrrd*), something common in virtuosic and energetic playing now. His wife was Ma Mahjuba. While the gender lines in gnawa music are extraordinarily firm, there are very rare examples that point to their permeability. Ma Mahjuba was not a muqaddima. She carried out some roles of the muqaddima when needed, but more importantly, she stood and played a tbal during the 'ada, the opening processions of her husband's ritual events. Of the two tbal parts described in chapter 4, Ma Mahjuba likely played the repeating accompaniment (the *fradi*), giving Ba Rami space to improvise rhythms on the other drum. After entering the house, according to Fatima, Ma Mahjuba sat and played the qaraqib along with the drari. Tbal playing goes to one of the more respected and experienced members of the ensemble, making Mahjuba's a significant position. I never witnessed nor heard of another woman performing with the qaraqib in ritual. More recently, women's gnawa groups have started to appear. 'Abd al-Rahim Amrani, the hamadsha leader, founded one that is exclusively for theatrical and festival performances. Yet Ma Mahjuba holds a unique place in Fez's gnawa history as the only woman to ever play qaraqib as a drari in a ritual ensemble, according to Fatima and others.

In conversation about the differences between marsawiyya and fassiyya gnawa style, I was invariably told that fassiyya is "slow," "cold," and "heavy." On a few occasions, knowledgeable m'allemin identified specific melodies that were different than their marsawi counterparts, such as those from M'allem Hamid, described in chapter 6. These types of demonstrations set fassiyya against the now common marsawiyya. Because few gnawa m'allemin continue to play the old fassiyya ritual styles, the small handful of fassiyya examples are rarely used to incite trance, nor are they reverently performed as part of a larger ceremony to remember saints. They exist on stages and as micro-demonstrations of something that used to be. Fassiyya tradition is not dead by any means—there is a market for it, and men like Aziz continue to work with it exclusively, though they do not achieve the fame and popularity of the most successful marsawi performers—but it is almost unknown, remembered only by the few who actively pursue it.

Fassiyya performance in Fez during the years that I was researching, then, carried nostalgic baggage. Conversations turned into laments as practitioners quietly remembered their youth or derided the changes that society had brought on their religious practices. For most m'allemin young and old who knew a sample of songs, fassiyya served a utilitarian purpose: it proved their reverence for and understanding of a repertoire that they believed to be somehow more authentic than what predominates today. I wanted to know how fassiyya style, as performed today at least, was colder than marsawiyya. I wanted to know how different the melodies were and how similar the lyrics were. I wanted to know what was slower and what was heavier.

To that end, I enlisted M'allem Aziz to perform a very short version of the ritual that I could record. Instead of requiring the elongation of songs as people went into trance, I asked him to move through the repertoire by playing examples of each of the songs and sets. There was an audience, but they were not particularly responsive and few knew how to react to this music. Those Moroccans unfamiliar with fassiyya found the style to be lacking due to the missing "hits" that they had expected. Aziz and his ensemble moved from one song to the next, completing each set and segment, generously giving me the recording. It was an artificial setting and says very little (if anything at all) about the relationship between music and trance. Fuson's (2009) coenunciation, the interactivity between instruments and dancing feet, was absent, but the group skillfully and confidently provided me with some fascinating and invaluable music.

My goal here is to look at what this one performance of fassiyya style, given by the man unanimously cited by Fez's gnawa community as the authoritative performer of this repertoire, says about its contemporary performance. My catalog of fassiyya melodies does not speak for the entirety of the repertoire, just as the previous marsawiyya analysis did not represent the diversity of potential performances. Two individual events provide rough observations about the ways in which repertoire labels are described and used now, in a contemporary context. There are some surprising disconnects between the ways in which people talk about fassiyya (in terms of marsawiyya) and the way that M'allem Aziz played the repertoire that day in Fez. This approach fleshes out, first, the influence of marsawiyya dominance on contemporary fassiyya performance practice and, second, the distinct musical ways in which popular aesthetics may have affected the wider contemporary performance of gnawa ritual.

In interviews, respondents cite the "heaviness" (*tqal*) of fassiyya performance practice in terms of tempo. When I set about arranging this fassiyya performance and recording with M'allem Aziz, he made it a point to say that the music is slow. He questioned me, making sure that this is what I wanted. His implication, confirmed later in a conversation during a break in the session, was that this music would be different from what I had ever heard, from marsawiyya. It was not entertainment, and he appeared concerned that, because of the differences, it might not be entertaining. He maintained a level of discomfort up until a younger member of his group who was more familiar with my project confirmed to him that a fassiyya recording was my goal.

After recording, listening to, and analyzing the music, I came across characteristics of the rhythmic cycles, the iqa', that surprised me. First, the hemiola rhythm was absent, as the march-like figure always moved directly into the heavy sixteenth-note pattern. Second, the heavy sixteenth-note figure itself featured an identifiably different pattern of articulations. Third, the average tempo for each figure was nearly identical to its *marsawi* version, as was average tempo of the entire performance. Lastly, the ranges between the initial slow tempi and the concluding fast ones were slightly smaller for Aziz's performance, meaning that it was 'Abd al-Rzaq's marsawiyya performance that actually contained the slowest tempi—and the largest swing of dramatic acceleration within each song.

In 'Abd al-Rzaq's marsawiyya performance, the hemiola pattern constituted the rhythmic accompaniment of ten percent of the songs, often serving as a short-lived intermediary between the march pattern and the heavy sixteenths. It is playable at a quicker tempo than the march, but as a set progresses, it adapts into the heavy sixteenths fairly quickly. It could be that the range for which the drari can maintain a stable articulation of the long-short-short-long figuration is relatively small. More likely, however, is that the hemiola is a frantic attempt to maintain the character of the march pattern at a high tempo before abandoning it for the more equidistant heavy sixteenths figure. The march pattern appears equally often between the two performances (see fig. 7.4), with the heavy sixteenths figure becoming far more common in the fassi version. The average tempo of the heavy sixteenths was lower in the fassiyya performance (see fig. 7.5), suggesting that the marsawiyya hemiola figure is a virtuosic show of speed, an opportunity to increase the intensity of the fastest march pattern-based songs. In performance, the hemiola pattern bears an aural relationship to sh'abi music's three-against-two rhythmic feel. This figure appears throughout the segments of the gnawa ceremony that feature female spirits, such as the songs dedicated to Lalla Malika described in chapter 6.

Perhaps more surprising, considering the incessant declamations that fassiyya was "heavy" and slow, was that the tempi of these two performances were very similar. The pace of the three-stroke rhythms were nearly identical with the duple pattern turning out to be a touch quicker in the fassiyya version than the marsawiyya one. These averages do not tell the entire story, however, as the standard deviation for the triplet pattern in the marsawiyya performance was twenty percent higher than that of the older style: 15 BPM compared to 12. This, and the larger range between the slowest and fastest iterations of each pattern in the marsawiyya repertoire mentioned above, shows that a far greater degree of acceleration dramatized the progression of each set of songs within the newer performance practice. This tells a similar story to that of the four-stroke rhythms described above. The clap rhythm is the only one in which there is a very large difference, and this is almost certainly due to the fact that it appears only once in Aziz's performance. A sample of one skews the average high and negates any real comparisons with marsawiyya practice, where the clap is used in multiple different settings. While the reality that these shortened performances provide only a skeletal outline of a diversity of ritual practices, these cursory statistics do point to new questions regarding the relationship between descriptions of the older traditions and their contemporary performances.

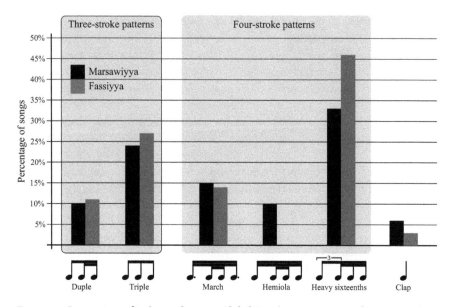

Figure 7.4. Comparison of iqa' usage between Abd al-Rzaq's marsawiyya performance and Aziz wuld Ba Blan's fassiyya performance.

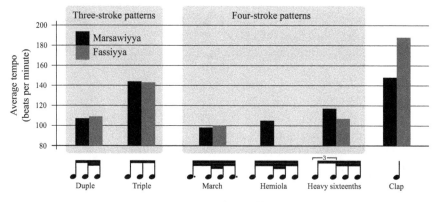

Figure 7.5. Comparison of each pattern's average tempo between Abd al-Rzaq's marsawiyya performance and Aziz wuld Ba Blan's fassiyya performance.

After hearing that marsawiyya was faster than fassiyya over and over again, I was surprised to find that these two performances did not display this allegedly central point of difference between the two repertoires. The average tempo for the marsawiyya performance was 120 BPM. This was less than 1.5 percent faster than the fassiyya version, which clocked in at 118 BPM. Furthermore, when I included the contentious women's segment in the calculation, M'allem Aziz's fassiyya version was actually faster on average than 'Abd al-Rzaq's marsawiyya iteration. There are some possible explanations that discount these observations. First, these are simply two performances, though I would argue that they are representative in that they are performed by respected and experienced m'allemin. Aziz's fassiyya version, which is faster than expected, is especially significant because no other similarly comprehensive recordings of the repertoire (even in this shortened form) are readily available. Second, it is very feasible that Aziz has been influenced by the increasing speeds of marsawiyya, making his iteration of fassiyya different than what may have been a past norm. If this is the case, then it is still noteworthy that what is described and even idolized as representative and authentic is so drastically changed. Without older recordings it is not possible to discern any certainty about this potential change in fassiyya style. The heaviness, on the other hand, may be a result of musical attributes other than speed. It could come in part from the adaptation and inclusion of the hemiola pattern in marsawiyya style. This rhythm, based within sh'abi tradition and familiar to audiences, alludes to popular music and dance styles, facilitating the "lighter" feel of the newer style.

Like the marsawiyya accompaniment patterns, the fassiyya hajhuj articulates melodic characteristics that develop over time, providing both cohesiveness and forward momentum within sets of songs. Whereas I had expected these to be somehow more "grounded" than the newer repertoire versions, weighing down the music to fit its description, they were just as likely to obscure the beat through syncopation and forward momentum. Looking at the same first segment of the ritual, that of the shurfa', the *mwima* patterns grow from simple to complex (example 7.2). The first song of the set, one of many with the ambiguous title of "Salatu al-Nabi" (Prayers for the Prophet), features a clear articulation of the duple pattern. There is little internal syncopation, but the last note anticipates the coming downbeat through a slight accent. As was the case with the flali rhythm, this is a common feel within Moroccan music. The next two songs feature similar contours, though the first, "Salatu al-Nab, Muhammad ya Rasul Allah," has a true mwima that moves underneath independent vocal melodies while the second, "Salatu al-Nabi," follows the vocal lines closely. "Salatu al-Nabi al-'Afu" is in three parts, transitioning from a duple to a triplet feel. The first part is a small rhythmic cycle, the second half of which expands—as a motive—to inform the second part. Here we see the same shifting two-against-three pattern that animates the women's portion of this tradition, and it only grows more ornate as the tempo increases in the third part of the song. The final two pieces of the set, "Jallala" and "Salatu al-Nabi La Illaha ila Allah," show a rise and fall in contour that audibly accents the second beat of the pattern. This has the effect of a clap or snare drum hit on two and four, propelling the musical motion forward. It is hardly the downward emphasis that I had expected when imagining a "heavy" musical style.

al-Shurfa: the white spirits

a) "Salatu al-Nabi"

b) "Salatu al-Nabi, Muhammed ya Rasul Allah"

c) "Salatu al-Nabi" (not a *mwima*)

d) "Salatu al-Nabi, al-ʿAfu"

e) "Salatu al-Nabi, al-ʿAfu" Part 2

f) "Salatu al-Nabi, al-ʿAfu" Part 3

g) "Jillala" h) Salatu al-Nabi, La Ilaha Illa Allah"

al-Kuhl: the black spirits

i) "Mimuna"

j) "Mimuna 2" (not a *mwima*)

k) "Ghumami"

l) "Marhaba"

m) "Marhaba 2"

Example 7.2. Accompaniment patterns from the first two sets of Mʿallem Aziz's fassiyya recording. This is a representation of fluid pitches and rhythms and suffers from the limitations of standard musical notation. Particularly, the pitches B and A-sharp change over the course of these songs as the mʿallem's hand occasionally moves higher or lower. While in some cases this is intention, it is often a result of the hajhuj tuning and setup. These changes should not be taken as an explicit change in modality.

The following set, dedicated to the black spirits called *al-kuhl*, acts similarly. These are the figures that draw the trancing body into self-mutilation with knives or hot wax. Ghumami, Sidi Mimun, and Mimuna strike fear into many gnawa participants. The patterns that accompany their songs, however, obscure the beat by pushing the boundaries of speed as they settle into upbeat grooves. The patterns in example 7.2 begin with two songs for Lalla Mimuna, both of which follow a similar contour, though the second loosely doubles the vocal lines that are trading back and forth above it. "Ghumami," which follows, has a slow syncopation thanks to the drop in tempo (a pause separates it from the previous two songs) and the repeated C-sharp that seems to bounce up and away from the cycle's initial beat. Mʿallem Aziz compared the song to riding a horse. The final two are similar to the last of the previous segment, as they flow up and down, drawing away from its initial beat before reaching a high point in the middle of the pattern. "Marhaba" does this by accenting the final stroke, again potentially borrowing a familiar rhythmic feel from elsewhere in Morocco's musical repertoire. The second "Marhaba" elongates into a three-beat cycle, leading into the third. Both obscure the downbeat by immediately moving away from the initial pitch, rocking down the instrument before rising back up. While all of these characteristics pull away from a slow musical "heaviness" implied by so many descriptions of fassiyya, there are a number of songs like the second "Salatu al-Nabi" and the second "Mimuna" here that closely track vocal melodies. These moments can be startling changes of musical texture that do, to my ears, elicit a sense of heft. That they do so melodically and not necessarily rhythmically speaks to the complexity and difficulty inherent in talking about music. The perceptions of musical content—things like heaviness—dramatically influence listeners' perceptions of things like authenticity. That older fassiyya styles may have transformed to meet the needs of newer audiences by speeding up to build excitement, or that perhaps they never were slower and more patient than more contemporary practices, becomes irrelevant because some other musical element can step in to contribute that necessary feeling of tqal, heaviness.

Later in the conversation that opened this chapter, the muqaddima Fatima described the segment of fassiyya ceremonies from her youth that invited female spirits into the room, and into the bodies of the possessed. They began with Lalla Hawa, Eve, who no longer shows up in marsawiyya ritual. The groups would then move into Lalla Mira, Malika, two other Malikas (Malika al-Arabiyya, the Arab, and Malika ash-Shilha, the Berber) before closing with songs referencing Aisha. The Aisha set did not include "Aisha Hamdushiyya," but it did include other songs for her that remain popular today. M'allem Aziz's performance featured many of these figures, as well as some others: Lalla Rqiyya, Lalla Mhaliyya, and songs referencing Sidi Ahmed Tijani and the *tijaniyya* brotherhood.

During the break before he played the women's segment, the m'allem approached me and told me to turn off my recording. This, he said, was because the women's segment was not part of the fassiyya mluk repertoire and therefore unrelated to my research. I told him that I was interested in hearing how he played the women's songs. He shrugged and let me continue recording. Just after the m'allem finished his performance, a Moroccan member of the audience came up to him and asked why he skipped "Aisha Hamdushiyya" and "Mulay Hamid," her two favorite pieces of gnawa music. He looked at her irritably—possibly because he had just finished playing and was preparing to head home—and simply said, "We don't play those songs." Aziz proceeded to gruffly explain that those were newer songs and were not a part of the repertoire that he was hired to play. He later told me that this often happens when he completes a fassiyya ritual, as few audience members understand the differences.

While casting innovations aside and questioning their validity during conversations, Aziz, Fatima, and others recognize their importance. Even though he did not play "Aisha Hamdushiyya," the m'allem had continued through the female spirits at a pace that exceeded what 'Abd al-Rzaq had demonstrated. (Aziz's versions of the music for the women's segment were 8 BPM faster than that of Rzaq's performance.) He clicked along, inviting the audience of his concert/ritual to stand and dance in front of the ensemble. An event that had passed through sunset and was flowing into the evening was reenergized with Aziz's Lalla Mira, his Lalla Malika, and others who were less familiar. What was austere until this point grew to a climax of moving bodies that were not possessed but were engaged and dancing.

Throughout this chapter, I have been hunting for tqal. The sheer consistency of comments pushing me to look to the music for weight—to look for a clear distinction between the old and the new—tempted me to note every descent, every arrival. Gnawa music sounds heavy in so many of its forms, old and new, just as it can defy this implied weightiness and push forward with agile figures and syncopated melodies. While I want to avoid a reductive approach with a predisposition to align this ritual music with power and potency, I do believe that there is a sense of weight in the music of the past that is distinct from what circulates through current ceremonies, at least to my ears. That so many described this difference to me confirms that I am not alone in this perception. It is a perspective that grows out of discourse, is seated within nostalgia, and requires a listener-centric view of the ritual. That this also implicates perceptions of the rituals themselves led me toward the narratives of history, authority, and authenticity that are threaded through these pages.

The following chapter looks more closely at the point between m'allem and listener, where personal expectations and values inform the perception of authenticity itself. It is difficult to fully recognize the depth and breadth of change affecting the gnawa community over the past generation, but Aziz's performance and the strategies undertaken by those described in the next chapter show that these shifts do not exist exclusively in the realm of the young and inexperienced. Those who dedicate their lives to maintaining an authentic gnawa tradition deploy many of the same strategies that they contest in an effort to educate audiences and push back against encroaching adaptation.

Notes

1. This innovation of a blond spirit highlights the appropriation of Western individuals in gnawa practice—young tourists dancing at a festival, for example—while also recognizing the presence of Moroccan youth who dye their hair brown or other colors (including blond) for fashion reasons. That a respected and feared spirit would be either from the West or aware of modern fashion trends is either a humorous aside or an audience-grabbing innovation. Humor is very present in ritual, making a combination of these two possibilities likely.

2. These terms are my own, but the organizational terms used by the gnawa are similarly inconsistent. *Trih*, for example, can be what I refer to as a song or a set depending on which m'allem is explaining the musical organization. These are more often performed than described, thanks in part to the lack of a "lesson"-oriented musical education. They are learned through experience and not explication, so I introduce these terms that I base in specific musical phenomena (instrumental interludes, resetting of tempi, and color/spirit change) to clarify my analytical points.

3. The word iqa' refers to a short repeated rhythm and is used to describe the percussion accompaniment in many musical genres throughout Morocco and the Middle East. While musicians of some genres have specific names for different iqa', gnawa musicians do not have native terms to describe these different rhythmic patterns as I define them.

4. Because I took the beginning and ending tempi of 'Abd al-Rzaq's performance from the points at which the group settled into a groove for the singing and the excessive (and sometimes frantic) acceleration near the end, respectively, the ending tempo of one song is not always identical to the listed beginning tempo of the next. Usually it is within 2 BPM, but some differences are much greater. This is due to the fact that sometimes groups continue to accelerate after beginning to sing and in other cases they settle into a slower tempo after "overshooting" during the *accelerando* of the previous song.

5. To best see how the order of the mluk ceremony differs between regions, see chart 6.1 in Timothy Fuson's dissertation (2009, 421). He outlines the standard progression as it exists in Marrakech. Notable differences include Lalla Aisha's presence in the middle of the ceremony as opposed to the closing moments of Fez's path, the earlier placement of the Buhali spirits (they are late in the evening in Fez and appear second in Marrakech), and the splitting of the white holy spirits into two sections in Marrakech. Many other variations appear across the country and the similarities or differences between them would be a fruitful avenue for future research. It is not clear how or why a sudani organization brought directly from Marrakech would have adapted to become the fassiyya organization that now dominates this city only. Furthermore, it is significant that while performance style shifted from fassiyya to marsawiyya, this local organization of songs has remained consistent.

8 Heritage and Hybridity

Wᴴɪʟᴇ ᴡᴀʟᴋɪɴɢ ᴛʜʀᴏᴜɢʜ a graveyard just east of Fez's old city on a beautiful spring day, M'allem 'Abd al-Rzaq pointed out the burial sites of local saints who appeared during the gnawa ritual. I had asked him to show me the resting places of those who populate and animate the ceremony. This was partly a "proof": after a few years of attempting to discern the identities of Lalla Mira, Sidi Mimun, and others, I yearned for a different approach, something that would say, once and for all, whether these figures were real people. The idea of taking a walk through a cemetery came one day when I was very, very lost in Rabat. Wandering down the coast in Salé, Rabat's sister city across the river, I stumbled onto a large shrine. The building's white qubba, the dome, rose up from behind a hill and stood out against the Atlantic Ocean. A woman at the door told me that it was dedicated to Sidi Musa and that each week religious groups and pilgrims came from the surrounding areas to pray, to supplicate, and to receive blessings. I realized that I had been mistaken in thinking that Sidi Musa, Moses, was that Moses: the one from the Qur'an, Bible, and other Abrahamic scriptures. Maybe his blue color and power over water did not speak to the parting of the Red Sea, where Moses delivered the Jews from slavery. Yet Moroccans make the same associations, spreading their hands to hold up imaginary sea walls as they described the saint. Here was a local figure, though, situated along the coast, with the same name and a relationship to water. This threw my ideas, and my hopes of ever getting firm answers about these sacred figures, into crisis. Which Musa appears in the gnawa ceremony? Both? Either? Who gets to decide?

So 'Abd al-Rzaq and I walked through the graveyard to structures dedicated to different spirits from gnawa tradition. He led me over walls, up tight and well-trodden paths that wound between the overcrowded resting places. Some destinations were large mausoleums, buildings that pilgrims can enter to make requests of a holy man or woman. Others were old and tiny, stones worn away by years of weather. Children played on the hillside, running up and down the trails, laughing, while families paid their respects to deceased loved ones. What followed, however, was striking. We left the graveyard and 'Abd al-Rzaq led me back to Bab Ftuh, the city gate that faced the hill. Built into the side of the city wall was another saint's site, though not one who appears in the gnawa ceremony. We went in the gate and turned a few corners that I had never taken before. Then we came upon a small whitewashed building tucked between two tall apartment buildings. The little home reminded me of photos that occasionally circulate online of a house whose *owner refused to sell, despite oncoming urban development, like a Seattle home that was compared to the house from the 2015 Pixar movie* Up.[1] *This was a shrine to Sidi Mimun, one of the most feared, and most mysterious, members of the gnawa pantheon. This spirit takes hold during the black segment and causes trancing bodies to dance with knives or lit candles. Stories abound of his possessed trancers eating glass. Was this building proof that Sidi Mimun was a person who had lived, perhaps as a pharmacist, as he was described by Mulay Tahir in a conversation in Tamesluht? I asked 'Abd al-Rzaq, only to get a shrug in response. Well, is he buried here? Don't know, he responded. There are shrines to Sidi Mimun all over the country, Rzaq explained. Some may have body parts, some may not. Maybe none do.*

This site, nestled between new apartment buildings, holding its own against urban sprawl—and 'Abd al-Rzaq's ambivalence toward what was buried there— symbolized the role of history in gnawa practice to me. It is tied up in a variety of state projects, commercial endeavors, and musical circulations. The identity of the spirits, even whether they were people who once lived, is fashioned into competing versions of the community's cultural heritage. In some cases, these identities inform different renderings of the history. The relationship between competing versions of this heritage tells a story of activists young and old working to define and protect a vision of gnawa-ness, of tgnawit, *in the twenty-first century.*

Authenticity through Listening

As argued in the previous chapters, authenticity is generated from many sources. It can rise up from lines of patrimony through sub-Saharan African lineage. Authenticity's literal fluidity can come from matriarchy, as seen in 'Abd al-Kabir Marshan's reflections on his black milk-mother. Powerful relationships built on family and teaching maintain the spiritual lives and careers of some of Morocco's most famous *m'allemin*. Success also breeds authenticity, as the power of audiences reinforces the importance of musical performers and innovators. Piety demonstrates the authenticity for those performers who go on pilgrimages, pray regularly, and otherwise serve as model Muslims from within, and not outside of, the gnawa community.

Each of these narratives of authenticity requires a certain negotiation. The authentic comes out of a relationship between performer and participant, something proven for most by the demonstrable presence of possessing spirits within the healing ritual, fitting into what Michelle Bigenho (2002) called "experiential authenticity." But there are other supporting "proofs." Pious behavior, popular success, and bloodlines each, in its own way, reinforces the authenticity of the performer; these traits show something to audiences that garners acceptance, and with that acceptance comes authority, respect, and paid work, akin to Bigenho's "cultural-historical authenticity." In this chapter, I turn toward that verification, the proof of authenticity, to ask how these measures of success find significance with different audiences. The ways in which elders themselves adapt, taking on didactic strategies to train audiences, exemplifies this process of claiming and negotiating authenticity. In girding the music and performance practice against what they see as destructive changes, they focus their efforts toward influencing audience expectations, showing that authenticity is firmly situated within this meeting between performer and listener.

The experience of listening has been the focus of much recent scholarship on Middle Eastern music and religious participation. Listening is an individual experience, but it is one that often happens communally and can carry a powerful ethical dimension (Gaffney 1994; Hirschkind 2006; Spadola 2014). Experienced religious sounds and musical entertainments are deeply embedded within context. They are both personal and interactive, sometimes with others who are similarly overwhelmed (or underwhelmed) by what is going on. Occasionally, as is the case with other Islamic religious practices, interaction is both outward and upward, with unseen spirits, God, or the extinction (*fana'*) of the self into the oneness of creation (*tawhid*). The religious listening experience, whether energetically entertaining or reflective and austere, involves moral expectations and values mixed with taste. There is a negotiation involved: Is the music appropriate? Is it appealing? Does it "speak" to me and to my conception of morality? And, in this case, does it "speak" to the invited spirits? I argue that the authentic experience, whether ritual or otherwise, emerges from this meeting of musical and extramusical performance with personal and communal tastes, expectations, and values. I engage the point of negotiation and ask how a multiplicity of authenticities reflects larger debates about cultural heritage, nostalgia, and the place of sacred music in Morocco today.

It is useful to think of these types of listening and performance experiences as forms of what Judith Becker (2004) called "deep listening." This mirrors an Arabic term, though one that is not generally used in the gnawa tradition: *sama'*. This word articulates a form of musical participation that invokes openness to spiritual inspiration. It is this listening—participating within the experience of gnawa music—that ensures an opportunity for authenticity. Within many Islamic practices, this listening widens far beyond musical appreciation and incorporates an eagerness, a fertility for the seeds of sacred experience. What remains important, however, is the recognition of individual personality and taste, even within deeply spiritual moments. Individuals practice religion and find the sacred through different avenues, so it should not be surprising that gnawa practitioners perform differently, with individual styles, values, abilities, and sounds. Listeners' personal experiences mediate and inform their understanding of those sounds. This mediation enables processes of meaning creation, of interpretation, of understanding and misunderstanding. Performer intent informs a physical sound that, in turn, falls on ears that are informed by dissimilar experiences, values, and expectations. It is not my aim here to enter into a semiotic analysis of gnawa music, but to point out that potential meanings do not necessarily follow sound from one place to another. A listener's perspective, which may be tangential to musical taste or ritual belief, plays an outsized interpretive role. Attitudes and ideologies both steer and are steered by musical listening. They also derive from and contribute to larger conceptions of identity and sacred experience.

I have proposed three interrelated but distinct narratives of gnawa authenticity that are in play throughout the ritual community and music industry. The first is that the narrative links authenticity to sub-Saharan lineage through blood, family, learning, proximity, and even skin color. The second situates piety as central to a practice that closely aligns with Sufism and notes dramatic change in ritual performance, considering many contemporary practices to be debased spectacles. These two narratives show how there is no singular conception of gnawa heritage in Morocco. Like the identities of the spirits whose graves dot the hillside I explored with ʿAbd al-Rzaq, the history of the music, musicians, and larger community falls directly into discourses of localized Islamic practice while simultaneously becoming wrapped into the Moroccan postcolonial nation-building project. Beyond these two versions of gnawa identity, other complex ideals percolate through globalizing trends, commodification, and regional difference. This ritual practice, with its traces of sub-Saharan musicality and spirituality, shares much with the religious tenants of Moroccan sainthood and Sufism. It serves the state by highlighting national diversity and inclusiveness. Over the last half-century it rose to become a stalwart part of the domestic popular music industry, bringing new interest and audiences. These two constructions of identity and identity maintenance pervade ritual and staged performance practice, personal piety, and even cultural memory—nostalgia—throughout the gnawa community.

The third narrative of authenticity that I propose throughout these pages highlights the validation of the commodity market as clients look to commercially successful performers as not only legitimate but also definitive symbols of authentic performance precisely because of their ability to demonstrate concrete skills and adeptness with audiences. Any given performer may draw different measures from each of these pools of authenticity: ʿAbd al-Rzaq in Fez cites his virtuosity and training while Marrakech's ʿAbd al-Latif Makhzumi laments the contemporary spectacle and impiety of young performers who perform at major festivals. The apparent contradictions between these three authenticities are flexible and productive. They open avenues both for individual opportunities and for perspectives from which one performer can question the authenticity of another, two important elements of a competitive ritual marketplace.

Just as performers utilize the opportunities presented by a variety of authenticities, listeners and clients recognize them as a space for choice. Metaphorically, consider the American recording industry's approach to audiences. Faced with changing demographics in the 1970s, industry leaders diversified their popular music offerings by dividing genres into increasingly specific subgenres. Country, for example, eventually gave way to the Nashville sound, the Bakersfield sound, bluegrass, old time, pop country, alt-country, Americana, and so on. While these genre subdivisions have had an undeniable impact on the demographics of listening for decades (Garofalo 1987), they also provide a service: they curate an oppressively large catalog for individual listeners' tastes. While the power structures and grassroots communities that inform these delineations is a conversation worth continuing, my purpose here is to note the multifaceted utility of increasingly specific genre distinctions.

Ritual clients and fans of gnawa music have their own sets of aesthetic preferences that connect with individual understandings of authenticity. In gnawa music, the differences are not so extreme as to warrant individual genre terminologies, and no one I spoke with expressed a desire to categorize beyond using lines of appropriate and inappropriate ritual practice. Performance practice, however, was closely aligned to listener taste when determinations of "true" or "pure" were tossed around by participants. Besides, if concerts can be rituals, rituals can also have informal genres based on diverse aesthetic values, markets, and audiences in ways similar to how we conceive of concerts. This is especially the case when rituals operate within the competitive demands of economic markets and results, in part, from the fact that ritual clients and fans of staged performances are not cohesive unified audiences. For example, because someone in need of healing may have only heard the gnawa on television or from the speakers of a CD seller's stall, he or she might bring tastes from the popular marketplace—with its own aesthetic priorities—into a ceremony. That there are only so many clients for the growing number of gnawa musicians who look to their ritual practice as a primary or secondary occupation makes competition, and therefore adaptation, an important reality.

As debates about history and identity percolate up from individuals, they increasingly inform popular conceptions of gnawa heritage. Whether from artists or audiences, ideals about who the gnawa were and are disseminate through loud ritual performances throughout the winding neighborhoods of Morocco's cities. Conceptions of identity based within differing ideals of authenticity and tgnawit come from both within and outside of the gnawa community. These various pulls from within and outside illuminate the polyphonic nature of heritage at play. I say polyphonic because they are not necessarily diametrically opposed, nor do they align snugly. There is overlap and contestation in how gnawa identity and history appear in various staged and ritual settings across the country. The idea that heritage is performed or produced is certainly not new; these contexts lay out strategies used by participants to perform against the grain, as they actively produce alternative heritages that stand against the ones that they grew up with or push back against the changes that they so passionately resist. In other words, this music facilitates an understanding of multiple heritages operating in polyphony with and against each other.

Institutionalizing Heritage

The strategies of various groups within the gnawa community underline the saliency of *Ethnicity, Inc.* (2009). In this book, John and Jean Comaroff show the legal and economic pressures on populations, national leaders, and flagship companies who work to demonstrate specialization (120–21) and stake a claim to heritage production. The types of events generated by this strategic push are both reflective of a focus on an intangible cultural heritage, one that Morocco is well positioned to preserve and share, and demonstrative of attempts to steer articulations of specific cultural values (Kirschenblatt-Gimblett 2004). Tolerance, cooperation, diversity, and fusion are frequent themes of the major festivals in Fez and Essaouira. The 2012 festival in Fez had the theme "Re-Enchanting the World," and 2013's was "Giving Soul to Globalization." The festival in 2010 was focused on connections and collaboration with "In Search of the Sacred Other" as its topic, and 2015's was "Fez, an African Reflection." That these and similar themes continue to reappear on festival banners year after year speaks to the active neoliberal and diplomatic projects that they front. These domestic and international messages, however, also carry political meaning: internally, they promote civility alongside antiterrorism signage and slogans across the country while externally, they forecast safety to tourists weary of instability in the Middle East and North Africa. A very specific form of gnawa heritage animates festivals and other large events, highlighting collaboration and African-ness. The gnawa coincide with a vision of Morocco that illuminates a diversity and openness running counter to rising fundamentalisms around the world. Narratives of exchange, engagement, interaction, and cooperation emphasize the national projects that underpin these festivals and, as such, gird the political aims of the country's tourism market. The music of the gnawa ritual plays a role in establishing Morocco as distinct from other troublesome potential vacation or investment destinations for international audiences. At the same time, the music teaches Moroccans, especially the young men who enjoy the massive outdoor events, that this country is diverse, it is tolerant.

Members of the gnawa community have similarly taken steps to advance their standing within the country through incorporation, both formal and informal. Some, like the major performers who banded together in 2009 to create the Yerma Gnawa Association, a group "for the promotion and dissemination of gnawa patrimony," ally with major festivals. The group is, from their website, "committed to the continuation of the Gnawa and World Music festival" and works to create residencies and other performance opportunities for its members. Abdessalam Alikane, a frequent performer on the Essaouira stage under the name Tyour Gnawa who was involved in the early stages of getting this organization started, relayed similar priorities to me in an interview. Simultaneously, it has taken steps to preserve "Gnaoui heritage" by planning a *mussem* pilgrimage event and undertaking a recording project to preserve and transcribe texts for regional variants of the ceremonial repertoire. The group has underwritten health insurance for a number of m'allemin and assisted major artists with international performance opportunities, including help with logistics like securing artists' cards for others (see the organization website[2]; see also Kapchan 2014: 8–9). This entry into the incorporated world of heritage preservation and maintenance is particularly powerful because it is aligned with a large music festival focused on gnawa music. This certainly helps it to capture the attention and support of national and international organizations. The potentially out-of-date website notes that "one of the main objectives of the Yerma Gnaoua Association is the classification of Gnaoua traditions with UNESCO as 'oral and intangible heritage of humanity.' The Moroccan Ministry of Culture has also pledged its support."

As seen throughout these pages, however, there are multiple voices projecting a variety of gnawa identities and authenticities across the country. Many who operate outside of the festival marketplace and focus solely on local ceremonies or are otherwise prevented from entering into this community of support—those like Yassine, for example, who advance outside of the standards of the apprenticeship system—have dissenting opinions of what gnawa heritage, history, and identity is, or at least should be. Certain elements of the sound and practice were adapted in order to establish a well-received form of gnawa music. This likely began well before tourism markets and national festivals were in play, but it did rise out of an increasingly competitive market space for gnawa performers. These pages have outlined many changes in ritual performance practice that resulted from the ritual's move from rare annual community event to a family or neighborhood ceremony focused on individual clients. Even though many from the ritual audience continue to trance at different points of the event, the ceremony's purpose is aimed directly at its host. Thus began a fight for clients and the professionalization of gnawa musicianship. Marketing and style grew in importance as clients were confronted with a choice between multiple local performance troupes. Authenticity ceased to be centralized and instead democratized through the meeting point between ritual leader and client. The definition of authenticity grew into an important part of the economic marketplace.

Because performance practice is so closely linked with ideals and identities within ritual and staged contexts, I argue that, following Daniel Herwitz, heritage is an aesthetic concern, one "about the quality and kind of *experience* afforded in late capitalist society, not simply a moral and political issue about recognition, reparation, and social power" (2012, 7–8). He notes that heritage is part of citizen-making, a process that stretches in many directions in this context. Gnawa heritage as African—and therefore representative of diversity—as presented by national interests on stages, is distinct from gnawa heritage as Muslim—and like but not necessarily identical to Sufism—as argued and performed by elders who recount a history before the transformative influences of professionalization. Herwitz identifies heritage as either bankable, something usable toward an end, or reflective, a vantage point for a critique of the present (see also Boym 2007). That members of the gnawa community engage in both modes of heritage maintenance is demonstrative of the complexity of this population's self-identification. While Yerma Gnaoua fully engages Comaroff and Comaroff's sense of "Ethnicity, Inc." through the models and institutions of neoliberalism to bank heritage, others react against these moves, refuting what they see as a manipulation of history and identity in the service of nonritual or nonreligious motivations. They critique this version of identity, the present, from a vantage point in the past.

The past and present fluidly interact within the memories and ideologies that engender nostalgia. I use the term as a conflation of memory and ideology, an active political force within the contemporary world that draws on narratives of personal and communal history. This nostalgia is individual, but like memories themselves, it is influenced by larger discourses of nation-building, religious piety, and ethnic struggle. In this way, nostalgia plays an important role in the negotiation of authenticity. Performers, listeners, and clients making choices about what to play, approve of, or pay for must determine for themselves what is authentic. For many, authenticity is in experience: authentic performance is the performance that most directly connects with listeners. The authentic experience may be the virtuosic style seen in rituals and on stages. It could also be purity: authentic performance might connect the listener, performer, and spirits to a sound and ritual devoid of these innovations, linking back to a time before the fame and fortune shifted *hajhuj* techniques and expanded the size of ensembles. An authenticity based in a sense of purity does not need any of this. The ritual worked without these distractions before, and it can still do so now.

In this way, nostalgia within the gnawa community is both preservationist and revisionist. In both senses, activism in the name of past truths are what Svetlana Boym describes as restorative, attempting "a transhistorical reconstruction of the lost home" (2007, 13). Similarly, it can be what Debbora Battaglia described as practical nostalgia, a "vehicle of knowledge" (1995, 77). Nostalgic listeners worry about the loss of older styles of performance and work to develop new listening audiences in order to maintain them against an encroaching commercialism. Simultaneously, the Moroccan state highlights a history of slavery that rings true for only a portion of the gnawa community—many gnawa performers and listeners are not direct descendants of sub-Saharan Africans—to introduce a view of the identity's history that is similarly preservationist *and* revisionist. Both perspectives are preserving something while pushing back against (or revising) something else. The nostalgia of these elders attempts to preserve a memory of the previous generation's perspectives by focusing on the recent past while the version of gnawa performance that appears on stages preserves and emphasizes a history of slavery. Both also actively revise the historical narrative: one acts as a corrective against what it sees as a degradation of the ritual and the other emphasizes cultural heritage while adapting performance practice for expanding audiences. These two forces, and many complex intermediaries that weave between them, produce the dynamic heritages of tgnawit that pervade ritual and staged events. Cultural heritage as a performed element of personal and communal history exists in varieties, some of which conflict. Within the experience of Morocco's diverse gnawa musicians, this heritage links to issues including ethnicity, piety, and memory. This chapter argues that, by listening to and performing gnawa music nostalgically, practitioners like 'Abd al-Latif strategically critique the broad definitions of "gnawa" and "Moroccan Islam," even of "Sufism," that circulate through the industry and major heritage festivals.

Rituals, like stages, are places for imagining cultural identity. Within these liminal spaces, nostalgia has a potency to assert versions of ethical, economic, spiritual, and national ideologies. Insofar as authenticity can be negotiated, its verification depends on a sense of recognition, a nod of agreement from clients and listeners. This nod invokes an individualized sense of nostalgia that comes to bear fruit within larger communal discourses. In a sense, all gnawa performances, whether ritual or representative in festivals (and, in a different way, fusion projects) look to evoke a sense of nostalgia. The content of that nostalgia within a given listener and performance context, however, can differ greatly. When a performance meets a listener's expectations, a powerful sense of authenticity envelopes the listening experience. This view of authenticity, in which nostalgia serves as verification, allows for a wide range of moralities, value systems, priorities, and aesthetic choices to "count." It also insinuates that preconceived, or at least impressionable, understandings of gnawa heritage are important to the definition of authenticity. Projecting your values to change minds, even educating listeners or young performers, is therefore of utmost importance. Clarifying and convincing others of what heritage is and was, of what their nostalgia should look like, is the battleground for preserving and/or revising ritual and musical identity.

In this sense of nationalism as cultural project, the gnawa context aligns with what Jonathan Shannon (2015) describes within the trans-Mediterranean music of al-Andalus. Nostalgia can be restorative, but the aims of the restoration are not universal. The ways in which the presentation of gnawa heritages serve national or cultural projects do not always align comfortably, just as Andalusian music in Spain, Morocco, and Syria both sound different and represent conflicting meanings or sentiments in each locale. In this way, recognizing nostalgia's significance within the present links its "politics . . . to the postmodern commodity sensibility" (Appadurai 1996, 30, citing Jameson 1983). For example, many performers are concerned by recent ritual adaptations aimed at meeting new audience demands. This only increases frustrations with the growing influence of a performed aesthetics imported, at least in part, from the priorities of world music circuits and state festivals (see Erlmann 1996). Competing ideologies of the past presented through recording studios and festival stages create and commoditize heritage within an opportunistic present, often through stubbornly persistent histories, at least from the perspective of those who disagree with the presentation.

Festival Pilgrims

It is difficult, if not impossible, to discern any causal relationship between the festival stages, gnawa music's popularity, and the continuity of ritual practice, but it is easy to see that gnawa music is doing at least two things: it is expanding and it is changing. I saw ritual events in the poorest homes and some of the wealthiest. The events were full. Folding chairs set up around the room were insufficient for the crowds of friends, family, and neighbors who came and went throughout the evening. Groups of adults and teens sat outside the door, smoking and listening while trying to avoid the crowds and the incense-infused sweat of the tiled rooms where men and women tranced. People were excited, dressed up, and eager to come to a neighborhood *lila*, even if only to watch, listen, and catch up with the community.

At the same time, the music is diversifying. Musicians work to differentiate themselves in a way that is allegedly new to the contemporary context. Whereas events were rare, austere, and secretive in the past, they are now loud, public, celebratory, and not cheap. The vocation of being a gnawa musician is now an occupational opportunity as well. Just as Sean Bellaviti (2015) describes the stylistic innovations required by professional musicians in Panama, gnawa performers balance novelty and adherence to genre expectations as they compete for ritual work. The music's popular success and attention in major festivals influence audience demands on musicians within ceremonies. While there is a cyclic relationship between what happens in intimate rituals and on public stages, the dualistic performances of heritage maintenance and innovative fusion that are so present within festivals reflect anxieties that do not always match those of local performers. On one hand, idealistic preservationism serves two goals: it simultaneously works to counter a lost performance practice while didactically moralizing on what is correct. The musicians work "toward broader recognition while fighting against being treated as 'ghostly fetishes of culture loss' [Ivy 1995, 10–11], hovering between the center and the margins" (Sharp 2014, xvii).

Down the metaphorical street, gnawa performers work with jazz artists, other Moroccan groups, rockers, or whomever else may participate to navigate their music into a global circulation of world music, into a media industry that plays by a different set of rules and derives value through sales, markets, and advertising instead of healing, piety, and reverence. Deborah Kapchan writes, referencing Barbara Kirschenblatt-Gimblett (1998), that "constructing the imminence of the death of tradition is thus necessary to the project of heritage" (2014, 181). The construction of this imminence plays out in a variety of ways, however. What is dying? What is disappearing? For many, the answer is reverence. To discern where that reverence is (or is not) being directed, I turn to questions of the ritual's contentious place in Islam's diverse practice within Morocco.

There are many literal and figurative stages across Morocco for the contestation of gnawa heritage. These dot the country's vast network of festivals and *muwasim* (s. *mussem*, pilgrimage). Hicham Aidi notes the abundance of these events, most of which benefit from state patronage if not organization. He writes that the government began organizing Sufi and Berber events about two decades ago to promote economic growth through tourism, display a "self-image" of diversity, and "activate various genres of Sufi music and Berber culture against the growing Islamist movement and the increased influence of Saudi Salafism and Iranian Shiism" (2014, 152; see also Kapchan 2008).[3] In short, he writes, "the sounds of fusion, it is hoped, will drown out the purist call of Salafism." Now, he estimates, seventy of these annual events operate as modernized pilgrimages. In my work, I have seen local and national government forces tame major and minor pilgrimage events, especially when representing them on camera for news agencies. Within a small town inundated by impoverished and middle-class adepts of local religious brotherhoods, corporatized boards of organizers gather to enjoy the music and "heritage" of traditions while presenting, even selectively curating, legendary histories for distribution across the country. There exists in Morocco a "gold rush" as representatives of various religious organizations navigate the opportunities presented by state sponsorship and media circulation. My research led me to *hamadsha*, *'issawa*, and *malhun* artists currently engaged in such projects, but all of them are floundering to keep up with the dramatic pathway to success carved out by a handful of gnawa musicians.

Where historical pilgrimage destinations are growing in importance as sites of this negotiation, the major cultural tourism festivals of the previous fifteen to twenty years sit at its center. The two most prominent, the Fez Festival of World Sacred Music and the Gnawa and World Music Festival in Essaouira, in all of their previous incarnations, have been the focus of a great deal of scholarly attention, and with good reason. They identify two dramatically different approaches to national messaging, marketing, and collaboration that appear to share many large-scale goals. Both also bear out concepts of hybridity within public culture that move beyond the reification of a simple "new national solidarity." Instead of catering to a "salvaged past," they open opportunities for national priorities and efforts that run counter to the organizers' goals within the same cultural performances (Guss 2000, 4). This discursive polyphony within festivals produces new relationships and meanings such that national, communal, and other identities themselves are "continually being reconfigured" (11–12; also see Schauert 2015). Further, it is not simply the performers or organizers who contribute to these negotiations; rather, it is audience members who, through tactics native to the very same neoliberal order that instigates the state's interest in such festivals, rise as authorities of the self and therefore contribute to the whole. They attend or skip events, cheer and complain, are engaged or bored. The participatory nature of performance becomes especially significant when representatives of communities like the gnawa take the stage, presenting themselves, their music, and perhaps a rendering of ritual, history, and identity.

Yet, as Deborah Kapchan writes regarding the Fez Festival of World Sacred Music, internationally focused festivals that are marketed as sacred create something distinctly different from pilgrimages. They incite a "public sentiment through the reappropriation and fetishization of the category of 'the sacred,' creating in the process a new form of pilgrimage in sacred tourism and a new kind of liturgy in world sacred music" (2008, 467). Again, it is within the experience of the audience and the perception of a shared intersubjectivity, here instigated by the promise of a universalizing ritual, that authenticity gains meaning. In Fez, the festival's purpose and structure facilitate this understanding and, in doing so, creates a sense of sacred purity, albeit one that exists tangentially to or even outside of local Islamic (and especially conservative) definitions of institutionalized religiosity. The strategic high stakes of this privately run (yet state-funded) festival activity are compounded because of the dual aims of national and international consumption. Furthermore, many concerts at the Festival of World Sacred Music require expensive tickets, effectively making it an event that targets higher-class Moroccans and tourists who may share an ideological interest in celebrating these elements of global cosmopolitanism.[4]

This "festive sacred" bleeds into Essaouira's major event, as well. Even though the city's Gnawa and World Music Festival targets different audiences—it largely comprises free events and draws a number of Moroccan, mostly male, youth— it remains of interest for both international and domestic listeners, increasing the touristic circulation of people, music, and ideologies. The relationship with sacred music in this event has historically focused on gnawa activities, highlighting ritual activity in some way or another. At the macro level, the event often opens with a procession through Essaouira's main central avenue, just as an evening ceremony would begin outside of the home. In recent iterations, organizers expanded the number and types of venues to accommodate ritual performances that sit, somewhat uncomfortably, between demonstrations and legitimate ceremonies. Timothy Fuson relates an experience from one of the first attempts at a festival ritual performance in 1999 when guards unfamiliar with the trance attempted to restrain members of the audience who rose to move forward and participate as they would in a ceremony (2009, 62). In my experiences, these two-to three-hour mini-rituals featured a small segment of the repertoire with paying tourists sitting on cushions throughout the room. Present Moroccans and some visitors usually stood along the sides or in the back dancing, often with those who were unaware of the expectations of gnawa trance watching and following the actions of community members, perhaps trancing, perhaps demonstrating, either way, enjoying themselves.

On the larger stages in main squares and on beaches across the small city, famous gnawa m'allemin perform segments of the repertoire while featuring their acrobatic ensemble members either by themselves or in collaboration with visiting international jazz, rock, blues, and sub-Saharan African artists. While some of these collective fusions come across as more interesting than others—I remember a fantastic performance with Wayne Shorter's ensemble particularly well—they address many identical concerns as those of the Fez Festival. A local understanding of the sacred becomes something universal through the shared experience of a musical performance. That this featured tradition is itself demonstrative of Moroccan ethnic and religious diversity only legitimizes the universality as it reaches—following the slave trade itself—across oceans to sound and somehow feel familiar to listeners from far and wide. Here the purity of tradition from each performer is operationalized alongside ideals of fusion and international collaboration.

With this staging comes innovations within performance practice. Maisie Sum (2011) describes the limitations on ritual repertoire as it appears in festival settings just as Schaefer (2009, 226) shares his experience with members of Dar Gnawa, a troupe based in Tangier and led by M'allem 'Abdulla al-Gourd, where performing in the event compares to undertaking a pilgrimage. Schaefer's analysis of the ensemble's engagement with this neo-mussem invokes issues of nostalgia: following Abrahams (1982, 171), festival activities become an attempt to recapture loss. Similarly, these fusion stages present openings for new Moroccan identities, what Aidi calls the "gnawittude" of contemporary gnawa reggae bands and their fans (2014, 142). Dreadlocks and the music of Bob Marley ("le Top Gnawi") are common sights and sounds accompanying the festival each year. With these "neo-gnawis" come novel orientations toward nationalist, corporate, and religious manifestations of heritage: new music circulates new youth (mostly male) identities.

The success of these two festivals shows a facility in navigating a wide range of priorities, especially given the instrumentality of the events themselves at the hands of performers, organizers, and audiences who use them to disseminate diverse understandings of heritage and identity. The stage's contemporary popularity was "unthinkable before the 1990's" (Fuson 2009, 62). Yet, even within a nostalgic love of the festival, there is a sense of loss at its hands. The primacy of music minimizes the extraordinary roles that women play within ritual (Kapchan 2014, 9). Sacred festivals are influencing ritual practices at older holy sites and blurring the relationship between domestic cultural tourism and religious pilgrimage. Despite the apparent democratic nature of these public performances, institutionalized structures continue to primarily support those in power. Finally, the growing audience's demands influence ritual practice outside of these staged settings, bringing unwelcome change to the ceremonies of established and conservative performers who disavow the quickening pace of adaptation since the Essaouira festival began in 1998.

The narratives of authenticity that bear fruit for festival audiences are not necessarily identical to those of ritual elders and their clients. To the contrary, as authenticity requires verification, the diversity of "authenticities" expands to fill the range of potential performers, listeners, and other authorities. Different groups portraying a variety of understandings of gnawa heritage, identity, and authenticity struggle to illuminate the veracity of their own directives (Guss 2000, 14). By situating the negotiation of authentic experience between the performer and listener, each has his or her own opportunity to claim and bestow verification whether in a festival or a neighborhood ritual. This is important because as Kapchan's "festive sacred" foregrounds an individual yet intersubjective authentic sonic experience, the arguments about gnawa identity take shape around larger questions of communal history and future. More so, changes to performance practice that result from the influence of festival stages leave many in the gnawa community nostalgic for the previous generation's aesthetic and ideological tastes and for the values of a very different gnawa heritage.

The Contentious Novelty of Spectacle

M'allem 'Abd al-Latif sits with me in his small home in Marrakech. The thin door opens from the busy street into a steep stairwell, which winds up to a tiny room. There is a refrigerator halfway up the next stairway, blankets on the floor, and a television high up on a dresser. A stereo with a pile of CDs and cassettes sits on the opposite side of the room, playing old gnawa recordings (quite loudly). 'Abd al-Latif is a m'allem of an older generation who wears his disdain for many other gnawa performers on his sleeve. He answers questions in paragraphs, winding in unexpected directions as he talks, yet weaving back to the same topics after each question. There is a dramatic passion in his stories. He is one of the old masters that claims to have taught many of the most prominent m'allemin throughout Morocco. Yet his concern, his vehement and recurring diatribe, is that they move on too quickly and neglect the years of work that used to be a requirement. Instead, he says, they learn a few songs with the intention of moving to Casablanca as quickly as possible. Casablanca, the home of Morocco's recording industry, represents an opportunity in the eyes of many aspiring musicians. It is a place where one goes in order to record, to achieve success in the music industry. They chase fame, money, women, drugs, and the other expected trappings of music stardom. To others, Casablanca is a place where the art of the gnawa reverts to commercial popular music, falling into a two dimensional representation that only allows for the gnawa to be something bought and sold, a marketable commodity. The criticism from ʿAbd al-Latif, shared by many other gnawa, centers on the commercial nature of younger musicians' career aspirations. When young gnawa musicians attempt to learn for the sake of going to Casablanca, they make changes, slight adjustments, which make their music more widely accessible or interesting.

The change, according to ʿAbd al-Latif and Mulay al-Tahir (introduced in chapter 3), came when certain mʿallemin attempted to monetize their knowledge and abilities, making what was once an occasional ceremony for the dispersion of blessing (*baraka*) and prayerful enchantment into an occupation. It is likely that there was a moment when there was a shift in how the lila worked: instead of attending one ceremony each year, every adept had to host an annual event in order to receive the baraka of their possessing saint. What caused this change remains unclear, but it, along with a moment in which these helpful saints became possessing spirits, led to a series of adjustments that, as they gathered momentum, made the business of being a gnawa mʿallem into a potentially lucrative career.

As the number of lila ceremonies increased, culminating with the contemporary musical climate in which a mʿallem may be able to work four or five evenings each week, competing mʿallemin began to fight for clients. Continuing with the narratives from Mulay al-Tahir and ʿAbd al-Latif, to do so, they added "magic" to their ceremonial performances for spectacle and marketing reasons. This, they say, is the point at which outrageous acts of possession entered into the event. In order to prove their adeptness and power over the spirits and the spirit world, mʿallemin would act out extravagantly performed trances. Suddenly, drari were cutting their arms with large knives (*jinwi*) while possessed by Sidi Mimun; they were drinking boiling water straight from the kettle or pouring hot wax from bundles of lit candles onto their naked backs. Furthermore, they did so as self-identified Africans, claiming an exotic power and control over these mysterious and magical spirits from their ancient homeland, sub-Saharan Africa.

While I struggled to get a complete account of the history of change from these older men (something that indeed warrants further research), Mulay al-Tahir in particular emphasized how certain spirits were individuals: they were living, breathing men and women from Morocco who lived holy lives and, especially in death, gained an inordinate amount of baraka. Known for their generosity and altruism, they heard the prayers of the gnawa adepts who gathered at annual ceremonies and prayed to Allah on their behalf. In this sense, they epitomize the idea of the local saint described in the now classic anthropological accounts of Moroccan Islam such as those by Eickelman (1976) and Geertz (1971) and in more recent scholarship such as Vincent Cornell's *Realm of the Saint* (1998). Small shrines to men of this stature dot the countryside. The two that Mulay al-Tahir emphasized during our conversation were Sidi Mimun and Sidi Hamu. These two are seen as two of the most "African" and violent spirits within the gnawa pantheon. Mimun, according to al-Tahir, was a generous physician who wandered the countryside administering remedies to the ill. Hamu, a butcher, was a similarly magnanimous member of the community, helping to feed the poor. Now, however, most consider both to be spirits hungering for sacrificial acts, demanding actual animal sacrifices from their adepts and causing them to, when in trance, fiercely self-mutilate. Sidi Hamu, due to his history as a butcher, is now accompanied in the ritual by the color red and occasionally by large amounts of blood (to the point where some drink the sacrificial blood during the possession, though a red juice-based beverage was used in each of the more than twenty ceremonies I attended between 2007 and 2013). The outpouring of kindness that, according to al-Tahir, defined the lives of these individuals has shifted drastically as they became savage spirits from exotic "Africa."

This emphasis on self-induced "otherness" moves the gnawa explicitly away from Sufism, and the parallel shift of ontology in the *mluk* gives the gnawa, highlighted as descendants of African slaves, a specific power over those African spirits. "Gatekeepers of a counter world," the gnawa move in the night and on the limits of the licit. Marked by a fundamental ambiguity, they are believed to be transgressors who can handle blood with impunity and can control the most dangerous of forces. Embodying a "troubling strangeness," these descendants of black slaves see themselves as invested with the most powerful supernatural abilities (Hell 1999, 160).

These types of statements, that they are "gatekeepers of a counter world" moving "on the limits of the licit" appear throughout journalism about the gnawa, and they also pepper the discourses from those who are outside the tradition. Someone with a condition that requires assistance from the spirit world knows that they now go to the gnawa, masters of that realm. They carry an authority that can be explicitly different than that of the Sufis, as they have the option, provided by the African potentialities of tgnawit, to operate outside of the standards of Islamic spirituality. While other Muslim groups avoid the jnun at all costs, the gnawa see some of these spirits as mluk or saints and encounter them on their own terms, as Africans and in the night. They enter into the depths of the spiritual world and come out victorious, successfully negotiating the darkest of the unseen alongside (and on behalf of) their clients.

El Hamel, in his historical study of slavery in Morocco, concludes that the gnawa are "not a mystical order per se since they do not seek the connection with the divine." Instead, he writes, songs "contain issues of displacement, dispossession, depravation, misery, nostalgia for a land and a former life" (2008, 255). The overpowering Africanist history of the gnawa places them outside of Sufism, which aims for *al-hal*, this condition of divine connection. Such representations take this narrative at its word and rarely describe the gnawa as members of the Islamic community.[5] In doing so, they neglect the strategies that performers use to orient their own identities while pushing the lived experiences of many gnawa practitioners, clients, and lovers (*muhibbin*) into the background. Elders like Mulay Tahir of Tamesluht, Aziz wuld Ba Blan of Fez, and 'Abd al-Latif Makhzumi of Marrakech reify older styles despite dwindling interest from audiences. Each engages the heritage industry differently. Their questioning of the "spectacle" of contemporary gnawa performances—in ritual and on stage—gives voice to an alternative, more local, version.

Negotiated Nostalgia

Gnawa performances across the country's festival stages and media circuits demonstrate innovative approaches to the ritual sound. Audio technology and collaborations tweak the content and its presentation. Nylon strings ring longer and more brightly than the twisted intestine ones that m'allemin dry out after a ritual sacrifice. Microphones help the hajhuj sound soar over the clangs of *qaraqib* and the shouting of milling audiences. Satellite television sends the sound of a Casablanca-based star into the homes of families across the country. YouTube and Facebook do the same for listeners in New York, Paris, and around the world. These forms of mass media are the realm of the proverbial "one percent": a small handful of stars exist as national and global tastemakers. Their adaptations quickly become the canon among listeners who love them or know little else. This is not necessarily an economic one percent, as fortune does not rise to match fame, but the prominence that comes from connections to state and commercial media interests prove influential.

The local gnawa practices of the nostalgic past, however, present an oppositional force. The debates surrounding heritage, aesthetics, identity, piety, and performance practice percolate through neighborhoods across Morocco. Aziz wuld Ba Blan of Fez or 'Abd al-Latif in Marrakech approach their style of playing in different ways. Yet they are joined by younger members of their groups who value their unique styles. They also earn the respect of younger m'allemin who see a value in maintaining local identity, even if they themselves do not find the time or the market for performing local ritual styles. Aziz's outspoken activism takes a simple approach. He plays for those who want an older style of ritual. This market is shrinking quickly, but he provides for himself through a day job. This also allows him to train younger drari, building a love of the musical style that his grandfather brought to Fez. 'Abd al-Latif, on the other hand, claims to have ceased playing rituals. Though he does still occasionally perform in ceremonial contexts despite his criticisms of the contemporary community, he is extraordinarily selective about which *muqaddimat* he allows to run his events. His respect is hard earned.

In their own ways, Aziz and ʿAbd al-Latif reject spectacle in ritual. Like Mulay al-Tahir, they strive for a specific type of reverence in ceremony. Contemporary reality, however, maintains its influence on these two musicians. When I enlisted Aziz to play a lila ceremony for me to record and analyze, he included many of the dance-influenced pieces from the segment devoted to female spirits (see chap. 7). This got people up and moving around. Later, he informed me that he includes these songs because even those who want the older style of ceremony still wait in anticipation for the ritual's conclusion of pop-influenced high-energy music. He refused to include the popular "Aisha Hamdushiyya," however. This borrowed spirit from Morocco's hamadsha brotherhood simply has no place in his ritual. When Rashida, a native of Fez and a close family friend who attended a recording session/concert that I had organized, requested this song, she was sharply refused and mildly scolded by the performers. This popular piece of music did not fit within Aziz's model of the lila ceremony. Not only was it newer than the ceremony that he held as central to the tradition, but its popularity served as a marker for adaptation, even bastardization. Aziz regularly performed for knowledgeable clients who hired him specifically for his older style of performance. Because of his uncompromising focus on the sacredness of his musical practice, and his attendant piety (he had just returned from the *hajj*, the pilgrimage to Mecca, when I spoke with him in 2014), he had a certain amount of disdain for gnawa fans and ritual participants who loved these newly added songs and spirits.

ʿAbd al-Latif, despite his semi-moratorium on ritual performances and frustrations with those who pursue fame, performs regularly at the Essaouira festival, most recently in 2013 and 2015. His performances are typically in the close quarters of an "intimate" concert. These take place in the Zawiya Sidna Bilal or a similarly small venue where audiences sit on the floor and enjoy a shortened version of the ritual over roughly two hours. Some Moroccans fall into trance, and a small number of foreign listeners often stand or move as the music, pregnant with the "festival sacred," as described earlier. ʿAbd al-Latif, by stepping into the festival circuits that he distrusts, finds an avenue for the presentation of his performative values.

In their own ways, these two performers discipline the sound of their ritual performance. They reclaim the music and context, even in situations far removed from a traditional ritual. Aziz's staunch refusal to perform "Aisha Hamdushiyya" in a concert setting and ʿAbd al-Latif's exception to his moratorium on events that did not meet his high standards transform these two performance contexts in the name of didactic presentation. Both artists bring their traditionalist and preservationist tendencies into contemporary contexts that appear, at first glance, to be problematic. They are not antimodernist, however. In working with researchers like myself and audiences made up of both Moroccans and foreigners, these two successfully represent a perspective in the debate about ritual authenticity, identity, and heritage. This perspective lives through their performative decisions. These choices, in turn, exist as part of a distinctly modern recognition of the importance of media and circulation. The tools provide opportunities to enter into the discussion, to push back against what they see as inappropriate innovations in instrument construction, performance practice, and "spectacle" that degrade gnawa practice. They also give Aziz, 'Abd al-Latif, and others who share their views direct access to listeners nationally, building a community of similarly minded gnawa participants.

As older styles of gnawa performance lose popularity in neighborhoods across the country, artists like Aziz and 'Abd al-Latif find larger national audiences with varying success. When 'Abd al-Latif makes this trek from Marrakech to nearby Essaouira, he enjoys his time with influential gnawa leaders, many of whom are old friends, as well as international musicians and travelers. His is a style that these tastemakers hold up as authentic and authoritative. Aziz, on the other hand, stays mostly within his neighborhood of Fez. He will leave the Mulay 'Abd Allah quarter to perform in nearby homes, but he does not appear on the national radar in quite the same way. Throughout the city, m'allemin reference him with respect as a source of ritual knowledge and authentic performance practice. His grandfather is said to have brought the gnawa ritual to Fez generations ago, after all. He works at the royal palace, situated between his neighborhood and nearby Fez Jdid, just outside of the old *medina*, where he is a driver and carries out odd jobs. Yet Aziz's post remains a day job, and when a recent major compilation of gnawa styles from across the country was recorded, the Yerma Gnaoua association who planned it chose M'allem Hamid from Fez Jdid to represent the local sound instead of Aziz, even though Hamid himself described Aziz to me as his teacher and superior on the older style of performance. Aziz's influence is radiating outward from his neighborhood, however. Despite the decreasing frequency, he continues to perform for select clients and when he does so, he brings a trusted crew of drari, some young and some older. The younger ensemble members, in their twenties and thirties, love and respect the fading practice and hope to continue it, even as they simultaneously take gigs with other ensembles. The voices arguing for local styles, local identities, and local values in gnawa ritual practice are not exclusively those of the elders. As such, Aziz, 'Abd al-Latif, and their peers use performance opportunities to build communities of focused listeners while training young performers in what they value and remember as gnawa heritage. Their navigation of contemporary festival markets and media opportunities helps them to perform and share their nostalgia, both as persevering preservationists and didactic revisionists.

Notes

1. See Oliver O'Connell, "The Real-Life 'Up' House Finally Faces Wrecking Ball as Developers Demolish Home of Senior Who Turned Down $1m to Move Out," Daily Mail, March 11, 2015, http://www.dailymail.co.uk/news/article-2990676/Elderly-woman-s-style-house -symbol-corporate-buyout-defiance-reluctant-folk-hero-finally-face-wrecking-ball.html.

2. See Festival D'Essaouira Gnaoua Musiques du Monde, http://festival-gnaoua.net/fr /association.

3. Aidi references two movements—Salafism and Shiism—that highlight different types of global Islamic conservatism. These are wrapped in specific national contexts but are being exported internationally through monetary investment and other forms of state support. Salafi movements are generally composed of conservative Sunni Muslims and are often seen as fundamentalist within the context of international discourse and news. They often contest Iranian Shiism politically, militarily, and religiously, especially in heterogeneous national contexts like in Iraq. While a few individuals and communities fit this mold, the negative and highly charged connotations that accompany this term are far from accurate or fair for most.

4. Previous chapters discuss the events at the Festival of World Sacred Music's Boujloud stage, which feature free concerts and target local audiences.

5. See Bertrand Hell's *Le Tourbillon Des Génies* (2002) for an example of a treatment that places the gnawa within the Islamic tradition.

9 New Authorities and Authenticities

A FEW WEEKS AGO, the spring weather was arriving. I was sitting at home, doing some work on my computer and watching my sad dog, a large black lab, who was perched on top of our couch, staring longingly out the window. Needing a break anyhow, I got up and starting getting things together to take her for a jog. I called up an album that I had saved on my phone a while back but had not yet listened to. By the time we turned the first corner, my mind was racing, imagining the fun that the producers of *Jah Gnawi* by a band called Gnawa Impulse[1] must have had in putting this recording together. Its songs stridently draw from reggae, EDM, funk, and rock. In "Marhaba," dance beats underscore a tune from the *gnawa* repertoire that I heard in virtually every event I saw while in Morocco over the past few years. This turned out to be perfect running music. When the track turned over to the next one, I actually laughed out loud from the unexpected juxtaposition of styles, prompting a confused glance from my (now very happily jogging) dog. "S'adi Bil Wali Jani" was one of my favorites from the songs that M'allem 'Abd al-Rzaq had taught me to play and sing. Something about this version, however, felt like a foggy reference from further back in my memory. The instrumental opening and timbre of the first vocal lines struck me, even shocked me, with their familiarity. After some hunting around, I can confidently say that my mind made a rough association to "Mmm Mmm Mmm Mmm," a 1993 hit from the Crash Test Dummies. I made my wife listen to it; she heard Third Eye Blind. Either way, the track pulled us both back to the 1990s.

In this book, I have not dealt much with ritual experience, nor have I addressed important issues of international collaborations. Much of the previous gnawa scholarship cited here focuses on these very concerns. It questions personal experience within trances and musical changes that take hold as the gnawa adapt for foreign stages and audiences. Instead, I wanted to look at aesthetic tastes, especially domestic ones that are informed by other sounds across Morocco. Those sounds invariably include foreign influence, but they also maintain some level of familiarity with the music of other local groups. This is even the case if a listener has only heard 'issawa music during news broadcasts or hamadsha sounds during Ramadan television specials.

Most clients of the gnawa, those who search out and hire musicians to host a healing ceremony, have some semblance of familiarity with the music, though it may also only come through exposure to domestic festival stages and more of those TV specials. The economic power of the clients' tastes makes me wonder if it is not so much that recent trends are changing the music of the ritual, but that the ceremony itself is coming to serve a new purpose, as evidenced in part by the Gnawa Impulse album that I was running to. It is hardly a far cry to claim that EDM-based clubs can provide a ritual experience (St. John 2015) or that listening deeply can manifest differently depending on personal background and expectations (Becker 2004). Disparagement within the gnawa community toward newer musical styles, commercial approaches, and educational pathways often focus on musical change or the experience of the performer. But an underlying concern persists: the ritual itself is eliding into something different. What used to count as sacred does not always count anymore and the old power structures of community elders who bestowed *tgnawit* has lost their exclusivity of control. Clients go rogue, selecting ritual leaders who lack what were once basic qualifications, and because these clients and performers can negotiate their own expectations for what the event should look and sound like, it works. The spirits come and heal. In one view, this could throw the entire system into a crisis of authenticity and authority. In another, however, this shows that the community has already made it through such a crisis and found a wealth of approaches that thrive within the contemporary world.

I have argued here that the aesthetic sensibilities of popular music are increasingly influential within gnawa ritual. Ideas about the sacred nature of the ritual are inextricably linked to the sounds that animate it. Those sounds, in turn, display the variety of economic and social pressures that orient the professional *m'allem*'s career. Because of a shifting relationship between audiences and musicians, a result of the increased professionalization of gnawa musicianship, audience requests and demands are triggering new trends in performance practice. People want to hear music that they find entertaining, and it follows that music that engages them is more likely to incite the desired results. It is more convincing. Musicians that can best involve their audiences are often very adept at bringing about trances in their clients. It is unlikely that this symbiosis is particularly new, but influences are quickly changing thanks to vast developments in the music industry and its modes of distribution.

As these changes codify through the omnipresence of *marsawiyya* performance practice, they influence how clients and listeners understand the ceremony. It becomes less an austere praise of local Muslim saints than a show of supernatural power through spectacle. The debates surrounding this slippage— and especially the backlash epitomized by the perspectives of Mulay al-Tahir, M'allem 'Abd al-Latif Makhzumi, and M'allem Aziz wuld Ba Blan—play a central role in legitimizing and delegitimizing contemporary performance practice styles. This a case where language about music (Feld and Fox 1994) sits alongside the performances themselves as demonstrations of authority, authenticity, and, more broadly, tgnawit.

This process arises through the fractures brought about by new modes of distribution. When the contexts of musical practice wear away, musicians and audiences gain the flexibility to reorient their production and consumption in novel ways. When Steven Feld discusses the concept of schizophonia, he describes the removal of context and the creation of new sounds within the internationally distributed global popular music market. What I discuss in the preceding pages works differently, however. Context is never removed entirely because these markets are local, domestic. The audiences know where the popular music influences are coming from. They often know that marsawiyya is created from the diverse forms of popular music that they hear when they attend weddings or that Lalla Aisha's content comes from the hamadsha history. This information is embedded into the names; the title "Aisha Hamdushiyya" makes the relationship explicit. Yet the increased flexibility is powerful, as music, through changing musical tastes, transcends the boundaries among Sufi brotherhoods, cosmologies, and healing practices as well as those that differentiate between the celebratory dance music of the wedding or night club and the ritual. Meaning does not disappear; it stratifies. Just as the self-imposed identity of a gnawa mʻallem is a layered set that includes African heritage, Muslim piety, and commercial viability, the identity of this music gains depth as it incorporates ideas and ideals from outside sources. It is ritual *and* entertainment, gnawa *and* hamadsha, mainstream *and* periphery. The shifts and simplifications bring the music to new audiences, out of the marginal and into the popular.

Chapter 8 opened with a walk as I saw the small shrine for Sidi Mimun tucked between new buildings in Fez. Mulay al-Tahir had described the saint as a pharmacist from the south who wandered the country and administered to the poor. Similar small burial sites throughout the country are a testament to his saintly stature, even as the fear that he and the other spirits clothed in black elicit within the gnawa ritual evoke the respect that many have for his power. The connection between the spiritual figure in ritual and the saint who wandered the country is all but absent in conversations about the ontology of the gnawa spirits. Scholars like Deborah Kapchan, who describes her own personal encounter with Sidi Mimun (2007, 109–10), contribute to this understanding of Sidi Mimun's identity without engaging with any history of his saintly activities. When I spoke with mʻallemin and asked about spirits like this one, I found a similar absence of any reference to their living histories; they were spirits from Africa, not holy men from Morocco. Tension between contemporary marsawiyya performance and a novel understanding of the coinciding ritual is threaded through the events that I have recounted. The interactions between music and spirit provide a spectacle—the use of candles and knives to perform self-mutilation acts are just one example—that was allegedly absent in *fassiyya* or other older performance practices. This change from saint veneration to "spectacle" is the primary route by which older practitioners criticize younger mʻallemin and their performances.

This spiritual heaviness has a musical counterpart. The patterns that accentuate a slow beat for Ghumami (a figure associated with Sidi Mimun whose music immediately follows), for example, sounds intimidating and overpowering. Whereas the march rhythms of slower portions of Sidi Musa's music feel agile by comparison, these rhythms sit oppressively over the room, mixing with the black incense and the anticipation of the audience, waiting for the knives to be blessed by the spirits, to see what the possessed body will do with them. As the rhythm accelerates toward a climax, spectators wonder if the knives will draw blood, gawking when the *maskun* circles the room showing off his or her new wounds.

These types of relationships between musical and ritual aesthetics continue throughout the ceremony. It is worth noting that this particular set, "Sidi Mimun Ghumami" to "Marhaba" to "Marhaba Sidi Mimun," contains three of the more well-known songs in the repertoire. That these three songs, commonly extracted from the ritual for public performance or recording, have witnessed a wide circulation is also likely related to the change in conception of these spirits. The perceived weight of the songs' rhythms, alongside the allegedly novel spectacle of their ritual context, makes them very clear examples of mysterious power. The popularity of the songs outside of the ceremony affects the performance in the ritual: excited adepts engage more directly and energetically by clapping or singing along.

This interdependence of musical aesthetic and ritual understanding also, however, makes clear that the histories of saints from across the gnawa pantheon are discursively formed and understood. In my experience, few m'allemin have substantial historical knowledge of the ceremony and its spirits. Those who can articulate the past do not always agree on details. Simultaneously, marsawiyya is a flexible practice that allows spaces for the ritual leaders to make minor adjustments that align their tastes and practices with the events—sacred or otherwise—as they see fit. The competitive sphere of commercial productivity—composed of stages, folkloric presentations, restaurants and hotels, and busking in the streets—leads to stylistic diversification. The performer/ritual leader accentuates his strengths. Some strong performers choose to highlight their knowledge of tradition through what they consider tasteful phrasing, an economy of playing that demonstrate their control of the voice and their instrument. Others foreground virtuosity. There are also, of course, weaker players who lack the knowledge or ability to compete. By charging less money for their services, they may continue to find work.

Performers participate in the circulation of popular forms by selling and sharing their own recordings. They also listen closely to those made available by other m'allemin, both local and national. Younger players are especially receptive to new ideas and trends. They scour YouTube, Facebook, and other social media sites for new material while making connections and cultivating friendships with other young performers across the country. Importantly, when they hear something that they like or that they feel the audience will like, regardless of its origin, they incorporate it into their own techniques. Such hybrid mixes of regional styles were not nearly as feasible before the advent of mass multimedia broadcasting. Now, however, with marsawiyya as a nationally resonant style that has all but dispelled other variations, these connections transcend geographical distance thanks in part to the resulting aesthetic consistency. Practically, marsawiyya brings a new generation of technologically and commercially savvy gnawa musicians into cohesive social and professional networks of their own.

Older generations, however, pride themselves on their own consistencies. M'allem 'Abd al-Rzaq is a strong player with technical virtuosity and a deft control over the musical dynamics of his rituals. In my work with the many m'allemin of Fez, he stood out as the strongest musician,[2] a quality that is related to, but not directly representative of, his ritual leadership. Because of his ability to play complex accompaniment patterns in all contexts and volumes, rituals led by him contain dynamic variety and nuance that I rarely witnessed among other leaders. His style is very much his own. He fills empty spaces with a constant sixteenth-note drone either above or below the melody, and his ability to continue his complex patterns at high speeds helps him to effectively engage both listeners and spirits. His playing creates an energy that animates the ritual space. His style has not changed over the five years that I have known him and while this may be a small sample of his life's career, he claims that his style is concrete and consistent. Going a step further, he asserts his consistency to the fact that he never practices. He once asked me, "Have you ever seen me playing when you entered here?" He learned to play well, he practiced hard as one of Bujma's *drari*, and now his style is his own. Practice and rehearsal as ways to improve his technique or to learn new ones, he claims, are therefore useless to him. Constant gigs keep him in shape.

Change, therefore, comes through the younger performers who are still learning. Marsawiyya took hold while members of 'Abd al-Rzaq's generation were still practicing, traveling the country, building friendships, and creating professional networks. When Rzaq attends pilgrimages in Sidi Ali or music festivals such as the one in Essaouira, he is sure to visit with old colleagues from Tangier and farther off cities. When current forty- to fifty-year-old m'allemin were drari themselves, they traveled, working with the previous generation's most respected players. That these networks could lead to a consistency of performance practice is not surprising, and the parallel with contemporary youth is striking. If marsawiyya came to dominance in the 1970s and 1980s as I have been told, the then young performers attempting to begin a career would have been very much influenced by the new trends. Television, radio, cassette tape distribution, and other forms of mass media were beginning to circulate the music of that period's popular gnawa musicians, mirroring the use of internet and individual recording technologies available in cell phones for today's younger generation. Marsawiyya, therefore, can be situated firmly within a context of technological change.

Wider distribution and the resulting specter of commercial success entered into a feedback loop with ritual content. Saints' histories and realities circulated alongside the musical ideas that fed into contemporaneous understandings (even misunderstandings) of the gnawa ritual. What was once a closed activity operating at an extremely local level was becoming a national network punctuated by international journalistic and world music representations. Musical aesthetics were filtered through retellings of fuzzy stories about generalized spiritual figures. Men and women who lived and are buried in Moroccan soil are increasingly understood as spirits imported from sub-Saharan Africa. Many m'allemin, from those who enjoy commercial fame (like Marrakech's 'Abd al-Kabir Marshan) to those who operate primarily in local ritual (like Fez's 'Abd al-Rzaq), do not attempt to answer my questions about who these spirits were, if they lived, or what they did. Instead, their attention is focused on healing through musical means. They invoke and depend on the spirits to heal clients, but knowing more than the most basic histories is unnecessary.

Musical knowledge, therefore, overtakes religious knowledge. The gnawa m'allem has moved away from being someone who might understand and diagnose problems to become a hired practitioner of musical healing. At the same time, certain personal issues have become so consistently "treated" through gnawa ritual activity that there are few who attempt to disentangle the saintly personalities from the healing practice; as this musical event continues to effectively heal, its efficacy is reinforced. Conversely, those who know the history of the saints in Morocco rarely deal directly with gnawa traditions, practices that they see as watered down or, at worst, bastardized Islam. The historical knowledge has therefore separated from the ritual knowledge, and it follows that the understanding of the gnawa's use of saints and spirits gets simplified. This change in focus is an important factor in the rise of professional or commercial success as a marker of tgnawit.

Performers and ritual leaders like Yassine from chapter 4 represent a very new model for navigating a career in what 'Abd al-Rzaq once called "the gnawa sciences." They see the commercial and monetary successes of the most prominent gnawa artists, those whose photos adorn CD sellers' walls and whose visages often appear on national television. Deciding to follow what appears to be a well-worn path, they pick up the *hajhuj* and begin. They play for their friends and start aligning themselves with as many elder m'allemin that they can. Instead of working with different master musicians for years to build an understanding of the ritual's depth, they allegedly learn only the songs. I met a number of younger self-identified m'allemin like this from across the country. The man from Agadir introduced in chapter 6, Yassine's friend, traveled to Meknes (around five hundred miles) so he could rent a garage and sound equipment to perform semi-informally with his troupe during the Sidi Ali pilgrimage. He, like Yassine, was eager to take photos and videos for his Facebook and YouTube pages. The two of them, good friends, began to share stories about different m'allemin with whom they worked. Once he saw my portable audio recorder, however, he immediately began to negotiate with me about a price for it. It held potential for him as a way to expand his collection of recordings of himself and his portfolio. The recorder dominated the remainder of our conversation.

These younger artists use novel strategies to run their professional lives like the eager small businessmen that they are. They hire and fire members of their troupes, they advertise and communicate using social media just as any striving bandleader pores over Facebook, YouTube, or Soundcloud.[3] They engage in endless self-promotion for staged or ritual gigs. Recordings are rarely purchased and sold but are instead traded on cell phone memory cards. Troupes will crowd together during breaks in rituals in order to hear the latest find on the tinny speakers of a member's phone. These self-identified m'allemin step well outside of the traditional forms of learning. They skip most phases of the apprenticeship and instead sit with recordings. They do not wait for the blessing of the local community to call themselves m'allemin. While many have incredible respect for the power of the ritual and go to great lengths to learn everything that they can about it, their apparent disregard for traditional systems of learning generates an incredible amount of disrespect from some elders, though others simply see them as commercial performers and give little energy or thought to questioning their practices. Yet the younger artists continue to perform in rituals and on stages. They work rarely and for little money, but like most poor youth in Morocco, they live cheaply and shrewdly. Their novel approach serves them well. Yassine's long hair, glasses, and garish dress make him easily identifiable, recognizable. He took every opportunity to start a conversation with strangers about the gnawa. By the time I was leaving, his band that I had played with had started gigging more and more often. This, alongside his ritual performances and a small shop he had recently opened to sell instruments, clothes, and other ritual paraphernalia, covered most of his low cost of living.

Yassine and others oriented their stature based on the number and types of performances that they had done. They talked about their skill as instrumentalists and singers more than their piety or any connections with a sub-Saharan heritage. They also worked hard in ritual to entertain as well as to incite possession. By harnessing the spectacle through dance, dress, and virtuosic performance, they validated themselves to their audiences as if they had been on stage. The ritual audience usually responded in kind, applauding, singing along, and occasionally dancing. Humor entered ritual in ways that I had never seen. Yassine would change and add words to ritual songs. He could bring a room of women who had just been heavily in possession to incredible laughter by weaving jokes and funny voices into his texts. While ritual incense burned in front of him, he would jovially or sarcastically mock his audience or his own status as a poor, single man looking for love and money. Despite or, better put, because of these innovations, his rituals were successful enough to incite possession and cause healing. His few clients hired him over and over again.

This is a new type of authenticity in the gnawa community. Yassine does not claim tgnawit because he is pious, though he makes sure to be pious enough. He does not claim to be a dark-skinned descendant of a slave, but he quickly points out that he, like all Moroccans, is African. Early in his life, he explored many musical traditions in Fez, drawn to the different songs and sounds. While he decided to learn the music and ritual of the gnawa, he regularly folds 'issawa and hamadsha songs into his gnawa ritual, citing these as equally powerful forms of worship and, therefore, posits himself as a versatile and valuable ritual leader.

Early on, I conceived of tgnawit as consisting of two sources that an individual m'allem might draw from to assert his identity, authenticity, and authority: Muslim piety and African heritage. As I continued to return to Morocco, I became aware of novel forms of gnawa activity and a new mode of participating in the ritual music economy. As such, I see popular success as a major source of tgnawit. It is a fount that, while far from being universally accepted, is actively present. Even the most traditionally minded m'allemin are beginning to keep records of their staged performances, showing me portfolio binders full of newspaper clippings or VCDs of televised performances. This mode of authenticating (making authentic) one's own validity as a ritual and popular music performer is not isolated to the youth. It is a powerful tool, recognized by the entire community. Some try to ignore it, but they actively engage it by playing in marsawiyya style, centering their ritual on the newly developed cannon of "hits," and including spectacular demonstrations in possession and dance. They actively blend the experience of ritual with one of didactic entertainment in festival settings or sponsored performances. Or in recording studios while creating the music that ends up on Spotify, accompanying my run. An expanded listening audience implies an equally expansionist conception of ritual context. I can better focus during a run thanks to Gnawa Impulse or one of the many similar groups whose music ends up on my iPhone. Listeners continue to return to Essaouira for music festivals year after year to experience a specific type of ritual that happens when Wayne Shorter or Pat Metheny joins gnawa musicians on stage. Grandmothers across Morocco allegedly fall into trance within the comfort of their living rooms thanks to television news reports about those very concerts.

The musical changes to the ritual aim to engage these new audiences, listeners who grow up with popularized versions of Islamic music, who yearn for entertainment, who live in a modern economic climate that makes weeklong ritual activity nearly impossible. Each m'allem meets his audience on these terms, allowing for as much change as he deems acceptable. This negotiation with audiences is drastically changing the content and sound of gnawa healing. Boundaries are proven to be porous as musical ideas swing between the gnawa and popular culture or as consistent strains of melody intersect between the varieties of religious brotherhoods that animate the pious lives of Moroccan believers. The soundtrack that gives depth to life's experiences penetrates both the sacred and the secular. It provides one example of how these two terms are not distinct spheres of reality. They are, or at least can be, indistinguishable, overlapping, and ever shifting in their relationship to each other.

Notes

1. Sadly, I do not own a hard copy of this album to confirm details, and Spotify is notoriously unclear when it comes to international artists. Gnawa Impulse appears to be a collaboration between a band from Morocco called Gnawa Halwa and two producers in Germany named David Beck and Jan-Claudius Rase. See https://www.womex.com/virtual/cross _culture_music/gnawa_impulse. Jan Rase's SoundCloud page has more recordings from the group as well, at https://soundcloud.com/jan-rase. At the time of this writing, however, the record label's website appears to be down.

2. By this statement, I refer to his ability to perform with a lightness of touch and subtly of variation that I rarely saw in other m'allemin. He was not the strongest in terms of adapting to new situations; Yassine was able to do this with ease, partially because of his eagerness to participate in new contexts. While my judgment of his musicianship came from my experiences and listening skills as a musician, he was also widely respected by other m'allemin in town, lending credence to my decision to work closely with him.

3. When I first arrived in Morocco in 2008, I actually found myself revisiting and updating my MySpace account. Facebook was the new rage in the United States at this point, and the mass migration of users from MySpace had been in full force. But it had not yet caught on in Morocco. By the time I last left Morocco in 2013, not a single person I knew continued to use MySpace. They had all converted to Facebook, which they called, using the English word in the middle of Arabic conversation, "the Face." These artists are constantly on top of the newest technologies and are some of the most active users of social media that I know. Constant access to things like Facebook drove two musician friends of mine to purchase old computers for their homes, a major expense that they deemed professionally worthwhile.

Bibliography

Abrahams, Roger D. 1982. "The Language of Festivals: Celebrating the Economy." In *Celebration: Studies in Festivity and Ritual*, edited by Victor Turner, 161–77. Washington, DC: Smithsonian Insitution Press.

Agawu, Kofi. 2003. *Representing African Music: Postcolonial Notes, Queries, Positions*. New York: Routledge.

Aidi, Hicham D. 2014. *Rebel Music: Race, Empire, and the New Muslim Youth Culture*. New York: Pantheon Books.

Appadurai, Arjun. 1996. *Modernity at Large: Cultural Dimensions of Globalization*. Minneapolis: University of Minnesota Press.

Armbrust, Walter. 2000. "Anxieties of Scale." In *Mass Mediations: New Approaches to Popular Culture in the Middle East and Beyond*, edited by Walter Armbrust, 1–31. Berkeley: University of California Press.

Asad, Talal. 1996. "The Idea of an Anthropology of Islam." In *The Social Philosophy of Ernest Gellner*, edited by J. Hall and I. Jarvie, 381–406. Amsterdam: Editions Rodopi.

Baldassarre, Antonio. 2003. "Moroccan World Beat through the Media." In *Mediterranean Mosaic*, edited by Goffredo Plastino, 79–100. New York: Routledge.

Barth, Fredrik. 1970. *Ethnic Groups and Boundaries*. Oslo: Johanses & Nielsen Boktrykkeri.

Battaglia, Debbora. 1995. "On Practical Nostalgia: Self-Prospecting among Urban Trobrianders." In *Rhetorics of Self-Making*, edited by Debbora Battaglia, 77–96. Berkeley: University of California Press.

Bayat, Asef. 2007. "Islamism and the Politics of Fun." *Public Culture* 19 (3): 433–59.

Becker, Cynthia. 2014. "Patchwork, Dreadlocks, and Cowries: Trancing the Trans-Saharan Journey of Moroccan Culture." In *Saharan Crossroads: Exploring Historical, Cultural, and Artistic Linkages between North and West Africa*, edited by Tara F. Deubel, Scott M. Youngstedt, and Hélène Tissières, 105–40. Newcastle upon Tyne, UK: Cambridge Scholars Press.

Becker, Judith. 2004. *Deep Listeners: Music, Emotion, and Trancing*. Bloomington: Indiana University Press.

Bellaviti, Sean. 2015. "Standing Out While Fitting In: Genre, Style, and Critical Differentiation among Panamanian Conjunto Musicians." *Ethnomusicology* 59 (3): 450–74.

Berriane, Johara. 2015. "Pilgrimage, Spiritual Tourism and the Shaping of Transnational 'Imagined Communities': The Case of the Tidjani Ziyara to Fez." *International Journal of Religious Tourism and Pilgrimage* 3 (2): article 4.

Bigenho, Michelle. 2002. *Sounding Indigenous: Authenticity in Bolivian Music Performance*. New York: Palgrave Macmillan.

Boym, Svetlana. 2007. "Nostalgia and Its Discontents." *Hedgehog Review* 9 (2): 7–18.

Buchanan, Donna. 2006. *Performing Democracy*. Chicago: University of Chicago Press.

Callen, Jeffrey. 2006. "French Fries in the Tagine: Re-Imagining Moroccan Popular Music." PhD dissertation, University of California, Los Angeles.

Charry, Eric. 1996. "Plucked Lutes in West Africa: An Historical Overview." *The Galpin Society Journal* 49: 3–37.

Chlyeh, Abdelhafid. 1998. *Les Gnaoua du Maroc: Itinéraires, initiatiques, transe et possession.* Casablanca: La Pensée Sauvage.

———, ed. 1999. *L'univers des Gnaoua.* Casablanca: La Pensée Sauvage.

Ciucci, Alessandra. 2010. "De-Orientalizing the 'Aita and Re-Orienting the Shikhat." In *French Orientalism: Culture, Politics, and the Imagined Other,* edited by Desmond Hosford and Chong J. Wojtkowski, 71–96. Newcastle upon Tyne, UK: Cambridge Scholars Press.

Comaroff, John L, and Jean Comaroff. 2009. *Ethnicity, Inc.* Chicago: University of Chicago Press.

Corbin, Alain. 1998. *Village Bells: Sound and Meaning in the Nineteenth-Century French Countryside.* New York: Columbia University Press.

Cornell, Vincent J. 1998. *Realm of the Saint: Power and Authority in Moroccan Sufism.* Austin: University of Texas Press.

Crapanzano, Vincent. 1981. *The Ḥamadsha: A Study in Moroccan Ethnopsychiatry.* Berkeley: University of California Press.

Crawford, David, and Rachel Newcomb, eds. 2013. *Encountering Morocco: Fieldwork and Cultural Understanding.* Bloomington: Indiana University Press.

Danielson, Virginia. 1987. "The 'Qur'an' and the 'Qasidah': Aspects of the Popularity of the Repertory Sung by Umm Kulthūm." *Asian Music* 19 (1): 26–45.

Dernouny, Mohamed, and Boujemâa Zoulef. 1980. "Naissance d'un chant prostestataire: Le groupe marocaine nass El Ghiwane." *Peuples méditerranéens* 12 (July–September): 3–31.

Ebron, Paulla A. 2002. *Performing Africa.* Princeton, NJ: Princeton University Press.

Eickelman, Dale F. 1976. *Moroccan Islam: Tradition and Society in a Pilgrimage Center.* Austin: University of Texas Press.

———. 1995. "The Art of Memory: Islamic Education and Its Social Reproduction." In *Comparing Muslim Societies: Knowledge and the State in a World Civilization,* edited by Juan R. I. Cole, 97–132. Ann Arbor: University of Michigan Press.

El Hamel, Chouki. 2008. "Constructing a Diasporic Identity: Tracing the Origins of the Gnawa Spiritual Group in Morocco." *Journal of African History* 49: 241–60.

———. 2013. *Black Morocco: A History of Slavery, Race, and Islam.* New York: Cambridge University Press.

el-Zein, Abdul Hamid. 1977. "Beyond Ideology and Theology: The Search for the Anthropology of Islam." *Annual Review of Anthropology* 6: 227–54.

Ennaji, M. 1999. *Serving the Master: Slavery and Society in Nineteenth-Century Morocco.* Translated by S. Graebner. New York: St. Martin's.

Erlmann, Veit. 1996. "The Aesthetics of the Global Imagination: Reflections on World Music in the 1990s." *Public Culture* 8 (3): 467–87.

———. 2004. "Resisting Sameness: À Propos Kofi Agawu's Representing African Music." *The Journal for the Society for Music Theory* 26 (2): 291–304.

Feld, Steven. 1994. "From Schizophonia to Schismogenesis: On the Discourses and Commodification Practices of 'World Music' and 'World Beat.'" In *Music Grooves,* edited by Steven Feld and Charles Keil, 257–89. Chicago: University of Chicago Press.

———. 1996. "Pygmy POP: A Genealogy of Schizophonic Mimesis." *Yearbook for Traditional Music* 28: 1–35.

Feld, Steven, and Aaron A. Fox. 1994. "Music and Language." *Annual Review of Anthropology* 23: 25–53.

Feriali, Kamal. 2009. "Music-Induced Spirit Possession Trance in Morocco: Implications for Anthropology and Allied Disciplines." PhD dissertation, University of Florida, Gainesville.

Fuson, Timothy Dale. 2009. "Musicking Moves and Ritual Grooves across the Moroccan *Gnawa* Night." PhD dissertation, University of California, Berkeley.

Gaffney, Patrick D. 1994. *The Prophet's Pulpit: Islamic Preaching in Contemporary Egypt.* Berkeley: University of California Press.

Garofalo, Reebee. 1987. "How Autonomous Is Relative: Popular Music, the Social Formation and Cultural Struggle." *Popular Music* 6 (1): 77–92.

Geertz, Clifford. 1971. *Islam Observed: Religious Development in Morocco and Indonesia.* Chicago: University of Chicago Press.

Gellner, Ernest. 1983. *Muslim Society.* Cambridge: Cambridge University Press.

Goodman, Jane. 2005. *Berber Culture on the World Stage: From Village to Video.* Bloomington: Indiana University Press.

Grame, Theodore C. 1970. "Music in the Jma Al-Fna of Marrakesh." *The Musical Quarterly* 56: 74–87.

Guilbault, Jocelyne. 1993. *Zouk: World Music in the West Indies.* Chicago: University of Chicago Press.

———. 1997. "Interpreting World Music: A Challenge in Theory and Practice." *Popular Music* 16 (1): 31–44.

Guss, David M. 2000. *The Festive State: Race, Ethnicity, and Nationalism as Cultural Performance.* Berkeley: University of California Press.

Hagedorn, Katherine J. 2001. *Divine Utterances: The Performance of Afro-Cuban Santería.* Washington, DC: Smithsonian Insitution Press.

Hell, Bertrand. 1999. *Possession et Chamanisme: Les Maîtres Du Désordre.* Paris: Flammarion.

———. 2002. *Le tourbillon des génies: Au Maroc avec les Gnawa.* Paris: Flammarion.

Herwitz, Daniel. 2012. *Heritage, Culture, and Politics in the Postcolony.* New York: Columbia University Press.

Hirschkind, Charles. 2006. *The Ethical Soundscape: Cassette Sermons and Islamic Counterpublics.* New York: Columbia University Press.

Ivy, Marilyn. 1995. *Discourses of the Vanishing: Modernity, Phantasm, Japan.* Chicago: University of Chicago Press.

Jameson, Fredric. 1983. "Postmodernism and Consumer Society." In *The Anti-Aesthetic: Essays on Postmodern Culture,* edited by Hal Foster, 111–25. Port Townsend, WA: Bay Press.

Jankowsky, Richard C. 2010. *Stambeli: Music, Trance, and Alterity in Tunisia.* Chicago: University of Chicago Press.

———. 2013. "Rhythmic Elasticity and Metric Transformation in Tunisian Stambeli." *Analytical Approaches to World Music* 3 (1): 34–61.

Kapchan, Deborah. 1996. *Gender on the Market: Moroccan Women and the Revoicing of Tradition.* Philadelphia: University of Pennsylvania Press.

———. 2003. "Nashat: The Gender of Musical Celebration in Morocco." In *Music and Gender: Perspectives from the Mediterranean,* edited by Tullia Magrini, 251–65. Chicago: University of Chicago Press.

———. 2007. *Traveling Spirit Masters: Moroccan Gnawa Trance and Music in the Global Marketplace.* Middletown, CT: Wesleyan University Press.

———. 2008. "The Promise of Sonic Translation: Performing the Festive Sacred in Morocco." *American Anthropologist* 110 (4): 467–83.

———. 2009. "Singing Community/Remembering in Common: Sufi Liturgy and North African Identity in Southern France." *International Journal of Community Music* 2 (1): 9–23.

———, ed. 2014. *Cultural Heritage in Transit: Intangible Rights as Human Rights.* Philadelphia: University of Pennsylvania Press.

Kapchan, Deborah A., and Pauline Turner Strong. 1999. "Theorizing the Hybrid." *The Journal of American Folklore* 112 (445): 239–53.

Kirchgassner, Andreas. 2007. "The Appeal of Moroccan Gnawa Music for Jazz and Pop: A Trancescendent Fusion." Translated by Charlotte Collins. Qantara. http://en.qantara.de/wcsite.php?wc_c=8824.

Kirschenblatt-Gimblett, Barbara. 1998. *Destination Culture: Tourism, Museums, and Heritage.* Berkeley: University of California Press.

———. 2004. "Intangible Heritage as Metacultural Production." *Museum International* 56 (1–2): 52–65.

Klein, Debra L. 2007. *Yorùbá Bàtá Goes Global: Artists, Culture Brokers, and Fans.* Chicago: University of Chicago Press.

Kriady, Marwan M. 2002. "Hybridity in Cultural Globalization." *Communication Theory* 12 (3): 316–39.

Lapassade, Georges. 1976. "Les Gnaoua d'Essaouira: Les rites de possession des anciens esclaves noirs au Maghreb, hier et aujourd'hui." *L'Homme et la société*, no. 39–40: 191–215.

Largey, Michael D. 2006. *Vodou Nation: Haitian Art Music and Cultural Nationalism.* Chicago: University of Chicago Press.

Larkin, Brian. 2008. *Signal and Noise: Media, Infrastructure, and Urban Culture in Nigeria.* Durham, NC: Duke University Press.

Lee, Tong Soon. 1999. "Technology and the Production of Islamic Space: The Call to Prayer in Singapoore." *Ethnomusicology* 43 (1): 86–100.

Lindholm, Charles. 2002. "Authenticity, Anthropology, and the Sacred." *Anthropological Quarterly* 75 (2): 331–38.

Lovejoy, Paul, ed. 2004. *Slavery on the Frontiers of Islam.* Princeton, NJ: Markus Wiener.

Magidow, Melanie Autumn. 2013. "Multicultural Solidarity: Performances of Malhun Poetry in Morocco." PhD dissertation, University of Texas, Austin.

Mahmood, Saba. 2005. *The Politics of Piety: The Islamic Revival and the Feminist Subject.* Princeton, NJ: Princeton University Press.

Masquelier, Adeline. 2001. *Prayer Has Spoiled Everything: Possession, Power, and Identity in an Islamic Town of Niger.* Durham, NC: Duke University Press.

Matory, J. Lorand. 2005. *Black Atlantic Religion: Tradition, Transnationalism, and Matriarchy in the Afro-Brazilian Condomblé.* Princeton, NJ: Princeton University Press.

Meintjes, Louise. 1990. "Paul Simon's Graceland, South Africa, and the Mediation of Musical Meaning." *Ethnomusicology* 34 (1): 37–73.

Munson, Henry, Jr. 1993. *Religion and Power in Morocco.* New Haven, CT: Yale University Press.

Nabti, Mehdi. 2006. "Soufisme, métissage culturel et commerce du sacré: Les aïssâwa Marocains dans la modernité." *Insaniyat: Revue Algérienne D'anthropologie et de Sciences Sociales Insaniyat* 10 (32/33): 173–95.

Nelson, Kristina. 2001. *The Art of Reciting the Qur'an.* Cairo: American University in Cairo Press.

Ong, Walter J. 2000. *The Presence of the Word: Some Prolegomena for Cultural and Religious History*. Minneapolis: University of Minnesota Press.

Ouaknine-Yekutieli, Orit. 2015. "Narrating a Pending Calamity: Artisanal Crisis in the Medina of Fes, Morocco." *International Journal of Middle East Studies* 47 (1): 109–29.

Panagia, Davide. 2009. *The Political Life of Sensation*. Durham, NC: Duke University Press.

Pâques, Viviana. 1964. *L'arbre cosmique dans la pensée populaire et dans la vie quotidienne du nord-ouest africain*. Paris: Institut d'ethnologie.

———. 1991. *La religion des esclaves: recherches sur la confrérie marocaine des Gnawa*. Bergamo: Moretti & Vitali.

Porcello, Thomas, Louise Meintjes, Ana Maria Ochoa, and David W. Samuels. 2010. "The Reorganization of the Sensory World." *Annual Review of Anthropology* 39: 51–66.

Rabinow, Paul. 1977. *Reflections on Fieldwork in Morocco*. Berkeley: University of California Press.

Racy, Ali Jihad. 2003. *Making Music in the Arab World: The Culture and Artistry of Tarab*. Cambridge: Cambridge University Press.

Rasmussen, Anne. 2010. *Women, the Recited Qur'an, and Islamic Music in Indonesia*. Berkeley: University of California Press.

Samuels, David W., Louise Meintjes, Ana Maria Ochoa, and Thomas Porcello. 2010. "Soundscapes: Toward a Sounded Anthropology." *Annual Review of Anthropology* 39: 329–45.

Sayed, Omar. 2011. *Nass El Ghiwane*. Borgaro Torinese, Italy: Senso Unico Editions.

Schaefer, John Philip Rode. 2009. "Moroccan Modern: Race, Aesthetics, and Identity in a Global Culture Market." PhD dissertation, University of Texas, Austin.

Schafer, R. Murray. 1994. *The Soundscape: Our Sonic Environment and the Tuning of the World*. Rochester, VT: Destiny.

Schauert, Paul. 2015. *Staging Ghana: Artistry and Nationalism in State Dance Ensembles*. Bloomington: Indiana University Press.

Schuyler, Philip Daniel. 2000. "Joujouka/Jajouka/Zahjoukah: Moroccan Music and the Euro-American Imagination." In *Mass Mediations: New Approaches to Popular Culture in the Middle East and Beyond*, edited by Walter Armbrust, 146–60. Berkeley: University of California Press.

Shannon, Jonathan. 2003. "Sultans of Spin: Syrian Sacred Music on the World Stage." *American Anthropologist*, New Series, 105 (2): 266–77.

———. 2006. *Among the Jasmine Trees: Music and Modernity in Contemporary Syria*. Middletown, CT: Wesleyan University Press.

———. 2011. "Suficized Musics of Syria at the Intersection of Heritage and the War on Terror; or, 'A Rumi with a View.'" In *Muslim Rap, Halal Soaps, and Revolutionary Theater: Artistic Developments in the Muslim World*, edited by Karin van Nieuwkerk, 257–74. Austin: University of Texas Press.

———. 2015. *Performing Al-Andalus: Music and Nostalgia across the Mediterranean*. Bloomington: Indiana University Press.

Sharp, Daniel B. 2014. *Between Nostalgia and Apocalypse: Popular Music and the Staging of Brazil*. Middletown, CT: Wesleyan University Press.

Silverman, Carol. 2012. *Romani Routes: Cultural Politics and Balkan Music in Diaspora*. Oxford: Oxford University Press.

Slyomovics, Susan. 2005. *The Performance of Human Rights in Morocco*. Philadelphia: University of Pennsylvania Press.

Small, Christopher. 1999. "Musicking—the Meanings of Performing and Listening. A Lecture." *Music Education Research* 1 (1): 9–21.

Spadola, Emilio. 2014. *The Calls of Islam: Sufis, Islamists, and Mass Mediation in Urban Morocco.* Bloomington: Indiana University Press.

Sterne, Jonathan. 2002. *The Audible Past: Cultural Origins of Sound Reproduction.* Durham, NC: Duke University Press.

St. John, Graham. 2015. "Introduction to Weekend Societies: EDM Festivals and Event-Cultures." *Dancecult: Journal of Electronic Dance Music Culture* 7 (1): 1–14.

Stokes, Martin. 1994. "Introduction: Ethnicity, Identity, and Music." In *Ethnicity, Identity, and Music: The Musical Construction of Place*, edited by Martin Stokes, 1–27. Oxford: Berg Publishers.

———. 2010. *The Republic of Love: Cultural Intimacy in Turkish Popular Music.* Chicago: University of Chicago Press.

Stoller, Paul. 1989. *Fusion of the Worlds: An Ethnography of Possession among the Songhay of Niger.* Chicago: University of Chicago Press.

Sum, Maisie. 2010. "Analysis of Sonic Structure in Gnawa Music." Presented at the First International Conference on Analytical Approaches to World Music, Univeristy of Massachusetts, Amherst.

———. 2011. "Staging the Sacred: Musical Structure and Processes of the Gnawa Lila in Morocco." *Ethnomusicology* 55 (1): 77–111.

———. 2013. "Music for the Unseen: Interaction between Two Realms during a Gnawa Lila." *African Music* 9 (3): 151–82.

Turner, Tamara Dee. 2012. "The Ethics and Aesthetics of Musical Speech: Sounding Moral Geographies in Moroccan Gnawa Music." MA thesis, Tufts University, Boston.

Wade, Peter. 2000. *Music, Race, and Nation: Música Tropical in Colombia.* Chicago: University of Chicago Press.

Waterbury, John. 1970. *Commander of the Faithful: The Moroccan Political Elite.* London: Weidenfeld & Nicolson.

Waugh, Earle H. 2005. *Memory, Music, and Religion: Morocco's Mystical Chanters.* Columbia: University of South Carolina Press.

Weiner, Isaac. 2009. "Religion Out Loud: Religious Sound, Public Space, and American Pluralism." PhD dissertation, University of North Carolina, Chapel Hill.

Weston, Randy, and Willard Jenkins. 2010. *African Rhythms: The Autobiography of Randy Weston.* Durham, NC: Duke University Press.

Willemont, Jaques, dir. 2011. *Gnawa: Music and Beyond.* Espaces. DVD.

Witulski, Christopher. 2016a. "The Gnawa Lions: Paths towards Learning Ritual Music in Contemporary Morocco." *The Journal of North African Studies* 21 (4): 599–622.

———. 2016b. "Light Rhythms and Heavy Spirits: Entertaining Listeners through Gnawa Musical and Ritual Adaptations in Morocco." *Ethnomusicology Forum* 25 (2): 172–90.

———. 2018. "Contentious Spectacle: Negotiated Authenticity within Morocco's Gnawa Ritual." *Ethnomusicology* 62 (1): 58–82.

Index

'Abd al-Latif wuld Sidi 'Umara.
See Makhzumi, 'Abd al-Latif
'Abd al-Rzaq, 'Abd al-Rahim, 1, 20, 40, 63,
140–1, 164; as hariqsa, 67; folklore performances, 128–9; in Sidi Ali, 96; training, 57
'ada, 1, 25–6, 45, 47, 95; Ma Mahjuba's
involvement in, 131
adhan, 3–4, 49
aesthetics. See fassiyya; marsawiyya; ritual,
aesthetics of
Africa (sub-Saharan): and memory of
slavery, 8; as identity, 4, 38–43, 45–7, 147;
as marker of authenticity, 10–11, 32, 52; as
negotiation, 6; as source of gnawa sprits,
6, 44, 155 (see also mluk); in ritual lyrics,
39–41. See also genealogy
Aisha. See Lalla Aisha
"Aisha Hamdushiyya." See Lalla Aisha
'aita, 99, 102
Alikane, Abdessalam, 146
al-kuhl. See Sidi Mimun
al-Qasri, Hamid, 11–2, 56, 120; and marsawiyya style, 99, 104, 117; referenced in
Sidi Ali concert, 111; rituals, 62–3
al-Tahir al-Hayat, Mulay, 43–4, 154, 157
Amrani, 'Abd al-Rahim, 107, description
of Lalla Malika, 104; efforts to broaden
hamadsha audiences, 109; relationship
to Yassine Boudouaia, 55, 71. See also
hamadsha
Andalusia, 25
apprenticeship. See juqay; training
artistry. See individual artists; fnan
'ashiyya, 60–1; as marker of ritual change,
101; differences from lila, 121; hamadsha
ritual, 95; in Meknes, 1, 25; negative opinions of, 74n1. See also lila
audience engagement, 10, 12, 162, 164–8;
importance in performance, 89, 110–3;
innovation and change, 90, 98–9, 161; in
ritual, 28–9, 37–8, 44, 60, 105–6; on stage,

72–3. See also authenticity, narratives of;
maskun; musical taste; spirit possession
authenticity, 4, 31–5, 90–2, 141–2, 164–8;
claiming, 12, 32, 47, 97–8; claims of inauthenticity, 6; from commercial success, 62;
narratives of, 7–10, 12–3, 44–7, 52–3, 56, 80,
141–5; negotiating, 5–6, 50, 162; on stage, 6;
performing, see performance of authenticity; state support for presentations of,
83. See also heritage; tgnawit
authority, 2, 164–8. See also authenticity;
elders; youth
awliya. See saints
Aziz wuld Ba Blan, 4, 36n10, 52, 129, 131–2;
role in fassiyya performance, 100, 137–8,
156–8. See also fassiyya

Ba Blan, 100, 113n6, 129. See also Aziz wuld
Ba Blan; fassiyya
Ba Bujma, 130. See also bin Bujma al-Flali,
Muhammad; Fez, gnawa history in
Ba Rami, 130–1. See also Fez, gnawa
history in
Bambara, 40
banjo, 6
baraka, 25, 27, 35n4, 107; ethnographic
description of, 38; in Sidi Ali procession,
94–5; transmitted by phone, 120
Bekkas, Majid, 56
bil-Khayat, 'Abd al-Hadi, 86–7
bin Bujma al-Flali, Muhammad, 57, 100,
129–30. See also Fez, gnawa history in
blan, 31
Bnat Gnawa, 19n3
bori, 10
Boudouaia, Yassine: career as example
of shifting authenticities, 61–2, 71–4,
91, 165–6; in Sidi Ali, 95; introduction to, 55–6; knowledge of fassiyya
style, 55; performance with his Gnawa
Lions, 72

CHRISTOPHER WITULSKI is an Instructor of Ethnomusicology at Bowling Green State University in Bowling Green, Ohio.

CPSIA information can be obtained
at www.ICGtesting.com
Printed in the USA
LVHW04s2234100918
589761LV00001B/198/P

9 780253 036759